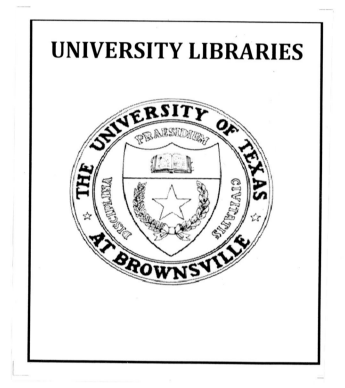

FROM
DEMOCRATS
TO KINGS

FROM DEMOCRATS TO KINGS

The Brutal Dawn of a New World
from the Downfall of Athens to the Rise
of Alexander the Great

MICHAEL SCOTT

THE OVERLOOK PRESS
New York

This edition first published in hardcover in the United States in 2010 by

The Overlook Press, Peter Mayer Publishers, Inc.
141 Wooster Street
New York, NY 10012
www.overlookpress.com
For bulk and special sales, please contact sales@overlookny.com

Copyright © 2009 by Dr. Michael Scott

Cataloging-in-Publication Data is available from the Library of Congress

Manufactured in the United States of America
ISBN 978-1-59020-391-0
FIRST EDITION
2 4 6 8 10 9 7 5 3 1

Contents

About the author

MICHAEL SCOTT is currently a Moses and Mary Finley Fellow in Ancient History at Darwin College, Cambridge, where he studies the ancient Greek and Roman worlds as well as teaching undergraduates and working with schools around the country.

Since 2007, he has been a regular guest lecturer aboard cruise tours of ancient Greece, has run the route of the ancient Marathon in Athens, and has been an on-screen historical consultant for several documentaries about the ancient world for the History Channel.

www.michaelcscott.com

*For Peter Wicker,
who taught me my first letters
of the ancient Greek alphabet*

Acknowledgements

The genesis of this book was in a series of lectures given to undergraduates at Cambridge University. My thanks go to the class of students who attended those lectures with good humour and grace, who gave me an opportunity to road test my ideas and who gave much helpful feedback. To the many friends and colleagues with whom I have enjoyed countless discussions about the subject of this book and about the ancient world in general, I offer my sincerest gratitude. I would especially like to thank Prof. Robin Osborne, Prof. Paul Cartledge, Prof. Pat Easterling, Dr Alastair Blanshard, James Watson, Ben Keim, Peter Agocs, Clare Killikelly and Kelly Agathos for their thoughts, wit and guidance. To the small team of 'veteran travellers' who willingly came with me to explore the 'dancing floor of Ares', its mysteries and delights (not least of which was the underrated modern town of Thebes), I say 'Suga!' To Davina Barron, who carefully and helpfully read earlier drafts, I offer my indebted thanks. To Darwin College, Cambridge and to the British School at Athens, two admirable research institutions, which have made me feel very much at home in Cambridge and Athens not just during the research and writing of this book but over the past several years, I offer my heartfelt gratitude and praise. To the people who make these two institutions what they are, and who are themselves so much more besides, I give my admiration and affection. To Moses and Mary Finley, towering greats in the scholarship of the ancient world, whose legacy funds my current position as Finley Research Fellow at the University of Cambridge, I offer my continued awe and thanks. For good advice on entering the world of history writing, my deepest appreciation goes to my agents Diane Banks and Sue Rider, my editor at Icon Simon Flynn, Duncan Heath and the rest of the team at Icon, and at Cambridge Prof. Mary Beard, Prof. Simon Goldhill and Dr Chris Kelly. Finally, to my family, who encouraged my desire to pursue this crazy classics thing many years ago: thank you. It has been a pleasure and an honour to write this book and to help bring the ancient world once more to life.

List of Illustrations

Maps

Plate section

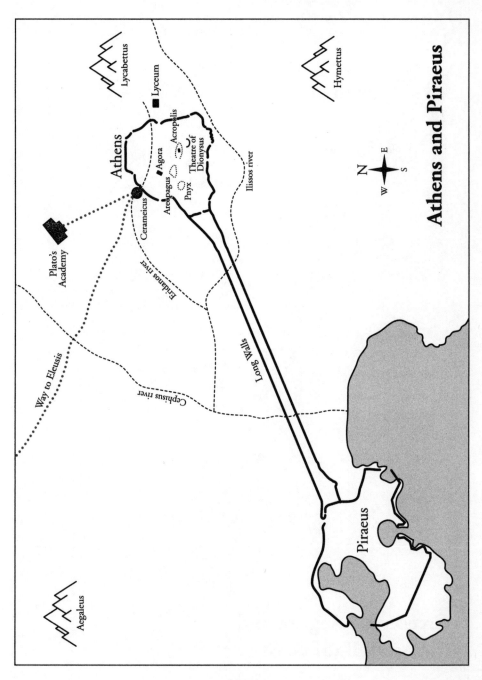

Map 1

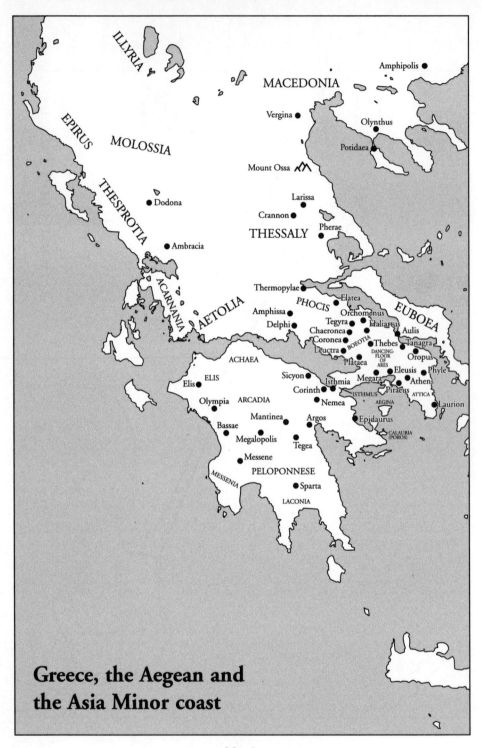

Greece, the Aegean and
the Asia Minor coast

Map 2

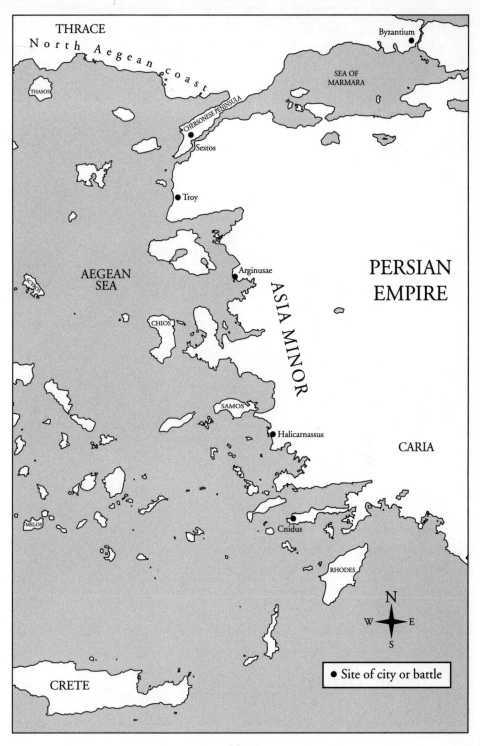

Map 2

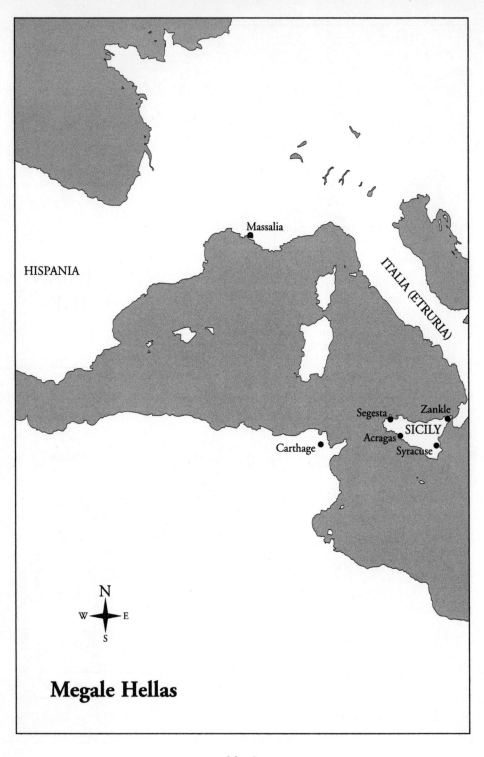

Megale Hellas

Map 3

Map 3

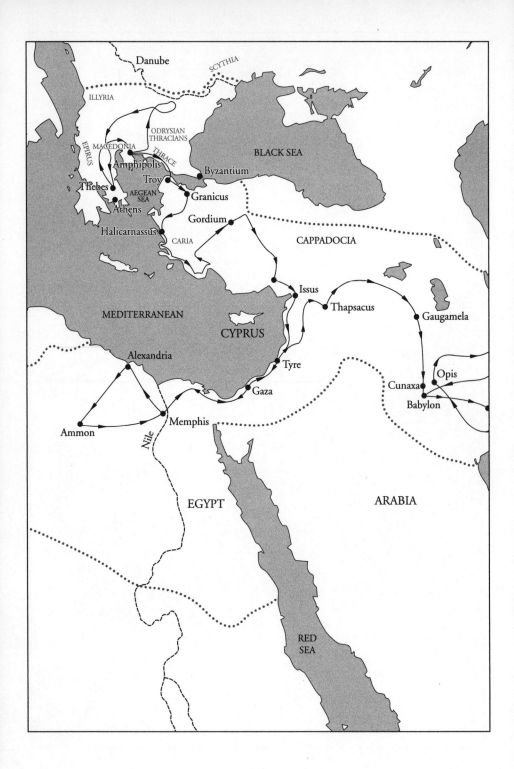

Map 4

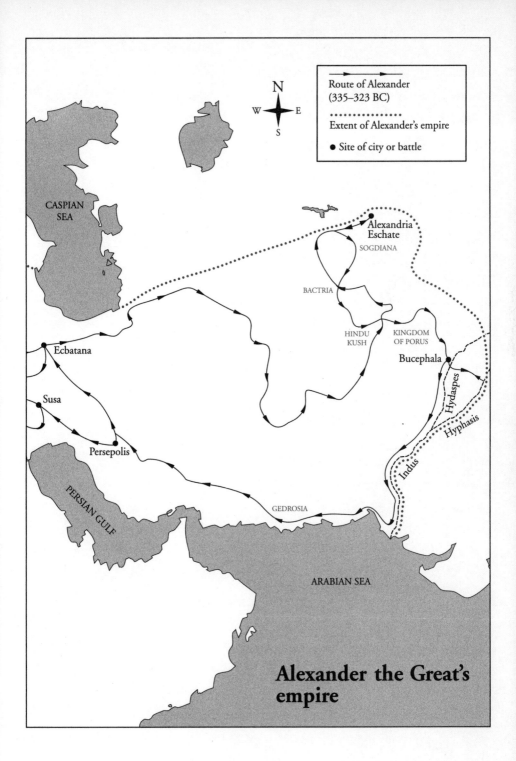

Alexander the Great's empire

Map 4

xvii

When you set out on the journey to Ithaca,
pray that the road be long,
full of adventures, full of knowledge.

C.P. Cavafy (1863–1933),
'Ithaca' (trans. E. Sachperoglou)

INTRODUCTION

One Man's Dream

In the year 339 BC, an old man forced himself up from his deathbed to undertake one final task. Struggling against the illness which had blighted him for the past three years of his life, encouraged by his friends and colleagues who were only too aware of the importance of what he was about to do, this 97-year-old man painstakingly put the finishing touches to the work he had been writing in the years before his illness had taken over. His name was Isocrates, from the city of Athens in ancient Greece, and his writing sought to save his city from itself.

Isocrates was an idealist. Throughout his extraordinarily long life, he had fought tirelessly to put Athens and the ancient Greek world on a better course, to remind its constituents of the dangers they all faced and to call on those with the necessary capabilities to lead Greece out of crisis. Now, as his own life started finally to fade, as he forced himself despite his illness to complete his final words of advice, he knew that Greece stood at a fundamental fork in the road. As he reflected on the gravity of the crisis, he was perhaps the only man left in Greece who had been alive long enough to see for himself how such a moment had come to pass.

Born back in the previous century, in 436 BC, when Athens was at the height of its power, Isocrates had been one of five children. His parents had been wealthy thanks to his father's flute-making business, which meant that as a child he had received an excellent education. Yet his idyllic childhood had been rudely interrupted by the savage wars that tore apart the Greek world in the last 30 years of the century and brought about Athens' fall from grace. His father's property and wealth were lost and Isocrates, for all his education, could look forward, like many others at the time, to little more than a hand-to-mouth existence. His only hope was to make a living by passing on his knowledge. Opening a school in the city of Athens, Isocrates began to teach. He was, by all accounts, a demanding but popular schoolmaster who, over his lifetime, amassed a fortune and shaped the minds of many who would play key roles in Athens' and Greece's future. He taught about the value of self-control, the fundamental importance of freedom and autonomy, the seductive nature of power, and the destructiveness of unfocused aggression.

But educating future leaders wasn't enough for Isocrates. Though he never wanted public office for himself, he did want to help shape the political world around him as it changed dramatically throughout the course of his life. His answer was to write. Isocrates became one of the first in a long line of political commentators and observers, dispensing his advice to cities and individuals across the ancient Greek world in the form of written political pamphlets. Though he never held any kind of official position, and probably never even delivered a public political speech in his life, his carefully thought-out exhortations endeavoured to influence the cities and individuals who attempted to dominate Greece. Starting to publish only in his fifties, Isocrates proceeded to cover nearly every one of the turbulent moments in Athens' and Greece's history during the second half of his life. Throughout those writings, two themes are always dominant. The first is his love for his home city, Athens. The second is his deep desire to see Hellas, the ill-defined community of often disparate and warring individual cities which made up ancient Greece, unified and dominant over the entire ancient world.

For the majority of his life, Isocrates envisaged with unremitting zeal a particular kind of future for Greece. As one scholar has put it, if mighty Hellas was a religion, then Athens was its central altar and Isocrates was its most outspoken prophet. All Isocrates' early writings spoke to Athens, encouraging his beloved city to better itself as it fought to keep its place in the shifting sands of international politics, to be worthy of its glorious reputation, to think past its normal political infighting and to step forward to lead Greece. But as time passed, Isocrates became more and more disillusioned with Athens' failure to live up to that reality. More and more, Isocrates sought out others, powerful individuals rather than cities, who might be more willing and able to bring his dream of a dominant Hellas to reality.

It was not until the final year of his life that he gave up on Athens. Rising from his deathbed, he forced himself to finish his parting words to his beloved city, encouraging it, one last time, to rise once again to glory. But those words were empty of hope. In the following year, 338 BC, months before his own death, Isocrates forsook Athens and found a new shrine for his religion of a greater Greece. Writing one last public letter to the new king of Macedon in northern Greece, whose armies were on the verge of taking control of much of the country and had just beaten those of Athens and its allies on the field of battle, Isocrates thanked the king for making 'some of the things I dreamed of in my youth come to pass'. He ended simply: 'I am hopeful the rest will follow.'

Isocrates died soon after. He was buried with his father and mother near the banks of the Ilissos river in Athens. He never knew what happened next. He never knew that Greece was on the verge of being ruled by its most powerful and successful father and son: Philip of Macedon and Alexander the Great, who would create the greatest empire the ancient world had ever seen. But Isocrates did die aware that Athens, and Greece, had come to a fundamental fork in their destinies. He knew better than anyone the turbulent tides of events, personalities, debates and decisions that had brought both Athens and Greece to this moment. In the final year of his life, his last two public pamphlets symbolised the change coming over Greece: a change in the balance of power from cities like democratic Athens to the king of Macedon. Isocrates had witnessed and played his part in the brutal dawn of a new world – from democrats to kings.

It's a safe bet that you will have heard of Alexander the Great (not least because of the Hollywood film with Colin Farrell and Angelina Jolie). It's a safe bet that you will have heard about Athenian democracy (not least because America recently celebrated the origins of its own democracy in Athenian democracy 2,500 years previously). But it's also a safe bet that you will not have heard of Isocrates or realised that these two extremes of the political spectrum, democracy and absolute monarchy, and the diametrically opposed societies and worlds they defined, were separated in the ancient world by just a single ancient lifetime: Isocrates' lifetime. Though there are many good history books available today to describe and explain the 'accident' of Athenian democracy and the heroic story of the ultimate over-achiever, Alexander the Great, there are few that focus on the single generation in between them. This book is about that time and the story of the dawn of a new world order that it contains.

But why should anyone care about such events in Isocrates' lifetime, which happened so many hundreds, indeed thousands of years ago?

First of all because this is a period still imperfectly understood even by specialists. Scholars of the ancient world have been quick to focus on Athenian democracy and subsequently to skip to Alexander the Great, without understanding how one gave way to the other. Even if they have studied the period between the two, they have often discarded it as a story of decline and decay after the glory days of the century preceding it (the glorious 5th century BC during which time the Parthenon was built and democratic Athens had its own empire). But every indication is that a story of decline and decay simply will not do. In fact, it is becoming clearer and clearer that an understanding of this period of dramatic transition may well be pivotal in developing a better understanding of the ancient world as a whole. This book makes the case for the importance of the period 'from democrats to kings' for everyone who is interested in ancient history. It tells this story of tumultuous change not as a succession of inevitable events like a timeline in a history textbook, but from the perspectives of the actual people involved, who were making decisions about how to react to the changing world around them with limited time, information and room for manoeuvre. It follows the decisions, debates and personalities that turned the Greek world on its head.

Such a story, however, is not only important for a better understanding of ancient history. I think that now is a more appropriate time than ever for this period of turbulent transition to be brought to the attention of the modern world. This book is a story of world change, of political and economic turmoil (even the banks in ancient Greece stopped lending at one point), of democracies being crushed and rebuilding themselves, of older and newer democracies teetering on the edge of imperialist ambitions, of faltering empires and hitherto backward states rising to prominence and suddenly becoming the powerhouses of the ancient world. It tells of a desperate, and ultimately delusional, struggle to maintain the status quo, and the triumph of new strategic thinking over stuck-in-the-mud tactical paralysis. It investigates the development of identity and a sense of self, at an individual, civic, national and even international level in the face of the integration of very different worlds, cultures, politics and religions. It follows population movement and the potential, as well as the traumas, of immigration. It puts the spotlight on a loosening of the class system and the creation of new wealth and celebrity. It shows how societies searched for new ways to conceptualise, regulate and police themselves and how individuals clamoured for reason, balance and the perfect life. It brings to light agreements behind closed doors and great debates among thousands. It is the story of a fight for natural resources and the persistent search for self-sufficiency, of treacherous transformation from face-to-face world into globalised society, in which individuals, as well as governments, could have a major impact. It is a celebration of people breaking the boundaries of the possible, of investigating uncertainty and discovering the intricacies of the world around them. Few people could find something in this list that does not speak to them and the world in which we all live right now. If history generally can provide a map of where we have been, a mirror to where we are right now, and perhaps even act as a guide to what we should do next, the story of the change from democrats to kings is perfectly suited to do just that in our times. It is a period of history that we would do well to think a little more about right now.

But perhaps the most important reason why we should care about this moment in the history of ancient Greece is the following: whether we like it or not, large parts of today's world are tied in tightly to the stories, values and paradigms of ancient Greece (America's cherished link to ancient Athenian democracy being only one example). The morals, practices, culture, philosophy, language, politics and identity of the ancient Greeks have, for a multitude of reasons, become embedded in our own, and ancient Greek examples have often been cited as justification for modern actions. The results have been both positive and negative. Ancient Greek tragedy has inspired generations of literary creativity. Yet Hitler justified his eugenics programme in part based on the heroic mentality of ancient Spartan warriors (those ones in the film *300*). As a result, our world has a great deal at stake in how we choose to understand the history of ancient Greece and how we choose to let others use it.

For me, the only solution to this dilemma is to improve our understanding of what happened in the ancient world so that everyone is better equipped to evaluate the appropriateness of its example and influence for our own world today. We cannot be blind to how unimaginably different the ancient world really was from ours. But at the same time, we should not be deaf to how little has changed, how much the ancients faced the same struggles and challenges as we do, and how much we can still learn from them. If the modern world is to evolve and feel more comfortable in its relationship to ancient Greece, and if ancient history, instead of being misappropriated, is to be as useful as it could be for our present and future, we need to understand better the game of proximity and distance that separates us from them. We all need to engage in the debate about the relationship between the ancient and modern worlds.

In our increasingly busy world, we have little time to take stock of where we are in our own lives, let alone where we are as families, communities, cities, nations and as humanity in comparison to our past. The story told in *From Democrats to Kings* can help in that task because it is a true story of change, of failure, of triumph, of distress and hope in the ancient world, but most of all because it is, ultimately, a story of being human.

CHAPTER 1

※

Flute Players and Pick Axes

In the year 404 BC, when Isocrates was 32 years of age, the democratic city of Athens and its great empire lay in the final throes of a slow and painful death. Athens had been at war for almost the entirety of Isocrates' life. The reason for this epic struggle was simple enough. After the cities of Greece had resisted the Persian invasion (and the 300 – in reality 301 – Spartans had fought so gloriously at Thermopylae) at the beginning of the century, the city of Athens had slowly moved to dominate much of ancient Greece. In the 440s BC, roughly 30 years after the heroic actions of the 301, as construction work on the great Parthenon temple in Athens was beginning and almost a decade before Isocrates was born, Athens' empire had grown to span much of the Greek world. Its unbeatable navy patrolled the Aegean and the Black Sea and often visited violent retribution on cities unwilling to accept its leadership, its taxes and its garrison outposts. Eventually the strain had become too much and the one city which had the strength to oppose Athens' stranglehold grip on Greece, Sparta, with its famous warrior citizens, had declared war in order to deliver what it called freedom once more to the Greeks. Athens, the celebrated democracy, was denounced as the tyrant of Greece by Sparta – a city, ironically enough, itself ruled by two kings. Gathering allies as it went, Sparta faced up against Athens in a war, which eventually enveloped much of mainland Greece, the islands of the Aegean and the coast of modern-day Turkey. This war, known as the Peloponnesian war, raged across Greece for much of the next

30 years. It consumed Isocrates' early life and wiped out his family's fortune, not to mention the lives of thousands.

Throughout those 30 long years, neither side could deliver the fatal blow. Yet by 404 BC, Athens was on its knees. Why? Partly, it was to do with factors beyond Athens' control. In an effort to protect its citizens, it had encouraged many who lived out in the vulnerable countryside to move into the city where they would be protected by Athens' stout city walls. But the effect of so many people crowded into a city, not best known for its public hygiene, was plague. Severe bouts of the plague struck the city three times, killing perhaps a third of its population. The plague bled the morale of the city, causing social and religious order to break down and taking the life of its most illustrious general, Athens' version of Winston Churchill, a man called Pericles. Without a clear leader, surrounded by funeral pyres whose scattered ashes seemed to symbolise the crumbling state of the once-proud city, Athens was ill prepared to continue fighting this debilitating conflict.

Yet Athens' fall from power was also due to its own mistakes. Too often, Athens' over-eager democratic assembly voted in haste for a particular mission which, not going to plan, they sought to blame on somebody else. The worst case was that of a sea battle at Arginusae in 406 BC, just two years before Athens' final defeat. Following the battle, in which they had actually been victorious, the Athenian admirals had been unable to pick up their dead from the water for fear of a storm, which threatened to take more Athenian lives in pursuit of those already dead. They returned home without the bodies of their compatriots, a serious breach of Athenian custom and religious obligation, but perhaps understandable given the circumstances. The Athenian assembly, standing together in session on the assembly hill, called the Pnyx, in the centre of the city (see Map 1), did not see it that way and voted to put on trial and eventually execute the offending admirals. In the midst of war, Athens killed its own successful military leaders. Athens left itself without a head, and with such a vengeful mob seemingly calling the shots, it's not surprising that it had difficulty finding talented men willing to take the place of the dead admirals.

But perhaps the final nail in the coffin for Athens during this great war was the Spartans' (perhaps surprising) willingness to think the unthinkable. For much of the current century, the cities of Greece had been at war with the great empire across the Aegean sea, Persia. Persia was the antithesis of everything Greek, and the successful repudiation of Persia's attempt to take over the cities of ancient Greece back in 490 and 480–479 BC secured not only the legendary status of Spartan warriors in the ancient world, but also Greece's freedom and the growing glory of the city of Athens. A Spartan could not even consider alliance with Persia. Yet the long years of the Peloponnesian war, and the fact that it was now the Greek city of Athens, not Persia, that was threatening Greece's freedom, seem to have prompted the Spartans to make a deal with the Persians. In return for military and financial aid, the Spartans promised the Persians control over the Greek cities dotted along the coast of modern-day Turkey (the borderlands of the Persian and Greek worlds), which had been a constant thorn in the Persian king's side. The Spartans, the descendants of the 301 who had held to their death the pass at Thermopylae against the invading Persian army, were now in bed with their one-time enemy. Against the combined army of Sparta and the financial and naval muscle of Persia, Athens didn't stand a chance.

In 404 BC, following a siege of the city of Athens and the blockade of its port, Piraeus (Map 1), which had provided the arterial life-blood of edible grain into the city, Athens accepted its defeat. The Athenian empire was dead. The Spartan general responsible for masterminding this final humiliation, Lysander, accepted Athens' peace envoy with great generosity, but also kept him waiting for an excruciating three months to agree terms. Three months in which exhausted Athenians waited to hear what lay in store for their battered city, like a victim of the guillotine waiting interminably for the sound of the blade sliding towards their neck. The terms that finally emerged were bludgeoning.

Athens had to surrender its crown jewel – its navy – except for a paltry twelve triremes (the ancient version of the battle-cruiser). It had to allow all supporters of oligarchy – rule by the few, the antithesis of democracy – back into the city. It had to become a friend and ally of Sparta and follow wherever it led. And if this wasn't enough, Athens had to pull down its own city walls, leaving itself naked to the world around it. Like a prisoner of war stripped naked in front of his captors, this was the final humiliation for the city that had been the glory of Greece.

In some ways, however, the peace agreement could have been much worse. It didn't, for instance, demand that Athens get rid of its system of democracy. In fact, Athens did that all by itself. In the assembly meeting on the Pnyx to hear the peace terms, some Athenians stepped forward to say that democracy had had its day and that what was needed now was strong, stable government by a small number of experienced men. This wasn't a new idea, since Athens had briefly tried a somewhat similar system of government seven years earlier but had thrown it out just as quickly as it had been brought in. This time, however, the movement was more serious. The man who had been sent by Athens to negotiate the peace terms (and, it was rumoured, enjoyed far too much the generosity of Sparta during those long three months of waiting) spoke in favour of appointing a board of 30 men to lead Athens in its dark hour. The victorious Spartan general himself, Lysander, sat on the platform in front of the Athenian assembly and *suggested* that, for Athens' good, the proposal be accepted. The opponents of the scheme, the die-hard democrats, walked out of the assembly in disgust at what they saw as the subversion of normal democratic procedures (fair enough, since Lysander's presence, and that of his army not far away, wasn't particularly conducive to democratic debate). In their absence, however, the motion's supporters continued the debate and won the day. On the same day as, 76 years earlier, democratic Athens with its allies had won its own famous victory against the Persians at the sea battle of Salamis, democratic Athens (somewhat) democratically voted itself out of existence.

In the nights following the adoption of Sparta's demands, its terms were brutally enforced. The most heart-rending of these was the destruction of the stout city walls that had defined and protected Athens. Every Spartan, every hater of Athens, was called on to hack down the walls with anything they could lay their hands on. In contrast to the tearing down of the Berlin Wall in 1989, which heralded the birth of unity in a splintered city, this tearing down signified a city's destruction. By day in the blistering sun and by night in the flicker of torch-fire, the rhythmic beat of metal against stone could be heard ringing out around the city. The Spartans, who marched to the tune of the flute, even installed flute players around the city to co-ordinate the work. The sad, rhythmical tune of the flute and the accompanying beat of the pickaxes heralded the final humiliation of a once proud city and, supposedly, the freeing of Greece from its tyrant.

The rule of the 30 (who would themselves later be branded the '30 Tyrants') was initially fairly mild and temperate. But one of their most controversial actions was to rebuild the Athenian assembly on the Pnyx. Since its inception, this open-air assembly area on top of one of the central hills of Athens had been structured so as to have the assembly members facing towards Athens' port, Piraeus, and the sea. The 30 Tyrants had it reversed so that the members now faced towards the land. Why? It is said that the 30 believed that Piraeus and the sea reminded the Athenians of democracy and empire (because rowing aboard Athens' fleet of triremes had been one of the great supports for democratic thinking in Athens: if you can defend the city by powering its warships, you should have a say in how the city is run). Pointing people towards the land, the thinking went, instead reminded people of landowners, aristocracy, and the 'traditional' order of things in which only the elites had a say. Putting the sea to their backs, the 30 Tyrants hoped that the Athenians would forget their love affair with democracy. You still can still visit the Pnyx today in Athens, set out in the same orientation as the 30 Tyrants left it in 403 BC (see Figure 2).

The 30's reign was fairly short, not simply because of their cosmetic attempts to eradicate many Athenians' deep-seated regard for democracy. By the winter of the same year in which they had come into power, competition between the 30 men chosen to lead Athens had led to a hardening of their positions. Theramenes, the man who had brokered the peace with Sparta and supported the 30's rule in the assembly, now questioned their motives and actions; he was exiled and a list of 3,000 people who were 'in' the club of Athenian citizenship was drawn up. Though always restrictive in who it gave citizenship to, democratic Athens, in the course of a couple of months, had now become an extremely exclusive members-only club. Supporters of the democracy and those not on this exclusive list fled the city to plot their revenge in neighbouring Greek cities like Thebes, Argos and Megara. By the end of the year, a revolutionary band of 70 men – both Athenian exiles and non-Athenians – was gathering in Thebes under the leadership of a man called Thrasyboulus. They struck out to occupy the town of Phyle on the border between the territories of Athens and Thebes. From there they moved to take Athens' port, Piraeus. This hotbed of democratic support had smouldered since the overthrow of democracy, despite the assembly men literally turning their backs to it, and was ignited by the arrival of Thrasyboulus and his heroic band. On the Munychia hill in Piraeus, Thrasyboulus and his by now vastly swollen numbers of resistance fighters met the advancing (and still larger) supporters of the 30 and the 'list of 3,000' in open battle for the future of Athens.

The result was inconclusive, but the insurrection did succeed in killing Critias, the most hard-line of the 30 Tyrants, and forced constitutional change. The exclusive list of 3,000 dispatched the 30 Tyrants, and, in an off-hand move to placate the democrats, installed ten people to govern the city of Athens and ten to govern Piraeus instead. Such moves only further angered the leaders of the rebellion, who threatened further military action. The ten and the 3,000 appealed in desperation and a good degree of panic to Sparta for more military help. But what would Sparta do?

We are more aware than ever today of the dangers and difficulties of interfering with another city or country's internal political affairs. Sparta too, despite its prominent position as de facto controller of Greece, was split in how to respond. The two sides of the debate were summed up by two of the city's leading figures. On the one hand, Lysander, the original architect of victory over Athens, wished to move in and crush the democratic rebellion once and for all. But one of Sparta's kings (Sparta had two of them at any one time) argued for restraint. The king pulled rank on the general Lysander. It was but another irony of Athens' history that its democracy, voted out of existence by its own democratic assembly, was reinstated by a settlement negotiated by the king of the city which had brought Athens to its knees just a year before.

Athens had been through turbulent times. In a single year, it had lost its empire, its pride, its city walls, its democracy, been reorganised into an oligarchic state, suffered internal civil war and had its democracy restored. In the summer of 403 BC, it was left with the gigantean task of rebuilding and healing itself – physically, politically and morally. The problem was this: how should Athens restore the democracy and punish those opposed to it, without making clear just how weak democracy had been? How should the city celebrate its victory without making clear how close it had come to defeat? Like Germany after the fall of Nazism, Athens had to work out how to move on from such a dark part of its history without forgetting the lessons that needed to be learnt from it.

The settlement the city struck on was one that brilliantly combined a selective remembering of the heroic moments and an equally important selective forgetting of the embarrassing ones. Athens allowed an amnesty to everyone except the 30 Tyrants, who were hunted down and punished. Athens, pushed by Sparta, offered a very attractive deal to anyone who didn't want to be part of a democratic Athens to go and live at Eleusis, a hugely important religious cult site about a day's walk from the city (Map 1). But most important of all, it agreed that no one would remember past wrongs: not just an amnesty from prosecution, but a deliberate wiping clean of the slate in the collective memory. The past never happened. The last year was nothing more than a hiccup in the graceful dance of democracy at work.

But before such a blanket could be drawn over the affair, democracy's heroes had to be honoured. With tacit acknowledgement of degrees of heroism, Athens reserved the ultimate honours for those brave few who had been willing to stand up to the 30 at the very beginning – the 70 men who had set out from Thebes under Thrasyboulus and occupied Phyle – with lesser honours for the larger numbers who had responded to Thrasyboulus' call at his arrival in Piraeus, and lesser honours still for the hordes who had flocked to Piraeus once it looked like he was a sure bet to win. The rewards for each were inscribed on a stone set up on the sacred hill at the centre of ancient Athens that dominated the city then as it does today, its Acropolis. Placed near the world-famous Parthenon temple, which sits astride this towering rock, the stone inscribed with the list of Athens' saviours, like the Parthenon itself, survives in part for us to read today.

The foreigners among the original heroes, the 'men of Phyle' as they became known, were granted the ultimate prize: citizenship of Athens for them and their descendants. In contrast, the non-Athenians who had only helped out in Piraeus were granted exemption from the tax imposed on foreigners by the city – to be considered a great honour but not quite such an honour as citizenship itself. The name of every man in each group was recorded with his employment for all to see. It reads like an inspiring report of a true, bottom-up, democratic revolution by the little man. 'Leptines the cook' and 'Hegesias the gardener', among others, fought for their democratic rights that day. Immortalised in stone, these humble cooks and gardeners became the heroes of Athens. Yet the inscription also reveals that, before anyone got onto that list, whether from Phyle or Piraeus, they all first had to provide witnesses to prove that they really had been where they claimed to have been. Athenian democracy, quite rightly, wanted proof of who its heroes really were.

After honouring the heroes, both in the inscription on the Acropolis and with graves in Athens' public cemetery, the Cerameicus (which was located in a highly visible position around the main entrance gate to the city so that you had to travel through the cemetery to reach Athens), the crucial task now was to paper over the gaps in war-torn Athenian society and to rebuild the democracy stronger than before. The men of Phyle and Piraeus were allowed one victory march to the Acropolis before they had to take their place anonymously with everyone else in the assembly and begin the slow process of rebuilding the offices of democracy. That process crucially involved a review of the laws of the city, many of which had been discarded by the 30 Tyrants. Soon enough, Athens would feel the result of this new underpinning of the rule of law. Its citizens were able to read the city's laws for themselves, set up on stone in the public space of the city's political market-place, the Agora, and to implement the law in new courtrooms also built in the same area. Athens moved quickly after 403 BC to make the democracy stronger, and more visible, than it had ever been before. The ultimate proof of this was the oath that all Athenians were forced to swear in the weeks after the settlement. Standing in the Agora, as one voice, they swore: 'I shall kill by word and by deed and by vote and by my own hand, if I can, anyone who overthrows the democracy at Athens.'

Every Athenian democratic citizen no longer just supported democracy with their voice and vote. They were now obliged by an oath, made before their gods, to go as far as killing anyone who attempted to overthrow it. An Athenian's allegiance was now ultimately not to friends or family but to the city. Democratic Athens, after the upheaval and revolution of 404–403 BC, was now a militant force of would-be killers.

It all seems a little too perfect: democracy faltered, was restored by the cooks and gardeners of Athens and returned stronger than ever before, with all past wrongs forgotten, and everyone lived happily ever after. In reality, of course, it didn't work like that. Whatever the official line, people could not forget so easily who had been supporters of the democracy and who had not. Partly this was to be expected. The settlement had laid out the bare bones of how post-revolution Athenian society was going to work, but it was up to the Athenians themselves to put nerves, ligaments and muscle on this skeleton framework. Here the law courts became paramount. They acted as the sites of discussion and debate for what was and what was not permissible to remember and to pursue. Slowly Athenian society groped its way towards a working political settlement. But there were casualties along the way. Even Thrasyboulus, the great hero who had led the revolution from Thebes and captained the men of Phyle and Piraeus, was not above the judicio-political intrigue of those difficult days after 403 BC. He was accused of illegally requesting too many honours for the revolutionary heroes (particularly the foreigners among them). 'Steady on', was the veiled call from the old guard, even for this hero of the democracy.

But the worst injustice of those turbulent years was reserved for a man who has kept on provoking history, thought and debate ever since. Athenian citizens could not accuse other citizens directly of supporting the 30 Tyrants in the newly built law courts (it was all forgive and forget, remember), but they could find some trumped-up charge to accuse them of and then load their speeches for the prosecution with thinly-veiled references to their past misdemeanours. Even as the mortar was drying in the law-court walls, Athens in 399 BC bore witness to an outpouring of vengeful double entendre and dubious accusation directed against one man: Socrates.

You probably already know what Socrates looked like, so iconic has his philosopher image become – short, tubby, with a receding hairline, an ugly face like that of a goat, pudgy eyes and a wagging finger. He had roved around Athens for many years, engaging high-flying politicians and citizens of all trades in discussion of what they thought they were doing. Among the close companions of Socrates was our future political commentator Isocrates, who, now in his late thirties, was earning himself a living as a teacher. Socrates had even prophesied Isocrates' glorious future. Yet the problem with Socrates was that, inevitably, his philosophical discussions ended up demonstrating only too clearly how the 'experts' he interrogated were not really experts at all. He was just the kind of fellow you didn't want at a party – the kind who doesn't let any statement go unchallenged, who punctures egos in public, who questions exactly what you meant by your flippant remark about 'freedom'. In short, a man who frustrated, annoyed and embarrassed a large number of the people he talked to.

But he was also a man whose arguments, teaching and search for real truth, knowledge, justice and the good life has challenged the course of our thinking across the ages. We are still struggling with the complexities of Socrates' arguments, and our world, just like the world of Athens, was, and is, better for it. But in 399 BC in ancient Athens, some people had had enough. Socrates, in the course of his baiting of powerful individuals, had come into contact with members of the 30 Tyrants. He had been their supporter and a member of the 'in-club' of 3,000. This, coupled with his difficult demeanour, was enough for his enemies to smell blood in the water. Officially the charges against the great thinker were those of introducing new gods, not honouring the gods that the city recognised, and corrupting the young (whatever that meant). But in reality, these charges were a front for an opportunity for revenge on the 30 and on Socrates as one of their supporters. Socrates' defence speech to the jury against these charges survives for us today in the writings of another of his philosophical disciples (and later a great philosopher in his own right), Plato. To the jury in front of him, Socrates defended his existence in Athens and his way of life by explaining an idea which has become the catch-phrase of thinkers throughout the ages: 'An unexamined life is not worth living for a human being.' But the jury, blind to the truth or rather blinded by a desire for vengeance, voted to convict.

The practice in Athenian law courts for this type of crime was for the jury to act also as judges and pass sentence. They did not, however, have free rein. The prosecution and defence, having heard the guilty verdict, could each suggest a punishment. The jury had to pick one of them – it had no third way. The prosecution, of course, claimed the ultimate punishment: execution by the drinking of poison. Socrates stood and claimed that instead of punishing him, the city should pick up all his bills – so much of a good thing was he for Athens. He later modified his stance by offering to pay a fine. The jury, left to choose between killing him and letting him off with a fine, chose to kill him.

A democratic Athenian jury sentenced Socrates to death in 399 BC. His final moments in prison, including his drinking of the poison (the dreaded hemlock which paralysed drinkers from their feet upwards so that they were aware of their approaching death, even as the poison stopped the lung muscles from moving so that the victim suffocated), are recorded for us once again by his disciple Plato. The most surprising part of this record of his last hours for me is that Socrates was given several chances to escape, but chose not to, such was his respect for the rule of law in Athens – however wrong that law may be. Socrates, the ugly warrior of truth, was killed by the bloodthirsty alter ego of Athens' new hard-line democracy in its blind groping for political reconciliation. It was an inglorious day in the history of democratic government.

*

Almost 2,500 kilometres east of Athens, another event was taking place that would change the face of the ancient world as it stood on the brink of a new century. In the same year that Athens was in the throes of losing and regaining its democracy, the Persian king, Darius II, lord over the immense Persian empire that spanned from modern-day Turkey to Afghanistan, died in his capital at Susa (Map 4). His death was immediately followed by the succession of one of his sons, Artaxerxes. But another son, Cyrus, watching events at Susa and later back at his base on the coast of Asia Minor (the ancient name for the western half of what is now Turkey), had other plans.

In previous times, such internal politicking for the throne may not have interested the cities of Greece that much. A Persian was a Persian – whatever name he had and under whichever king he served. But now Sparta had taken Persian money (indeed Cyrus' money) to help win its war with Athens, and promised Persia in return the Greek cities on the

Asia Minor coast. Sparta, and with it Greece, now had a stake in Persian affairs, especially since the pretender to the throne, Cyrus, was sitting on that very coast. The gamble was this: if Sparta helped Cyrus in his plot to steal the throne of Persia and Cyrus succeeded, the new Persian king would forever be in Sparta's debt. But if Cyrus failed, Sparta, and Greece, would have to deal with a Persian king whom they had actively tried to assassinate. The temptation of power and influence over the greatest empire in the ancient world was too much. Sparta sent one of its own generals to aid Cyrus, and together they put out a call for Greek warriors who would fight as mercenaries.

But fight for what? They couldn't possibly announce their intention to march on the newly crowned Persian king, giving him ample time to raise an army and squash the insurrection before it had started. Instead, Cyrus and his Spartan adjutant called for Greek mercenaries to fight in a local war against a rebellious tribe. Cyrus, it was claimed, was doing his brother, the king, a favour in dealing with local insurrection. While Cyrus gathered a native force on the coast of Asia Minor, Greeks from many cities flocked to the mercenary call: they were battle-hardened warriors of a 30-year war and, more importantly, were in need of the high pay that Cyrus would offer for their fighting services.

One of the men who didn't need the money, but who instead needed a reason to leave Athens, was Xenophon, a rich young Athenian not best pleased with the democratic reversal of fortunes in 403 BC. He consulted the wise Socrates (who was soon to suffer his own terrible fate) on whether he should go and serve with Cyrus. Socrates advised him to consult the great oracle at the sanctuary of Delphi, hidden high up in the Parnassian mountains of central Greece. Xenophon, eager young man that he was, asked the oracle not first of all whether he should go, but, going, to which gods he should sacrifice to do well on his adventure. His mind made up, he left to join Cyrus on that fateful expedition to the innards of the Persian empire.

It was not until they had gone so far inland that it was difficult even to remember what home looked like that Cyrus announced to his assembled troops his real intention: to fight his brother for the throne of Persia. What could the Greek mercenaries do? Turn around and wander homewards alone in the midst of a foreign, enemy country? Cyrus knew he had them cornered: they had to stay and fight with him for the throne of Persia. At Cunaxa near Babylon in modern-day southern Iraq in 401 BC (Map 4), a dust cloud appeared on the horizon, soon to be filled with the flashing glints of weaponry, announcing the arrival of the real Persian king and his forces. The battle for the future of Persia was soon under way.

It was short-lived. Cyrus, himself too eager for a man-to-man face-off between himself and his brother, dived into the Persian throng and was killed. Greek mercenaries didn't fight for a cause but for money, and the man who paid them was dead. They had no interest in continuing the battle. But they were left with one small problem. How should they get home? Indeed, surrounded by the land mass of Asia and out of sight of the sea, which way was home? Suddenly these 10,000 or so Greek mercenaries must have felt very alone. They were unwelcome strangers in a foreign land, facing the most powerful ruler in the ancient world whom they had just tried to kill.

With impressive honesty, they explained their situation to the now undisputed Persian king (an argument along the lines of 'business is business, no hard feelings') and made an agreement with his henchman, a man called Tissaphernes, to head home. Initially the gambit seemed to have worked. The deal was reached, provisions were bought and the 10,000 started off, watched by the hawk-eyed Tissaphernes every step of the way. But as they progressed homewards, Tissaphernes' intentions to harass them became clearer and clearer. Why wouldn't he? Ten thousand highly-trained Greek mercenaries had come once to Persia – why wouldn't they do so again if the money was right? Better to kill them off than let them live to fight another day. In a daring and outrageous subversion of normal custom, Tissaphernes killed the Greek generals who had come to see him under a truce to negotiate their continued march. The Greek mercenary army, now leaderless, still stuck deep in enemy territory, was a sitting duck.

It was at this time of crisis that Xenophon, that young, rich, eager Athenian who had responded to Cyrus' call – and who would later be hailed as the first 'horse whisperer' for his skill with horses – came into his own. In a march that he was later to recount in his own published writing (and which, rumours tell, is soon to be made into a Hollywood movie), Xenophon led those brave 10,000 warriors through the midst of the enemy, through the barbarous mountains of the Persian empire, all the way to the Black Sea (Map 4). His account says that when they first sighted the sea after months and months of nothing but unending dry land, the Greeks, a people born with sea water in their veins, cried out as one voice with heart-rending simplicity: '*Thalatta! Thalatta!*' ('The sea! The sea!') Their great journey had come to an end. Xenophon returned to Athens as the other Greeks did to their home cities. But the die had been cast. The cities of Greece, after an uneasy truce with the Persians during the Peloponnesian war, had been caught red-handed betting the wrong way against the new Persian king. What's more, it appeared that Sparta was now not so keen to give Persia the Greek cities in Asia Minor it had promised them. And from the Greek perspective, the Persians had proved once again that they could not be trusted: Cyrus had deceived them and Tissaphernes had broken all rules of common god-fearing behaviour. The new century had begun, after a brief entente, with a ten-fold increase in mutual distrust and dislike between the two major powers in the ancient world, a distrust that would echo down the decades to come.

*

While Athens was in the throes of revolution and Persia in a succession crisis, another part of the ancient world was also in the grip of significant upheaval. The island of Sicily had been home to Greek colonies for the past 300 years (Map 3). It was a difficult and treacherous place. The Greek cities there, with their own eclectic populations formed as a result of being major emporia on the international trade network, shared the island with a large selection of native tribes, as well as with Carthaginians, leaders of a powerful naval empire centred around the city of Carthage in north Africa. Sicily, just as it is today, was a melting pot of ethnicities, identities and political affiliations. In 406 BC, just two years before Athens lost the Peloponnesian war, Carthage had made a concerted push to capitalise on that unstable dynamic. Carthage's target was the wealthy Sicilian Greek city of Acragas. The fall of Acragas into Carthaginian hands set off city-wide panic in another major Greek city on the Sicilian coast, Syracuse. At the assembly in the city, no one knew what to do next. In the midst of confusion, a lone man stepped forward: Dionysius. He was just 35 years old and he knew how to play the crowd. He first attacked the politicians and generals of the city for their poor handling of the crisis so far. Everyone loves to know whom to blame. The people loved it. He taunted the city into electing new generals. A fresh start – everyone loves that. He claimed that he needed sole power to be able to deal with the threat – that he alone could lead Syracuse and Sicily to safety in its dark hour. Everyone loves a hero. Dionysius, by working the crowd, and with his flair for theatre (he staged a fake attack on his life to push the people into supporting him further), became sole general – *strategos autokrator* – of Syracuse. Dionysius I was born.

His first year was tumultuous. He conscripted all men under 40 in the city to fight. He led this army against the Carthaginians, only to be pushed back. The fickle crowd, turning against him, let the city's cavalry wreck his home and force his wife to commit suicide. But somehow Dionysius maintained control (of himself and the city). The Carthaginians were pushed back and the island of Sicily was divided: half to Syracuse and half to Carthage. But such a settlement was never supposed to last. Mustering his strength and dismissing his own thoughts of suicide, desperate to prove himself worthy of the title *strategos autokrator* and to hang on to power, Dionysius set off to take back Sicily. By 401 BC, just as Cyrus was killed at Cunaxa in Persia, Dionysius, himself acting now not so differently from a Persian monarch, had every Greek city in Sicily but one under his own personal rule. For the next 30 years, he would continue unceasingly his battle to enlarge his personal dominion, more than once almost losing it all, but in the end taking the fight both to Carthage in north Africa and to the cities in the heel of mainland Italy. Not for nothing did Dionysius I of Syracuse become known as the 'warlord' of Sicily.

What was this man like? Modern-day scholars, just like the ancient sources, are polarised between describing him as the strong man who did what was necessary in the circumstances and the brutal dictator who butchered a nation. He certainly wanted king-like rule over Syracuse for himself and his descendants (he even mentioned it in a treaty with Athens in later decades). He uncompromisingly married his children off in politically advantageous alliances; forced Syracusans to work solely on military projects, and taxed them heavily to pay for his war machine. Syracuse under his rule became the first example of the military-industrial complex – a city whose economic strength depended largely on it continuing to bristle with arms. He forced people from neigh-bouring cities to move to Syracuse to swell the numbers of workers and fighters. He was condemned openly at the Olympic games of 388 BC by the Athenian orator Lysias for being too much like the Persian king. Yet he wrote poetry from the writing desk of the great tragedian Aeschylus and used the pen of Euripides for inspiration. Athens would put up a statue of him in its own Agora in recognition of his achievements in defending Greek cities from the invading Carthaginians. Syracuse entered a period of unrivalled safety and prosperity under his control. Even Isocrates, our watchful political commentator who, by the end of Dionysius I's reign, had begun to write his pamphlets encouraging Athens to step up its game, was tempted by what this man had to offer. Although Isocrates taught his students to loathe the pursuit of power and aggression, he admired this man's ability to use that power to unite and lead. In 368 BC, as Dionysius neared the end of his life, Isocrates sent him a public letter, begging him to save the rest of Greece with his strong-arm tactics. Dionysius I – hero or villain? People of the time, just as we do today, had to decide for themselves.

As the 4th century BC dawned, a very different ancient world had emerged from the one everyone had known and understood just a decade before in the final years of the previous century. Key theatres of operation were in severe flux. Athens was defeated and in the grip of revolution, counter-revolution and self-flagellation. Sparta was now top dog in mainland Greece. The Persian empire was in a succession crisis. Sicily was being torn apart. From the depths of these conflicts, new politics were being born. From Athens rose a democracy more hard-line and uncompromising than ever before. From Persia, a king increasingly distrustful of Greece and a Greece even more distrustful of the king. From Sicily, a powerful king-like individual who, to some, offered the only hope of salvation not just for Sicily, but for some of Greece.

What made this world all the more terrifying was the difficulty in telling friend from foe. A Persian army could have a Spartan general or an Athenian admiral at its head, and Greek mercenary soldiers in its ranks, and still be Greece's enemy. Dionysius I might have been attacking and capturing Greek colonies but he did so with Greek mercenaries and was honoured for it in Athens and courted by Sparta. The rules of the game had changed, but no one was quite sure what the new rules were. Who was your friend and who was your enemy? As the peoples of the ancient world faced up to the new century, no one could be sure who to count on or what would happen next.

CHAPTER 2

~~~

The City of (Crass) Long-Haired Warriors

Who were these people who had managed to bring Athens to its knees, get into bed with Persia and support the pretender Cyrus in his quest for the Persian throne? Who were these Spartans, these warriors of ancient legend and Hollywood fame? Renowned for growing their hair long and combing it before battle, for shunning worldly goods, for teaching their children to be warriors by putting them through constant military training and making them steal and kill, the Spartans were a people as intoxicating and unfathomable to other Greeks as they are to us today. Throughout the ages, their uncompromising manliness and blinkered pursuit of the ultimate warrior lifestyle, which led them to encourage wife-swapping and the exposure of sickly children, has both inspired and horrified. The Spartans make you feel desire, revulsion or grudging admiration mixed with disdain, but never passive disinterest.

They were also not the most diplomatic of people. Put aside their (Hollywood) reputation in earlier periods for pushing messengers into deep wells, their penchant for the austere warrior lifestyle, or even their 'tonight we dine in hell' mentality. The real test of men, some say, is how they deal with success. And the Spartans, at the dawn of the new century, did not measure up so well.

Sparta was now the undisputed power in mainland Greece. With Athens undergoing a revolution, it was the Spartan military machine that everyone now looked to. This was an unusual position for Sparta. It had always been known for its military prowess. But its foreign policy had nearly always been that of an ostrich stuck with its head in the sand. Not for nothing was Sparta the only Greek city still to regard anyone from outside its own walls as foreigners (regardless of whether they came from the next town or Persia). Sparta was isolationist in the extreme, and had been entreated out of its cosy hideaway in the southern Peloponnese only on rare occasions in the preceding century: to defend all of Greece against the Persians and to take on Athens when it threatened Spartan liberty and the Spartan way of life. In short, Sparta was just not used to being in the position Athens had relished: the leading power in Greece and, as a result, Greece's policeman.

The first signs of Sparta's uncouth occupation of the top dog position came soon after its final defeat of Athens. A victory in battle required a monument to commemorate the event. The normal choice for such an important victory was to erect a monument not only at the battle site and in one's home town, but also at the international religious sanctuaries of Delphi or Olympia (Figs 5 and 6) – places where, at regular points, the Greek world gathered for the Olympic games or the Delphic oracle – where the new monument celebrating the victory would be seen by many in all its glory. These two sanctuaries over time became littered with thousands of expensive offerings that, together, provided a material documentary of Greece's history. At Delphi, the ragged crags of the Parnassian mountains, which formed the backdrop to the sanctuary sitting perched on its steep slopes, held in their clutches hoards of glinting gold, silver and bronze. Sparta had always frowned in the past on this kind of showy display (whereas Athens had gone in for it at every opportunity). The Spartans were men who drank blood broth for breakfast, lunch and dinner and weren't allowed to own items of value or use money. Their own city, laid out at the foot of the dramatic, cloud-gathering Taygetus mountain range deep in the southern

Peloponnese (Fig. 4), was famed in the ancient world for being singularly un-ornate and unimpressive. With a spear and shield in their hands, what use had the Spartans for fancy marble and gold sculpted by some big-shot artist – at home or abroad? Sparta itself was a 'spartan' place and the city had never put up an official civic monument at Delphi or Olympia in its history.

But the Spartans were now the lords of mainland Greece – heir to the Athenian crown and the remnants of Athenian empire – and they had to act like it. One can imagine those Spartan ambassadors sent to Delphi by Lysander, the victorious Spartan general, to conduct the negotiations for a victory monument, scratching their heads when confronted with the bewildering array of choices for their victory offering. Delphi was home to thousands of statues, treasuries and offerings in a myriad of designs, materials and sizes, all oscillating around the central temple of Apollo and his oracle, famed throughout the Greek and indeed the known world. What should they pick?

In the end, the Spartan answer was devastatingly simple and unsubtle: let's have everything. We beat the Athenians – we want something like the Athenians have, but bigger. They put up a statue group? Then we'll put one up too, but three times as big. Where? Well, let's put it right next to the Athenian statue group. The Athenians put up a marble colonnaded portico? We'll have one of those too. Let's put it right opposite our statue group. The Athenians had a treasure house? Well, let's rename one of the current treasure houses to honour some of our own heroic warriors. Oh, and let's have some statues of our heroes too, like Lysander, dotted about the sanctuary. Job done. Pass the blood broth, please …

Visiting Delphi today, its impressive remains nestled into the snow-capped mountains, the comparison between the subtle finery of Athenian monuments and the brute, showy force of the Spartan offerings is still palpable. But Sparta had more problems than just its artistic choices. Power at Sparta was split between its two kings, its military generals, its senior advisers and a council of elders. We have already seen how these different branches of government could disagree, when the general Lysander wanted to crush Athens' democratic revolution and the king Pausanias instead wanted to broker a settlement. That stand-off now continued over the question of what Sparta should do next. Should it gracefully retreat, having removed the Athenian threat, to its ostrich-in-the-sand policy or should it step up to lead a new empire? Sparta had fought the war against Athens to free the Greeks from the Athenian empire and Athenian tyranny, and here they were now debating whether to become empire-builders themselves.

Lysander was all for empire. A famous biographer from the ancient world, Plutarch, would later write a life of Lysander. He didn't paint a flattering picture (and Plutarch liked, if at all possible, to paint a flattering picture since his biographies were supposed to be moral lessons to future generations in how to lead a good life). Lysander, Plutarch commented, was not born in the royal line at Sparta, and carried a chip on his shoulder his whole life as a result. His hallmark was ambition, and he would stop at nothing to win. As a boy, he would cheat while playing with other boys their favourite game of knuckle-bones. As a man, he would think nothing of going back on oaths he had sworn. One of the worst insults in ancient Greece was to be called a Cretan – it meant you were a liar and cheat – and Lysander, Plutarch claims, was the ultimate Cretan. He was also, as success courted him, an increasingly vain man. He was the first man to be worshipped with altars and sacrifices like a god while still alive, and the first to have songs of triumph sung about him.

It is no surprise that, in the demise of the Athenian empire, Lysander saw an opportunity to increase his fan base and personal power. He continued to sail around the Aegean sea after his victory over Athens, and wherever Athens had ruled, he stepped in to impose his rule (supposedly in the name of Sparta). Throwing out the present government in whichever city he came to, he substituted each of them with a small group of ten friends. As Plutarch would say, Lysander became more powerful than any Greek before him. Great haughtiness and vicious severity invaded his character, so that he wouldn't hesitate in giving absolute power over cities to his friends and ordering death for every one of his enemies. Sparta was embarrassed enough with Lysander's pursuit of personal empire that it called him back to Sparta soon after.

Lysander's reputation did Sparta no good in its own quest to find a suitable role for itself as the new power in mainland Greece. Lysander had even put friends in charge of cities on the coast of Asia Minor – those same cities that Sparta had sworn to give over to Persia in exchange for Persian aid during the Peloponnesian war. But it was not only Lysander's fault. In the first years of the new century, Sparta managed to alienate not only Persia, but also its many allies back home in Greece. The city of Thebes, for instance, which had fought with Sparta against Athens in 404 BC, was happy to house and cultivate the Athenian democratic revolutionaries later that same year, so aggravated had it been by Sparta's unfair sharing out of the riches taken in war. Sparta did no better in its diplomatic dealing with the small city of Elis, which ran the international sanctuary of Olympia. Locked in a dispute for many years with Elis, Sparta now took advantage of its position as the major power in Greece simply to force admittance to the sanctuary against Elean wishes. Such action against such a sanctuary did not go down very well among the Greeks. The following year, Sparta was called in to settle civil strife in a small settlement in central Greece and did so by simply executing all the troublemakers on both sides. Not long after, the Spartan general who had been serving with Cyrus, the pretender to the Persian throne, now at a loss at what to do since Cyrus was dead, decided to try to compete with Lysander for glory and set off to occupy the rich trading city of Byzantium (modern-day Istanbul). So embarrassed was Sparta by this loose cannon on deck that it had to send a military force to remove its own general from the city.

But perhaps most surprising was Sparta's attitude towards Persia. Sparta, for all its blustering about its military might, and for all that its ego must have been inflated by defeating Athens and taking over the Athenian empire, was one small city with a limited number of warriors.

Persia on the other hand was a mighty empire with virtually limitless supplies of men. Caution was the order of the day. But Sparta not only reneged on its promises to hand over the Greek cities to Persia, not only got caught betting the wrong way in the battle for the Persian throne, but also decided that this was the right time to send an invasion force to protect and extend Greek influence on the coast of Asia Minor. A small exploratory force sent in 400 BC was replaced with a much larger force in 396. It's a sure bet that one of the prime moving forces behind this foreign policy disaster was Lysander, who had been cooling his heels back at Sparta. But he would never have managed to convince the different branches of Spartan government, and particularly to overcome the resistance of king Pausanias, without a clever bit of political manoeuvring. Lysander could never be king, but he could be a king-maker. A few years before, the death of Pausanias' co-king had left an opening for a new king. The dead co-king already had a son who was the natural choice for the throne, but rumours began to circulate that the son might not be Spartan at all, but – shockingly – the illegitimate son of the Spartan queen and an Athenian. That would never do. The only other option was the dead king's half-brother, a man named Agesilaus, who just happened to be a great friend (and most probably the one-time male lover) of Lysander. At age 40, never having expected to be king, Agesilaus was vaulted onto the throne with Lysander standing right behind him. Lysander had himself a puppet king to support his plans for conquest.

Agesilaus needed little convincing. He was all for taking on the might of the Persian empire. In 396 BC, he set sail with Lysander for Persia to square up against the same Persian henchman who had threatened the survival of the 10,000 Greek mercenaries who had escaped Persia a couple of years earlier: Tissaphernes. So deluded was Agesilaus in his quest that he attempted to start the voyage by proclaiming himself the new king Agamemnon, off to take 'Troy' in a new 'Trojan war'. He marched to Aulis, the jumping-off point for the Trojan expedition, and prepared to sacrifice as Agamemnon had done. But the Thebans, who were no longer fans of Sparta and who controlled the area around Aulis, refused him the right to sacrifice and hurried him on his way. Despite this rather inelegant start, Agesilaus and Lysander arrived on the coast of Asia Minor to begin operations against Tissaphernes. They were confronted not only by a Persian army of some strength but also by a Persian navy of even greater strength. What's more, it was a Persian navy commanded by a top Athenian admiral, and the Athenians knew more than anyone about war at sea. Before long, Lysander and Agesilaus, bosom buddies all their lives, were at each other's throats. Lysander was demoted from general to the position of Agesilaus' 'carver of meats', and subsequently sent home in disgrace.

Sparta had not done well in its first years as lords of Greece. Every major city in mainland Greece, which had fought against Athens in the Peloponnesian war less than ten years before, was now in league with Athens against Sparta. Plutarch later commented on Sparta's position by twisting the tale of a comic poet who had joked that Sparta was just like a tavern wench. Sure, Plutarch said, she had given Greece a taste of the fine wine of freedom, but she had then mixed it with so much vinegar you wished you had never drunk it at all.

You might think that, so soon after the 30-year-long Peloponnesian war, no city in Greece would be eager for more conflict. But such was the brutality of Spartan leadership that many Greek cities, themselves so sensitive to the notion of their 'liberty' and anything that threatened it, took to the battlefield once more. It was a war Sparta could never win, not least because it was simultaneously conducted on two fronts: the coast of Asia Minor and the heartland of central Greece. The only way to get from one to the other was to sail, row or march – and it was a long way to go: roughly 500 kilometres, in fact (and that's as the crow flies). Sparta, a city with limited resources, stuck down in the southern tip of Greece (Map 2), was now ludicrously overstretched in its commitment to a two-front ancient world war.

On the coast of Asia Minor, the Spartans continued to face the gathering forces of the Persian Tissaphernes, backed up if necessary by forces from the Persian king himself. In central Greece, Sparta faced the combined forces of the Boeotians, the Thebans, the Corinthians, the Athenians and the Argives, backed up, it was whispered, by Persian gold. Persia might even have bribed the Greek cities to start the war in the first place in order to confront Sparta, already in Asia Minor, with the difficulty of a two-front conflict. Once again, Persian gold, which had been flowing to the Spartans during the Peloponnesian war, swept through Greece, this time to Sparta's enemies. The tables had been turned on Sparta. It had gone from top dog to out-manoeuvred, over-stretched combatant in no time at all. But in true Spartan style, worthy of the men who had blindly held the pass at Thermopylae against the invading Persians 85 years before, the Spartans were not deterred. Led by their new king Agesilaus, thirsty for war and an opportunity to prove himself, they entered the war with, as one scholar has put it, 'the far-sightedness of moles'. They had no strategy for victory and certainly no exit plan. But they knew what Spartans did best: they fought – to the death.

The Spartans were in trouble even before the war really began. Their general Lysander, the hero of the Peloponnesian war turned personal ruler of the Aegean, king-maker and puppet-string puller of the new Spartan king Agesilaus, had been sent home in disgrace by his old friend when they had fallen out while on campaign in Asia Minor. Lysander was never to see his protégé again. Now stuck at home with little to do, it was rumoured that he grew unhappy with Agesilaus' thirst for con-quest, unsatisfied with his lot in life, and unwilling to accept what was going on around him (once you have been honoured as a living god, it's hard to settle for anything less). His thoughts turned, according to Plutarch, to revolution. The details of the plot are shady – many did not emerge until after his death. For in an early battle with the Thebans in 395 BC, Lysander was killed. The fall-out from the death of this Spartan hero-turned-embarrassment-turned-hero-again was twofold. In the immediate aftermath, the war-weary and peace-loving second Spartan king Pausanias, who had counselled a diplomatic approach to Athens and to Persia, was accused of not fighting hard enough to recover the hero Lysander's body from the battlefield. For such dishonourable conduct, Pausanias was put on trial in Sparta and condemned to death. Escaping from his captors, he was forced to flee in disgrace to the nearby city of Tegea and end his days as a refugee claiming sanctuary in the temple of the goddess Athena. It was a sad end for a sane voice in the midst of madmen.

The second outcome of Lysander's death was the rejuvenation of his reputation. Instead of being filthy rich, as many Spartans had suspected (and detested), he was found to be incredibly poor. The Spartans loved him for it – all except his daughter's fiancé, who broke off the engagement when he realised there would be no dowry. At the same time, however, documents came to light that betrayed Lysander's role in plotting a revolution at Sparta. The question was – what to do with them. With Sparta engaged in a war on two fronts, and heavily in need of some heroes to rally the troops, it was decided to bury, quite literally, the evidence with his body and to proclaim him the unblemished hero of Sparta. In the cruel fate of war, the man who promoted peace died a disgraced death in exile and the egotistical revolutionary became a civic legend.

Sparta thus had its hero, but it had also lost two of the most powerful voices in the Spartan command, and most importantly, it had lost the counter-point to Agesilaus' war-trumpeting rhetoric. In the following year, the reality of its position fighting this two-front conflict was to be made painfully apparent. First, off the coast of Asia Minor, the newly arrived Spartan navy was engaged by the Persian navy in what became known as the battle of Cnidus. The Spartans were first and foremost soldiers of the land, not sailors of the seas (their home city was land-locked). The Persian navy, on the other hand, was one of the largest ever seen in the ancient world, knew the coastal waters like the back of its rowing blades, and, as we have seen, was led by an Athenian admiral, battle-hardened from years of Athenian supremacy at sea. The result was little more than a foregone conclusion. Conon, the Athenian admiral leading a Persian fleet, comprehensively beat the Spartan navy. The Athenians, cheering their man from afar despite the fact that he now worked for the Persians, erected a statue of him in the political heart of their city – the Agora. They were so moved by the efforts also of the king of Cyprus to fight Sparta that they put up a statue of the Cypriot king too for good measure. At the heart of newly-reformed democratic Athens, alongside the statues of its old political heroes, now stood the statues of heroes of a very different world: the Athenian working for the Persians and a foreign king.

The loss of control of the sea effectively shut down the war in Asia Minor for Sparta – its troops on land were far too exposed to both Persian troops on land and to Persian raids from the sea. King Agesilaus was, humiliatingly, already on his way back from this theatre of war: Sparta would now concentrate on winning the war at home. Agesilaus, for all his shortcomings, wasn't lacking in military ability. He managed the march back from Asia Minor to mainland Greece in 30 days (which works out at approximately 52 kilometres per day – more than a marathon distance with his army every day). His arrival back in Greece later in the same year as the ill-fated battle of Cnidus, 394 BC, provoked a major confrontation with Sparta's enemies. It was almost as if everyone had been biding their time until Agesilaus arrived.

War in the ancient Greek world was a strange thing, unlike anything we know today. In the ancient world, there was very little in the way of a professional army – in most cities, the people who voted for war picked up their spears and went to war. Mercenary soldiers were a fairly new entity, created as a result of the long civil war in which Greece had recently been embroiled. In most wars, there was a campaigning season curtailed by the cold winter on the one hand, which made movement impossible, and by the agricultural calendar on the other, which mandated when soldiers – farmers in armour – needed to be in the fields attending to their harvests which were their main source of income and sustenance. Campaigns were carefully timed short forays into enemy territory. Battles were balletic engagements in which sides would draw up and subsequently march towards one another. The killing was savage and real enough. However, strict rules covered each side's right to recover their dead and to bury them in due order. Unlike today's world of shock and awe, covert ops, terrorist activity and 24/7 warfare conducted by a professional military, warfare in the ancient world was both more real for average citizens, as they were the ones who fought, and at the same time, given the strict rules and seasons of combat, more distant.

The Spartans had a set routine before battle – it had become part of the Spartan legend and was as important in frightening the enemy as their prowess on the battlefield. As the two sides drew up on 14 August 394 BC in the middle of mainland Greece, the Spartans began their customary preparations. Their flute players began to play and every Spartan warrior put a wreath around his head. Each warrior sat in quiet contemplation of the ensuing mêlée, combing his long hair, taking care to smile and look completely at ease with the situation. They combed their hair, it was whispered, so that they could be sure they looked good in battle. They need not have worried. As they put on their battle dress – the famous crimson cloak, the bronze-covered shield which their mothers told them to come home either holding (alive) or on top of (dead) – and took up their spears, their long hair would have blown about them in the wind like a modern-day shampoo advert. Xenophon, the rich young Athenian who had fought with Cyrus in Persia and subsequently led the 10,000 Greeks out of Asia, said that they dressed that way and left their hair long because it made them 'look taller, more dignified and more terrifying'. Without a doubt, despite their long observation of Spartan ways and their long history of war with them, the other Greek cities must have felt a chill through their spines as the flute players' music was carried to them on the breeze that day, telling them that the Spartans were preparing to do what they did best.

Xenophon himself was present at the battle. He describes the way in which the Spartans lined up in battle order against the combined forces of the Athenians, the Thebans and the Argives. He describes how the two armies marched towards one another in complete silence, the only sounds the heavy chink of their armour and the crisp crunch of sandal on dry grass. When they were only 200 metres apart, the Thebans were the first to raise the war cry – an undulating throaty roar – and began to run headlong at the Spartans. The Spartans held their ground. The Thebans crashed into the Spartan warriors to engage in hand-to-hand combat. The Athenians and the Argives, however, losing their nerve against the Spartan military machine, turned to flee. The Spartans pursued them and inflicted heavy losses. But the Thebans had managed to get through the Spartan ranks all the way to their baggage train and supplies, which were weakly defended, and wrought havoc. When the dust settled, it was hard to know who had won. Xenophon later surveyed the scene of conflict, describing 'the earth stained with blood, friend and enemy lying dead side by side, shields smashed to pieces, spears snapped in two, daggers out of their sheaths – some lying on the ground, others embedded deep in bodies, others still gripped by lifeless hands.' Agesilaus himself, who had made a heroic dash towards the centre of the enemy, was 'wounded in every part of his body with every sort of weapon'. The battle of Coronea, as it became known, was a victory for neither side.

King Agesilaus of Sparta is a hard man to sum up, not least because we have competing ancient sources which give us very different interpretations of the same events. It's like reading about a particular occurrence in today's newspapers, with each paper putting its own spin on the same facts, turning heroes into villains and vice versa. For Plutarch, he was a lame little man of unimposing presence who would bend all the rules for his friends, even if that meant sacrificing the best chances of his city in war. Xenophon, in contrast, argues that, though the course of action he adopted might not always have been the best in hindsight, his motives should never be questioned. Xenophon recounts Agesilaus' heroic qualities (his religious attitude, his sensible handling of money, his courage, his wisdom, his patriotism, his urbanity, the list goes on …)

and then for good measure, repeats them all again, 'so that his praise may be more easily remembered'.

He also had a famous and courageous sister – Cynisca – the first woman to sidestep the rules that only men could compete at the Olympic games, who won the four-horse chariot race twice, in 396 and 392 BC. We often don't hear much about women in the stories of war and politics in the ancient world, not least because they weren't allowed to fight and were denied voting rights in most cities – even democratic Athens did not give women the vote. Women did, though, often play extremely important roles in the home, in religious festivals and in the stories of Greek myth, which, together, governed and structured Greek society. Such positions mirrored the important role of the female gods in the ancient Greek world. The oracle at the great sanctuary at Delphi, for example, was always a woman, and one of the highest religious offices on the Acropolis in Athens was that of the priestess of the temple to Athena. Women were also often the focus of tragedies put on in the theatres at Athens and subsequently across Greece. Pick up any surviving Greek tragedy and it will almost certainly have a female protagonist (even if they are playing either a virgin or a villain, although they had much more varied roles in Athenian comedy). The irony is that we aren't even sure if women were allowed into the theatres in Athens and other parts of Greece to see these plays. In northern Greece, and on the coast of Asia Minor, however, things could be different. As we shall see in later chapters, in these places women could play real-life critical political and military roles, either as the power behind the throne or indeed by being on the throne themselves. As the 4th century BC progressed, women would also start to gain a foothold in other parts of society, even in central Greece: the philosopher Epicurus, born in 340 BC, for example, would be the first to invite women into his school of philosophy in Athens. But at the beginning of the century, among the women of mainland Greece, the women of Sparta were already a special case. Though they had little say in politics and war, they were trained in their own gymnasia to become strong, fit and healthy mothers of

Spartan fighting men. It is no surprise that the first woman to break the Olympic taboo was a Spartan woman.

But whether or not we think his sister's brave actions redeem Agesilaus, or even if we approve of Agesilaus' own intentions and actions, what is certain is that we have not heard the last of him. He recovered from his wounds in battle that day and served as Sparta's king for many years to come. His actions, and his motives, will many times more have to be put in the spotlight.

The result of the battle of Coronea in mainland Greece and the battle of Cnidus off the coast of Asia Minor in 394 BC was that the struggle turned from real conflict into phoney war. In Asia Minor, the Spartan forces were withdrawn and a hurried (and white-washed) peace with Persia was agreed. In mainland Greece, neither side could afford another large set-piece battle – the losses were too great. Both sides were reduced to lightning-strike skirmish tactics, picking at one another like pigeons grabbing crumbs from a picnic table. Agesilaus, despite his injuries, had to march his men back to Sparta right past the newly erected hero-tomb to his one-time lover, supporter for the king-ship, betrayer and now newly-crowned Spartan legend, Lysander. How galling it must have been for this most proud of Spartan men.

But the opposition alliance of the Greek cities of Corinth, Argos, Thebes and Athens was faring no better. Only the Thebans had distinguished themselves at the battle of Coronea; everyone else had shown ever so publicly how little stomach they had for a fight. In typical Greek fashion, this tenuous alliance of cities, held together only by their mutual fear of Sparta, now began to turn upon itself. In particular, Corinth lost its nerve for the fight, so Argos forced a coup in which Corinth lost its right to decide anything and became a satellite of the city of Argos. Far from succeeding in extricating itself from the war, Corinth's attempted retreat only made the city the epicentre of the fight. Sparta carried on gnawing at Corinth's land and defences like a dog with its bone, now helped by some Corinthians who objected to Argos' takeover, and even by some Thebans who were annoyed at Argos throwing its weight around. The war picked up an element of black comedy as the two sides disintegrated into multiple factions fighting over symbolic victories. In June 390 BC, Agesilaus had the temerity to take over the running of the athletic games taking place at the Corinthian sanctuary of Isthmia, to which all Greeks were invited, and set up honours to the winners. As he left, Argos came in to take back the sanctuary, re-held the games and set up a second winners' list as if Agesilaus had never been there.

Into this mess was injected still further Persian capital. Concerned that the cities of mainland Greece were not harrying Sparta enough, the Persians sent the Athenian admiral Conon with his Persian fleet to Greece. The conquering hero showed up with a huge armada in one hand and the offer of more gold in the other. The alliance against Sparta was stuck between the devil and the deep blue sea. They remembered all too well the lethal combination of Spartan and Persian forces from the Peloponnesian war. But they had little stomach for taking Persia's money to continue the fight now against Sparta. They opted, of course, for the lesser of the two evils, Persian money. From the Persian perspective, the objective was to quieten Sparta down and not, in the process, to allow any other Greek city to become so strong that it in turn might contemplate taking the fight to Persia. As a result, the war turned from black comedy to bedroom farce. Persian ambassadors dashed around Greece, making bold promises, exiting from one city through one gate just as Spartan ambassadors turned up at another gate with equally bold offers. Who would end up in bed with whom?

Athens benefited most from this game of bed-hopping. It managed to rekindle important contacts and alliances on the coast of Asia Minor and to extract enough money and Persian assistance to begin to rebuild its city walls, humiliatingly torn down in the difficult days of 404 BC, so that now, once again, they safely cocooned the city and its harbour. But in 391 BC, in the middle of this phoney-war-turned-bedroom-farce, a real opportunity for peace emerged. Sparta, Thebes and Persia were on board. Argos and Corinth were against it. Athens held the deciding hand. The city was divided on what to do. Could it get better terms if

it continued to play the dangerous game of courting Persia and fighting Sparta? Debate in the assembly at Athens raged on for hours. In
the end, Athens voted not only to reject the treaty, but to indict all the
negotiating team who had been involved with it and defy the wishes of
both Sparta and Persia. Athens, it seems, had become – once again – a
little too big for its boots.

CHAPTER 3

❦

Dancing with the Persian King

A fter any battle, each city mourned its dead. For Athenians, one of the most important parts of that process was the eulogy given back at home. This was not simply a speech given at each warrior's funeral by a close relative or friend – this was a speech given for all the fallen men in a particular battle or campaign by one man chosen to represent the city. Crowded into the public graveyard of Athens, situated just outside the city walls by one of its most important ceremonial entrance gates (Map 1; Fig. 3), Athenians gathered to hear this speech. It was given by a man thought worthy of the occasion, someone who had played an important role in the city's affairs and who carried the authority to deliver such a key-note address. Great men had been chosen to give this speech. Pericles – the heroic leader of Athens during the height of its empire who had finally succumbed to plague during the Peloponnesian war – had used this speech not just to honour the Athenian dead, but to outline the very nature of the democracy they had been fighting for. Excerpts from his speech that day were plastered on the sides of buses in London in the run-up to the First World War to inspire the nation, and his words are still today one of the primary texts for anyone keen to understand what democracy means and how it can be achieved. The eulogy speech was thus a chance to reiterate what Athens was, what it wanted to be, and despite the hardships and the losses, the progress it was making. This eulogy was not just a reflection on the past, it was a mandate for the future. It was a vital linchpin in the business of showing what Athens was about.

With so much riding on this one speech, it was an understandably double-edged sword for anyone given the honour of delivering it. This was one man trying to sum up, capture and inspire the mood of an entire city, before an expectant and ill-tempered crowd surrounded by the ancestral dead of Athens. During the ill-fated, farcical war with Sparta at the beginning of the 4th century, a man called Lysias was chosen to give the eulogy. His job was unenviable. Athens was a new militant democracy with the scars of oligarchy and revolution still scabbing, engaged in a pointless and draining war with its old adversary, now caught up in a new world of warfare across continents in which Athenians fought for their former arch-enemy the Persians and took their money. Lysias, a survivor of those revolutions in Athens and now a practising orator in the law courts, somehow had to make sense of all this, make sense of the loss of Athens' proud sons, give comfort to their grieving widows and families, and at the same time inspire and reassure them that Athens was heading in the right direction, that it was bravely and forcefully fighting for its place in this new world.

Whether they liked it or not, Athens' world was about to get a whole lot stranger. Their bellicose rejection of the peace negotiations in 391 BC had left a very sour taste in the mouth of the Persian king. For all his power and might, he did not want this conflict with Sparta to carry on for much longer. He had bigger fish to fry. The much larger, more profitable land of Egypt was causing trouble and the Persian king wanted to focus all of his attentions – and forces – against them. Moreover, he could do with some battle-hardened Greek mercenaries to fill out his forces. After all, he had been in a prime position to see not only their effectiveness when they had marched into Asia under the command of his brother Cyrus, trying to kill him and take his throne, but also their tenacity in being able to march out of Asia again despite his best efforts. But Greek mercenaries were unavailable because many were engaged in this persistent and debilitating war in Greece. A settlement to the

Greek problem would enable the Persian king to recruit them for his campaign against Egypt.

This, combined with the Athenians' rather arrogant rejection of the peace of 391 BC, encouraged the Persian king to listen more attentively to the Spartan ambassadors than he had before. The Persian court worked very differently to the Athenian assembly. In Athens, everything was debated out in the open, everyone could have a say, everyone voted on the course of action and everyone could see each other's decision. In the Persian court, however, everything was done behind closed doors. Decisions were taken with a nod of the king's head, a whisper in his ear, a discreet to-ing and fro-ing of courtiers and ambassadors from one room to another. Here intrigue, patronage and flattery were the weapons of choice in the decision-making battle. And here, for once, the Spartans had a man up to the task. His name was Antalcidas. Skilfully and carefully he poured poison into the king's ear about the Athenian actions. Without skipping a beat, he poured an equal amount of honey over the wounds caused by Sparta's own rash actions against the Persian king. Before long, the Athenian admiral who had so successfully led the Persian navy to victory against the Spartans was in prison. Before much longer, the Persian king and all his henchmen were dancing to Antalcidas' tune.

There was only one problem: one man, Pharnabazus, a Persian who was still holding out against Antalcidas' magic words and who argued that Persia should not trust the Spartans. His opinion couldn't simply be ignored – he had been part of Persia's most successful naval and military engagements in recent years. Nor could he simply be killed without first pinning some crime on him. But for Antalcidas' plan to work, this man had to be neutralised. The Persian king provided the solution. Recalling this obstinate man from the front line of battle to the court of the king, the Persian monarch proposed to honour him for his services with the offer of his own daughter's hand in marriage. If he refused, it would be an insult that could not go unpunished. If he accepted, marriage and a permanent home deep within the Persian empire would mean that he could do little to affect politics on the front line with Greece. Either way, he was taken out of the equation.

Now that Persia was in bed with Sparta, Athens' position looked very different. The whole balance of world power around them had changed again in a matter of months after little more than a series of whispered discussions behind closed doors. But Antalcidas knew that it would take more than this to bring the Athenians to the negotiating table. He encouraged the Persian and Spartan navy to harass Athens' vital strategic interests in the Aegean sea. His plan was little short of genius. With a hint of misdirection and a pinch of trickery, Antalcidas cornered the Athenian fleet in a trap. They surrendered without a fight. Without losing a ship, but with only his own winged words in a few well-chosen ears, Antalcidas had brought the war to an end.

Now came the greatest surprise of all. In any normal Greek conflict, the sides would gather to hammer out the peace terms (most normally a return to the status quo). But this was no normal Greek conflict and this would be no normal settlement. The Persian king wanted matters sorted out and so, behind closed doors, the peace terms were decided, not in Greece, but in the Persian capital. In 386 BC, one of the king's henchmen sailed to Greece and arrived in the city of Sparta, not to negotiate terms, but to announce them – the Persian king dictating the terms of a Greek peace. In the memories of those few still alive who had fought against the Persian invasion of Greece in the century before, it was the end of the world as they knew it: where had the liberty of Greece been lost on this road? The whole of Greece was now dancing to the Persian king's tune.

The meeting to hear the terms of the peace was attended by ambassadors from all cities of Greece involved in the war. But perhaps surprisingly, the man who had so brilliantly manipulated the Persians and ended the war, Antalcidas, who had himself been instrumental in agreeing the peace terms with the Persian king, took no public role in its pronouncement. He preferred to stay in the shady background, well aware of the furore it would produce and wanting no part of it. The man who stepped forward instead to orchestrate this charade was none other than the Spartan king Agesilaus – the lame, unimposing little man who had taken the fight to Persia and been recalled to Greece to face up against the Thebans, only to limp home badly injured to confront the growing legend of his one-time lover and best friend Lysander. Now fully recovered, and still eager for war, this most undiplomatic of men undertook to chair one of the most diplomatically important meetings Sparta ever hosted.

The text of the Persian king's ultimatum for peace was read out and Xenophon, the rich young Athenian general who had marched the 10,000 out of Asia back in 401 BC, and who keenly followed Spartan politics, later recorded the terms in his history of the Greek world. The tone of the decree was stunning. It began not with 'The Persian king would like to entreat the Greeks to agree …', but quite simply: 'The Persian king thinks …' The Greek cities on the coast of Asia Minor, which he had been promised by the Spartans for the last 30 years, would be his. So would Cyprus. The Athenians could have three little islands in the Aegean. Every other city in the Greek world was to be autonomous. Everyone was to lay down their weapons and anyone who broke the terms of the peace was to be visited by the full rage and military wrath of the Persian king himself.

The crux of this peace diktat was not, as it might appear at first reading, the Persian king's tone, or even his taking of the Greek cities in Asia Minor. The provision that sent shock waves through Greece and that changed Greek politics for the rest of the century was the stipulation that all Greek cities were to be autonomous. On the face of it, that doesn't seem much. Had not all Greek cities been fighting one another for the sake of their freedom and liberty over the last 50–60 years? The problem, as ever in international treaties, was what was meant by 'autonomous'. Empire was certainly out – never more could something like the Athenian empire of the previous century be realised. But what about alliance? Or federation? Just how legal was any kind of political organisation involving more than one city, if every city was mandated to remain 'autonomous'? What made the ambiguity of the treaty worse was that Sparta, as Persia's new best friend, was appointed de facto enforcer of the treaty's terms, with recourse to Persia if things went seriously wrong. The most ambiguous of terms – which went right to the essence of Greek politics, identity and inter-city relations – was in the hands of the most unambiguously undiplomatic of cities, and more specifically in the hands of the most unsubtle, and unfair, of men – Agesilaus.

His reign as the Persian king's peace enforcer did not start well. Thebes objected immediately. It was the centre of a loose alliance of cities called the Boeotian confederacy – a little like the federal union of the USA today. Sparta, and more specifically Agesilaus, demanded that Thebes disband the confederacy as it contravened the terms of the peace. Thebes' protests were muted as Agesilaus sent his army imme- diately marching towards it. The city of Argos too protested that the treaty's terms meant the loss of its influence at Corinth. The Spartan army was sent also to Argos to silence the protest. But did the Spartans disband their own control over the cities and peoples immediately surrounding Sparta, from which they had been press-ganging whole communities into Spartan slavedom for generations? No, they did not. The enforcers of the king of Persia's peace were also its most grievous violators.

More than that, they were outright manipulators of the peace for their own ends on the national stage. Not content with one rule for them and a different rule for everyone else, Agesilaus used his new- found role as 'peace enforcer' as a cover for a not-so-secret war of aggression and domination over the rest of Greece. Nearby cities were forced to tear down their walls, dismantle their city infrastructure and submit to Spartan will. Cities at the other end of Greece were attacked on the flimsiest of excuses. But most serious of all, Agesilaus used the king's peace to get even with the enemy that had so badly damaged his reputation and left his body – and more importantly his pride – full of holes: Thebes. Marching north from Sparta on the pretence of attacking a city in northern Greece for breaching the peace, the Spartan army just so happened to pick a road that led them by Thebes. While passing, it just so happened that some upstanding Theban citizens (read pro-Spartan informants) informed them that Thebes was thinking about (just thinking about ...) infringing the terms of the king's peace. The Spartan army needed nothing more. The Thebans, in the middle of celebrating an important religious festival, looked up from their sacrifices to find the Spartan army invading and occupying their city in the name of the king's peace, which insisted on the right of every Greek city to be autonomous. In the name of freedom, Sparta installed a garrison of soldiers in the centre of downtown Thebes and forced a puppet government of pro-Spartans on the city.

Sparta's playground bully tactics did not endear it to the rest of Greece. In part, such tactics were the direct result of the bullish leaders whom the Spartan citizens chose to listen to. They had listened to the battle-enthusiast Lysander rather than the much more sensible, conciliatory king Pausanias, whom they had eventually attempted to execute. They now listened to the even more battle-crazed, ego-bruised Agesilaus, rather than those within the Spartan system who called for Sparta's enforcement of the king's peace to be more gentle and diplomatic. Antalcidas, the diplomatic dancer who had so brilliantly won over the Persian king and orchestrated the peace deal, was now swept aside along with his calls for moderation and care. Listening to men like Lysander and Agesilaus had brought Sparta out of isolationism and won them control of Greece; but now it also threatened to undermine their position, as opposition to their chosen tactics hardened across Greece. Even Xenophon, the Athenian general who led the 10,000 out of Asia, who loved Sparta and Spartan ways more than he did his own city of Athens, who was at that very moment in the process of moving to Sparta and putting his own children into the Spartan education system, would later comment that, while in the old days, the cities of Greece would call upon Sparta to lead them against evil, now those same cities called upon each other to rid themselves of the evil of Sparta.

There is a limit, however, to how much you can blame the leaders alone for Sparta's actions. After all, the Spartan system of government was a complicated one, and an individual Spartan could do little unless the different branches of government agreed. Men like Agesilaus got their way only because they were able to convince their fellow Spartans that theirs was the right course of action for Sparta. But what the Spartans failed to realise in those years after the king's peace was that they were slowly digging their own grave. Almost constant warfare against Athens, followed by a war on two continents, now followed by a prolonged period of acting as Greece's policeman, put incredible stress on a small society which, in the past, had normally refused to get involved outside of its boundaries.

The first tell-tale sign of such stress was Spartan numbers. Sparta was an elite warrior society which allowed only the healthiest boys and girls to survive, in order to breed the best fighters and mothers of fighters. It resisted almost all attempts at immigration from other Greek cities and saw everyone else as foreigners. It is no surprise that, as more and more Spartans died in battle, it became harder and harder for Sparta to replenish its battle-lines. Rearing a Spartan warrior was a lengthy business, and even with every Spartan woman and every Spartan man doing their bit, the numbers of elite soldiers that Sparta could send out to battle steadily decreased, at the same time as Spartan deployment was being increased due to their (self-imposed) role as Greece's policeman (or as most other cities saw it, Greece's playground bully). A thinning population was being spread ever more thinly in an increasingly hostile world.

But there were other, perhaps even more serious, signs of fatal flaws in the Spartan machine. Sparta was a society based on the principle of equality. If you made it to become a Spartan, you were equal with your fellow Spartans (with the exception of the kings of course). This sense of equality was driven into Spartan skulls in every possible way. It is perhaps no accident, given Sparta's dislike of spotlighting the individual, that, despite their successes, no portrait of Lysander or Agesilaus survives from the ancient world. Such an emphasis on collective equality was reflected also in the fact that no Spartan was allowed to amass personal wealth. Every Spartan male belonged to one of a number of dining clubs, in which all members, regardless of their role in the government, sat together for every meal and ate the same food. In theory, this equality demonstrated what bonded Sparta together against the rest of the world. But in the early years of the 4th century BC, that equality came under huge strain. As Sparta took over the remains of the Athenian empire and continued to play a central role in Greek affairs, not to mention being in league with Persia, money started to roll into the city. It was impossible to stop people hoarding it. The rules of Spartan society, laid down some 300 years before, bent under the pressure and Spartans were allowed to keep money – at least for 'public use', whatever that was supposed to mean. High-profile scandals of individuals who gathered vast wealth followed. Spartan men were even said to be heard boasting of their material possessions – an insult to the Spartan way of thinking and moral code. And the biggest problem with this inrush of wealth was where it went: not to every Spartan citizen, but as money has a tendency to do, it pooled in the pockets of an elite few. Spartan society, which preached equality, was being undermined by the irrepressible flow of money, gathering around small inequalities in the system, eventually creating an unmissable wealthy elite. The fabric of Spartan society was being rotted away as a result of Sparta's own success on the international stage.

This increasing sense of inequality created by the influx of wealth was coupled with the impact of inequalities built into the Spartan system. In Sparta, unlike most cities in ancient Greece, both men and women could inherit land. More importantly, unlike many other cities, land had to be split equally between all children. It was part and parcel of the code of equality that guided the Spartan ideal. But, as time progressed, it meant that a large amount of Spartan land came to be owned by women (about 40 per cent in the 4th century) and the plots of land owned by Spartan men and women got smaller and smaller, as they were divided and divided over the generations. This created a real problem for the Spartan male. A Spartan male had to produce a certain amount of food from his own land to bring to his male-only dining club. Without it, he couldn't be a member. And if he wasn't a member of a dining club, he wasn't a Spartan citizen. The ever-reducing size and number of plots of land available to Spartan men placed enormous stress on many Spartans' ability to fulfil the obligations of citizenship. Spartan men increasingly fell out of the privileged circle of citizenship. The poor got poorer, just as the rich were getting richer thanks to the influx of foreign wealth into Sparta. The gap between rich and poor became wider and more noticeable, placing even more strain on the apparent 'equality' of Spartan society. It also further depleted Spartan military numbers. Spartans who failed in their obligations to the dining clubs were no longer Spartan citizens and thus couldn't fight as Spartan warriors. Sparta was killing off its military strength thanks to its own inheritance rules.

Sparta was thus, despite its apparent strength in Greece in the 380s BC, despite its sabre-rattling and playground bully tactics, slowly dying as its society was being torn apart at its very core. The Spartans were not totally unaware of their increasing vulnerability. To help boost their numbers, they accepted help in 387 BC from the warlord of Sicily, Dionysius I, who had been so effective in taking control of many of the cities in that perilous country. But Sparta's most critical headache wasn't the other cities of mainland Greece, it was much closer to home. For generations, Sparta had forced the people living in the region around Sparta to serve as its slaves. This made them very different from most other Greek cities, whose slave populations were non-Greeks enslaved following conquest outside of Greece. The Spartan slaves, or helots as they were called, from the area around Sparta called Messenia (Map 2), were Greeks with a single ethnic background. They were one people, one community, with a common identity. This unity and sense of identity made the helots very difficult to keep under control. Sparta saw itself, rightly, as surrounded by an enslaved army of Greeks who would try to rebel at any moment. To counter this ever-present fear of rebellion, Sparta attempted to repeatedly bludgeon the message of Spartan supremacy into the helots. All Spartan males when they came of age were required to kill a helot as proof of their manhood. Culls of the bravest helot males would occasionally be undertaken. But Sparta was unable to quell either its own fears or the helots' appetite for revolt. Several times in the previous century, the helots had revolted, always attacking when Sparta was at its weakest. Sparta had tried to insulate itself by inserting into any peace treaty it signed with other Greek cities a clause which forced those cities to come to Spartan aid if the helots rebelled. But now Sparta was more afraid than ever before. Spartan soldiers were away from home for increasingly long periods of time acting as Greece's policeman/bully, leaving the back door of their own city undefended. Sparta was suffering from an acute shortage of men and a rising tide of social inequality. It was relying on the helots more and more in battle (there would soon be seven helots for every one Spartan in their battle lines). And it had fewer and fewer friends to call upon if the helots did rise up. Sparta, for all of its bravado, was growing weaker by the year and it feared that the helots could smell blood in the water.

Sparta wasn't the only city in Greece to feel the strain of the wars that gutted Greece in the first decades of the 4th century BC. Athens too, of course, had had its own share of revolution and was also struggling with the difficulties of increasing social inequality. Certain individuals grew wealthier and displayed their wealth in more and more obvious ways, such as by erecting large individualised gravestones for themselves in the same public cemetery in which Lysias had offered his civic eulogy for all the Athenian war dead (Fig. 3). Such an expensive way of focusing on an individual's death ran contrary to Athenian democratic ideology, which mandated that all citizens had an equal say and carried equal weight, and served only to make obvious the growing gap between the haves and the have-nots. Many other Greek cities similarly experienced social instability, falling prone to what the Greeks called *stasis* – internal civil strife.

It was in this turbulent world that our future political commentator, Isocrates, opened his school of education in 390 BC and that Plato, who, like Isocrates, had been a disciple of the unfortunate Socrates, began his own philosophy school, the Academy, in Athens in 387 BC (Map 1). It was into these fraught times that the philosopher Aristotle, who would challenge the Greeks', not to mention our own, conceptions of the world, was born in 384 BC in northern Greece. And in the very same year but at the opposite end of Greece, the Athenian orator Demosthenes was born, who was to prove so crucial in framing Greece's response to critical shifts in the balance of power in the ancient world. The formative experience of these two great thinkers and political actors, growing up at different ends of the country, was the difficult and dangerous world of Greece under the auspices of the king's peace, brutally and unfairly enforced by a city walking, not even blindly, towards its own destruction.

In the midst of this confusion, two voices evoked clearly the difficult world in which the Greeks found themselves. Both sought a platform that would enable them to speak to all of Greece, to move above the stasis and inter-city squabbles that divided them and to reach out instead to what united them. They came to the sanctuary of Olympia when the Olympic games were in full swing (Fig. 6). The Olympics was a special time for ancient Greece. All wars stopped. Everyone had the right to travel free from hindrance. Members of every Greek city, whatever their differences, came to the religious sanctuary of Olympia in southern Greece to stand shoulder to shoulder, competing and watching the athletic triumphs. It was a unique opportunity in which to address the Greek world free from the fetters of normal politics. On the steps of the temple of Zeus at the heart of the sanctuary, two men stood in the place where the father of history, Herodotus, had, 40 years before, supposedly read out his history of the Greek world and argued, among other things, for what the Greeks had in common. The first of these men was none other than the Athenian Lysias, who had been called upon to deliver the eulogy for the Athenian dead during the recent debilitating conflict with Sparta. Not content with speaking to Athenians, he sought to take his message to the wider Greek world. His words offered a warning: beware the power of the warlord Dionysius I in Sicily and the Persian king. For Lysias, Greece's path to destruction lay in the megalomaniac desires of these powerful individuals, with which Greece was becoming more and more closely entwined.

Eight years later, our political commentator and overseer of the age, Isocrates, also stepped forward at the Olympic games. In 380 BC, at the height of the confusion and social instability sweeping Greece, as resentment against Sparta came to a head and as people began to believe that traditional models of Greek politics were dying a death, Isocrates stepped forward to publish his argument that it was time for a new course. It was perhaps the finest moment of his life. Athens and Sparta must stop their suicidal wars and recognise each other's potential and past glories. Greece must unite in a combined war against Persia. The message was clear: the only war that was worth more than peace was a war against their old enemy Persia.

Greece's dilemma was encapsulated in those two speeches. Should it cling to the traditional politics of the day, in which cities vied with each other for supremacy in Greece, or should it unite once more, reject the increasing influence of Persia and engage on a war to end all wars? We don't know who was listening that day in Olympia. We don't know what the reaction to either of these speeches was like. But we do know now, as the Greeks listening to Isocrates in that hot summer of 380 BC could not, that the balance of power in Greece was about to undergo another seismic shift, as rebellion against Spartan supremacy got under way.

CHAPTER 4

~∾~

'Serious Business for Tomorrow'

G oing north from Athens, the modern traveller is immediately hit by how quickly the landscape of Greece changes. Gone are the dry, dusty hillsides around Athens, to be replaced by a lush greenness that could easily be mistaken in parts for English countryside. This area of Greece, Boeotia, is a land of immense, green fertile valleys punctuated by high mountains, which clean the mind and lungs after the physical and mental assault of the frenzied activity of modern-day Athens. Boeotia's main city, then as now, is Thebes. Visitors to Greece today don't pay much attention to Thebes. The guidebooks describe it as an area only for the 'veteran traveller'. Landlocked, the city has no beaches to offer and few archaeological sites to compare with other treasures like Delphi, Olympia and Athens. Speeding north on the main motorway, it is easy to miss and quickly forgotten.

2,400 years or so ago, however, Thebes was quickly becoming one of the most powerful cities in one of the most strategically important areas of ancient Greece. Thanks to vast valley plains, natural lakes and fertile soils, this area of Greece had the potential to fuel a self-sufficient prosperity hard to match elsewhere. It was a prize worth fighting for. More importantly, Boeotia occupied the middle ground between south-ern Greece, the home of cities like Athens and Sparta, and northern Greece, the home of powerful communities like the Thessalians and the more shadowy, exotic, but potentially equally powerful Macedonians and Illyrians. As a result of its position in the centre of Greece, Boeotia had often served as the key battle ground for wars between north and south, between Athens, Sparta and their respective allies during the Peloponnesian war, but also for Greece's stands against the invading Persians in the previous century. Here in Boeotia can be found the sites of famous battles that changed the course of Greek history – Plataea, Tanagra, Leuctra and Chaeronea among them. To walk the fertile fields and valleys of Boeotia is to walk in the footsteps, and over the forgotten bones, of thousands of soldiers who died there to preserve the freedom of their own cities and that of Greece itself. To stand there is to stand in the place where the fate of Greece was decided time and time again. In the ancient world it was known simply as the dance-floor of Ares, the god of war (Map 2).

Thebes itself had an odd reputation in ancient Greece. Watch any self-respecting Greek tragedy (most of which were written to be performed in Athens), and Thebes is always a problem town. If brothers are killing brothers, fathers driving their sons to suicide, or, worst of all, sons killing their fathers and sleeping with their mothers, it's a safe bet that such action is set in Thebes. But in the first decades of the 4th century BC, Thebes had quickly gained a more hard-nosed military reputation. It had fought with Sparta against Athens in the Peloponnesian war, quickly become disgusted with Spartan imperial behaviour, dumped its former ally, and housed the Athenian revolutionaries who launched their attempt to restore Athenian democracy from Thebes. Theban warriors had been the only ones, in the recent war with Sparta, to distinguish themselves in battle – pushing through the Spartan ranks while others turned tail and fled. Thebes had been responsible for the death of the Spartan hero Lysander and inflicted serious wounds on the Spartan king Agesilaus. Thebes had later attempted to stand up to Agesilaus' imposition of the king's peace and his forcing of Thebes to disband the confederacy of cities in Boeotia over which Thebes presided. In return, Sparta had sent an army on the flimsiest of pretexts to occupy Thebes, and sentenced to death those in the city who dared to speak out against Sparta.

In the summer of 380 BC, it seemed, for all Sparta's weaknesses and Thebes' efforts, that Sparta was unstoppable. Sparta's control over southern and central Greece seemed firm and irreversible to almost everyone. But that was not the case for a small group of Theban rebels. A handful of anti-Spartan conspirators had managed to flee Thebes and had found refuge in none other than the city of Athens, whose own revolutionaries had been welcomed by Thebes 24 years earlier. These Thebans used their time in Athens to plot their revenge on Sparta. It was a dangerous time to be anti-Spartan – even in Athens. The puppet government installed in Thebes by Sparta was well aware of these men hiding in Athens and sent spies to keep an eye on them. Deciding they were too much of a threat, the pro-Spartan government sent assassins under cover to Athens to exterminate the plotters. But, by sheer fortune or clever evasion, the assassins managed to eliminate only one of them.

Throughout the early part of the following year, 379 BC, with the constant threat of assassination hanging over them, this small band, hidden deep under cover in Athens, continued to lay their plans for revolution at Thebes. By winter 379 BC, they were ready to put their plans into action. One day in December, this small number of would-be heroes slipped out at dawn from the city of Athens. Fearing that their every move was being watched, they attempted to disguise their true purpose by dressing up in long cloaks and taking with them hunting dogs and nets, so that anyone might think they were simply going out of the city to hunt. They were no more than twelve men – twelve men walking to Thebes to topple a puppet government and, in turn, to rebel against the military dictator of Greece.

They were not, of course, completely alone. They had managed to keep up secret communication with sympathisers still within the city of Thebes. These sympathisers had promised them their loyalty if they made it back into the city, especially if they brought with them promises of Athenian support for the rebellion. This the group of Thebans, walking slowly towards their home town, now had. Athens had promised, if the rebellion was successful, to support it with Athenian troops on the ground to protect Thebes against Spartan reprisals. This rebellion was no longer intended simply to free Thebes; it was the start of something much larger – a general uprising of the cities of Greece against the now much-hated Spartan supremacy. These men were the touch-paper for the fire of Greek revolution. As those twelve men walked towards Thebes, nervously avoiding anyone they met on the roads in case their disguise failed to hide their true intentions, they must have realised they were carrying with them the hopes not just of their own city, but of many. On the shoulders of these twelve lay the dream of escape from Spartan tyranny and a new beginning for Greece.

They would never know how close they came to being thwarted before they had even begun. On the day before they were supposed to set out from Athens, one of the sympathisers inside the city of Thebes had panicked and ordered a message be sent to Athens to tell them not to come. The messenger went to his house to fetch his horse to ride post-haste to Athens. But he couldn't find his horse's bridle. Searching high and low for it all over his house, he finally asked his wife if she had seen it. She replied that she had, that their neighbour's wife had asked her if they could borrow it and, given that she didn't think her husband needed it, she had lent it willingly. The messenger was stunned. Without a bridle he couldn't ride; without riding he couldn't deliver his message in time. And given the secrecy of the communication, he couldn't simply go round Thebes asking to borrow a bridle because he had an urgent message to deliver to Athens. Screaming abuse at his wife for doing something without his authority, to which she probably replied with equal venom that she wasn't a mind-reader and that it was only a stupid bridle, their squabble ended in a public brawl from which he stormed off, believing the only solution to be not to deliver the message at all. The message was never delivered, so the plotters left Athens on the appointed day and the wheels of revolution were set in motion thanks to an unknown woman who had chosen to do her neighbour a favour the day before.

The conspirators finally arrived at Thebes late in the day to be greeted by a cold wind swirling round the city walls. To avoid detection, they split up and, ditching their hunting costume for peasant clothes, each entered the city through a different gate. The cold wind aided their secret entry, giving each man good reason to draw his cloak high across his face to protect himself from the wind and mask his identity. Making their way through the back streets of Thebes, they arrived at the house of a man called Charon. Charon had bravely offered his home as a safe house and meeting place for the conspirators, from where they would launch their attack on the four main leaders of the pro-Spartan puppet government. If they could kill these four men, they reckoned, and take control, the rest of Thebes would follow them. With the Theban citizenry on their side, and Athens' troops not far behind, they thought they could take on the Spartan military garrison lodged in the city.

The four targets were at two different locations that night. But the conspirators had one ace up their sleeve – a double agent working for the pro-Spartan leaders, someone whom the pro-Spartans trusted implicitly. This man had arranged a drinking party for two of the pro-Spartans that very night, and would ensure that they were incredibly drunk by the time the conspirators arrived, making them easy prey. But the other two leaders would not be so easy to catch, particularly as one of them was the cleverest of all the pro-Spartans. Trusting no one, and refusing alcohol in case it dulled his wits, he remained well protected at home, as did his fellow leader in a nearby house. The conspirators would have to storm both of these houses, overpower the guards and servants, and get to the leaders before they had a chance to escape.

Forty-eight men gathered in the house of Charon that night to take part in the coup. As they were passing out weapons and armour, a knock came at the door. They froze in silence as Charon went to open it. Outside was a messenger from the two pro-Spartan leaders at the drinking party. They summoned Charon immediately, the messenger said. Charon had no choice but to go. Collecting his thoughts before leaving, he told the 48 men hidden in his house his worst fears: that news of the plot had leaked. The men looked back at him, knowing that they had gone past the point of no return. Their only hope lay in Charon being able to convince the rulers that there was no truth to the charges. Charon was no coward, but even he was scared by what lay ahead of him. So deep, though, was his commitment to his friends and to their revolutionary cause that he left them in charge of his handsome fifteen-year-old son, with orders to kill him if his father should betray his friends that night.

Appearing in front of the pro-Spartan leaders in the middle of their drinking banquet, Charon answered their questions on hazy rumours that had reached them of the return of the anti-Spartan exiles to Thebes. He resolutely denied everything, making light of the claims and of the stupidity of anyone who would dare to threaten the Spartans. The double agent, who was supervising the drinking party, now intervened to add his ridicule to the report of the return of the exiles and to encourage the men back to their drinking. They agreed to let it go and sent Charon on his way.

The conspirators, who had not known whether the next knock on the door would be Charon returning or the Spartan garrison arriving to kill them all, rejoiced at Charon's news and immediately set out to put the plot in motion before any more reports of their presence in Thebes could be fed back to the leaders. Heading out into the bitter wind, now mixed with snow and drizzle, they divided into two groups, one to take the two drunken banqueters, the other to take the houses where the last two leaders lived. As they marched quickly through the streets, they couldn't know that their plan once again hung on a knife-edge. A messenger, unannounced, had arrived from Athens and managed to slip past the double agent overseeing the banquet, to place a letter directly into the hands of one of the pro-Spartan leaders. This letter contained the details of the entire plot and even the name of the double agent. Someone back in Athens, it seems, clearly well connected with the conspirators, had decided to betray them. Putting the letter into one of the leaders' hands, the messenger told him that it contained serious matters for his immediate attention. The double agent, unable to do anything without arousing suspicion, looked on waiting to see what the leader would do. His life, and those of his fellow conspirators, lay in the hands of the half-drunk pro-Spartan. Time must have frozen as the leader looked at the letter in his hand. Crying out in intoxicated laughter, he replied to the messenger with a smile, 'Serious business for tomorrow', slipped the letter under his pillow and returned to his drink. The powers of alcohol had saved the Theban revolutionaries and their rebellion. For evermore in the ancient world, 'Serious business for tomorrow' would become a proverb of warning never to put off for tomorrow what should be done today.

The conspirators gathered outside the room where the drinking party was taking place. Putting women's dresses over their armour and thick garlands of pine and fir over their heads to resemble women's hair and to hide their stubbly faces, they entered the banqueting room. The drunken banqueters heralded their arrival with delighted cheers, thinking that they were the dancing girls and courtesans they had been so eagerly awaiting. But their cries of laughter soon turned to cries of anguish, as, flinging off their wigs and taking their swords out from underneath their skirts, these cross-dressing heroes of the rebellion slaughtered them to a man.

Across town, at much the same time, a very similar scene of murder was unfolding. The conspirators had dressed up, some as women, some as drunken revellers, to avoid detection in the streets, taking no obvious weapons but only one concealed knife each. The plan of attack was simple: to knock on the front door of both of the leaders' houses and to force entry when the slave came to answer it. Overpowering the guards, the conspirators managed to force their way into both houses and began to search for their prey. In the first house, one of the pro-Spartans, the one who never drank wine, snatched up a weapon to defend himself. His advantage was his knowledge of the house layout, but, instead of extinguishing the lights so that his attackers would be thrown into confusion in the darkness, he attacked in the glare of full lamplight and fell upon the conspirators, fighting for his life. Locked in hand-to-hand combat on the narrow stairwell of his house, the pro-Spartan finally fell, his body slumping on top of that of a conspirator he had managed to strike down seconds before, whose last vision in this world was of his hated enemy's body lying defeated across his own. In the other house, the last leader alive, instead of standing to fight his ground, had attempted to escape by hiding in his neighbour's house until he was found, dragged out and murdered.

As night gave way to dawn, the surviving conspirators gathered in the streets. Their task was only half complete. The pro-Spartan leaders had been killed. But there was still a Spartan military garrison installed in the centre of the city and Sparta was sure to send more troops as soon as it heard the news. Messengers were sent anxiously to the ranks of other Theban exiles massing outside Thebes to return as quickly as possible, and to Athens to send in the promised troops. The jail was broken into and all the anti-Spartan prisoners released. The news of the murders began to spread across the city and people filled the streets, anxious to know what might happen next. Realising the danger of their predicament, they broke into the city's armouries, handing out weapons to every able-bodied citizen, even raiding the shops of metal-workers for anything that could be used in battle. Armed as best they could, the citizens of Thebes gathered in the city's assembly to see what the dawn would bring. They must have been all too aware on that cold December morning that the rebellion, their freedom, and with it the fate of Greece, hung in the balance.

CHAPTER 5

❦

The Vegetarian Philosopher and the Body-Building Philanthropist

S tanding among the crowd of armed Thebans that cold December morning in 379 BC were two men who had been central to the rebellion effort thus far. The first was a man called Pelopidas. He had been one of the anti-Spartans chased out of Thebes who had taken refuge in Athens, had escaped repeated assassination attempts, and who, with his band of twelve hero brothers, had set out from Athens to slip into Thebes to begin the rebellion. He had been in the house of Charon that night and had led the second group of attackers in the much more difficult assassination attempt on the two leaders walled up in their own homes. Indeed, Pelopidas had been one of the men who engaged the teetotal pro-Spartan leader in hand-to-hand combat, and, more importantly, had been the man who managed to land the killer blow. Pelopidas was a hero of the rebellion.

The second man worthy of note that frosty morning was Epaminondas. Unlike Pelopidas, Epaminondas had been allowed to remain in Thebes and so had become part of the underground resistance in the city. Epaminondas and his fellow resistance fighters had communicated with Pelopidas and his exiled brothers and co-ordinated the safe house, men and arms for the attack the night before. He was the face known to the people of Thebes and, as he brought Pelopidas before the armed assembly the next morning, it was his calming presence, accompanied by a number of priests, that encouraged the people of Thebes to accept the rebels' actions and steeled their nerves for the forthcoming confrontation with the Spartan garrison still lodged within the city.

These two men, heroes of the rebellion, were great friends. They were to be the two most powerful men in Thebes for more than the next decade. They were also a very unlikely and odd combination. Pelopidas was a rich aristocrat who liked to spread his wealth around philanthropically as much as he could so that he, as he himself said, seemed like the master of his own wealth, rather than its slave. He married and had many children. He was physically very strong and capable but he disliked reading and intellectual pursuits. His favourite place was not the library but the gym, where he was an avid body-builder. He was the life and soul of the party and, as a consequence, had been a high-profile target for the pro-Spartans when they had taken over the city in 380 BC.

Epaminondas, on the other hand, was the only man who would not take one drachma of Pelopidas' wealth. He came from an impoverished aristocratic family, wore modest attire and ate a meagre diet. Invited to a dinner party and seeing the sumptuous spread in front of him, he walked out, saying he had thought this was supposed to be a meal, not a display of arrogance. He remained single all his life and had no children. He became devoted to a new kind of religious observance called Pythagoreanism, which, among other things, insisted on the avoidance of blood sacrifice and meat consumption. He was a strong fighter but, instead of devoting his time to the gym, he preferred reading and became intensely interested in philosophy. He was allowed to remain in Thebes by the pro-Spartan government because, as Plutarch would later comment, 'his philosophy ensured he was looked down on as a recluse, and his poverty as impotent'.

Yet these two men, the vegetarian philosopher and the body-building philanthropist, had a friendship which had been forged in the heat of battle a decade earlier. Pelopidas, in the front line of fighting, had been wounded seven times and left for dead on a heap of other corpses. But Epaminondas would not leave his body and kept fighting against the advancing enemy single-handedly, until he too was injured in the chest by a spear and in the arm by a sword. Determined to die rather than leave Pelopidas' body to the enemy, he refused to retreat. The two of them would not have survived that day if the Spartan king, on whose side they were fighting at the time, had not brought a relief force to save them both. Pelopidas and Epaminondas never forgot that day. But I wonder if, when the Spartan kings heard the news of the Theban rebellion and the names of its leaders, and when, over the next two decades, they faced up against them again and again in battle, they realised, and regretted, that it was their own royal Spartan predecessor who had once saved both the Thebans' lives? For in that single decision in the heat of battle, Sparta had created for itself a wasps' nest of trouble.

For the other thing that bonded Pelopidas and Epaminondas together was their unity of purpose: the desire to see their city become more powerful and glorious during their lifetimes than ever before. Standing in the assembly in Thebes that cold December morning, they must have realised that their 'Theban project' now had its best chance of success. This was Thebes' moment and it couldn't risk a second's hesitation. The Spartan military garrison, installed within the city, had failed to retaliate against the coup during the night. Spurred on by such a tactical error, Pelopidas and Epaminondas, now at the head of a semi-organised and armed citizenry, pressed home their advantage and forced the garrison – Spartan soldiers no less – to surrender their positions and to leave the city.

They were just in time. No more than a couple of days later, the Spartan garrison, marching home defeated and red-faced, met with reinforcements who had hurriedly been sent north from Sparta to help put down the rebellion. It cannot have been a pleasant meeting for those proud Spartans, who were much more used to defeating the enemy than being defeated themselves. Turning around, this combined force now moved to launch an all-out attack on Thebes. Thebes' rebellion and the lives of its citizens, not to mention Pelopidas' and Epaminondas' Theban project, hung in the balance. There was no way that Thebes could hold off the full onslaught of Sparta. Everything rested on whether the Athenians would keep to their promise to send in troops to support Thebes. Would the Athenians keep their word?

Athens' army hung on the border between Attica, the territory of Athens, and Boeotia like a boulder balanced on a mountain ridge. A tense stand-off followed and, in what can only be described as surprisingly acute Spartan tactics, it was Sparta that blinked first. Realising that winter was upon them and a lengthy siege campaign far from home wasn't an option, reluctant to risk all-out war with Thebes and Athens, especially with only a hurriedly gathered relief force and a garrison of proven incompetents to put into the field, Sparta decided to withdraw. Leaving a permanent garrison of soldiers at a town not far from Thebes, Sparta moved the rest of its men back home and waited for winter to pass. Thebes must have breathed a collective sigh of relief. But Pelopidas and Epaminondas must also have known that the battle wasn't over. With spring and summer would come a full-scale attack from the best Sparta had to offer.

Sparta did not spend the winter solely licking its wounds and preparing its army. In a bold diplomatic move, it sent ambassadors to Athens. Their message was simple. Do you, Athenians, really want to risk outright war with Sparta (and perhaps also with Persia) because of Thebes? What do you owe Thebes that it becomes worth risking your own lives? The Athenian assembly, standing nervously on the Pnyx hill, wavered (Map 1; Fig. 2). Still feeling the psychological effects of the Peloponnesian war, revolution, and their own recent poor performances on the battlefield against Sparta, the assembly voted to withdraw support from Thebes. They even voted to condemn the military generals who had led the force to support the city. Athens had performed a complete U-turn in policy. The Spartan ambassadors, their job done, returned home, much more confident of what the next year would bring. Thebes now stood alone. When the campaigning season began, there was nothing to stop Sparta garrotting the city. The countdown to Theban annihilation had begun.

However, as spring gave way to summer in the following year, 378 BC, a strange thing happened. Sparta's garrison of men, left near Thebes through the winter, acted as a reminder of Sparta's power to both Thebes and Athens. This garrison was commanded by a man called Sphodrias, whose orders, one presumes, were to hold the fort during the winter and wait for the arrival of the Spartan army. But one night in April or May 378, Sphodrias, it seems, decided on an alternative plan. Setting out from Theban territory, he made a lightning dash towards Athens with his troops. His goal was to capture the Athenian port of Piraeus by morning, which would cut off the Athenian food supply and render the city effectively powerless to resist any Spartan demands. It all sounds good in theory. But in practice it was nothing short of a fool's errand. Sphodrias was attempting to cover over 70 kilometres on foot in a single night through enemy territory in a terrain that was far from flat (Map 2). There was no way he would make it there by dawn – which was his only hope, given that, as soon as he was spotted, Athenians would be on the march to protect the port. The attack wasn't a daring gamble. It was a suicide mission.

So why did Sphodrias attempt such a ridiculous coup that night? And against Athens, which had already agreed to withdraw its troops and no longer posed any threat to Sparta? What possible upside was there to this mission? Was Sphodrias bored with playing caretaker of the Spartan garrison through the long winter and after his own piece of the glory? Plutarch thought so, summing up Sphodrias as a man weak in judgement, full of vain hopes and senseless ambition. But such an act of flagrant order-breaking would go against every fibre of Spartan military training. On the other hand, what if Sphodrias had been encouraged to do it? Rumours in the ancient sources point the finger at a number of different cities. Did some in the Spartan camp secretly want a good pretext to take up war not only against Thebes but also against Athens? By invading Athenian territory, they knew it was likely that Athens would renew its animosity to Sparta. But equally likely, the ancient sources argue, it could have been some in the Athenian camp who wanted war with Sparta and disagreed with Athens' decision to abandon their Theban allies. By encouraging Sphodrias, perhaps with reports of how badly defended Piraeus was, the pro-war Athenians could have intended to force Athens' hand. Most likely, however, is that this was the brainchild of one of the Theban leaders, perhaps Pelopidas or Epaminondas themselves. Thebes was alone. It couldn't win against Sparta. Its only hope was to get Athens back on side before the Spartan army arrived that summer, and the best way to do that was to provoke a diplomatic incident between Athens and Sparta by tricking or bribing Sphodrias into this outrageous endeavour. This may well have been Thebes' biggest gamble – and it paid off in bounteous terms.

Sphodrias – a poor pawn in a much larger game of chess – was sent back to Sparta for trial, and it was here in Sparta that the Spartan kings made their biggest tactical error. Athens could still have been mollified if Sphodrias had been appropriately punished and Sparta had made loud noises to distance itself from his actions. But king Agesilaus saw it differently. This man, who had blundered about Greece acting the bully and who had taken the fight to Thebes as part of his personal need for revenge, still held the reins in Sparta. Indeed, he seems to have been such a brute force of nature that, despite his many injuries, he had already outlived two fellow kings and was now onto his third. Agesilaus believed in doing harm to his enemies and good to his friends – a very traditional Greek way of thinking, but dangerous when that harm and good came irrespective of the consequences for the city as a whole. Sphodrias was a Spartan and Agesilaus had no intention of punishing a Spartan to appease the Athenians. Sphodrias was let off with little more than a smack on the back of his hand. Athens was outraged and insulted. Before the Spartan army had time to march out for the campaigning season of 378 BC, Athens had performed another U-turn in its foreign policy and was back supporting Thebes again. Just eight years after the king of Persia's peace had been signed, which was supposed to have ushered in a new era of concord and order, the stage was set for another war between the cities of Greece. Ares had taken to his dancing-floor once more.

Athens and Thebes played a very clever game. Sparta had a vastly superior force – some 30,000 men – swarming into Boeotia that summer. Athens and Thebes couldn't risk an outright set-piece battle, but they had the advantage of knowing the territory. By keeping to the hills and mountains of Boeotia, they denied Sparta the big victory they had hoped for out on the open plains, denied them the advantage of their superior numbers, and kept picking at the Spartan column in small guerrilla raids for the next three years. Every campaign season, Sparta had to march all the way up through the Peloponnese to Boeotia and supply its troops at long distance, all the time never having the enemy fully in their sights – a problem well known to commanders in Iraq and Afghanistan in recent years. Athens and Thebes were content to play this game of cat and mouse – it cost them little in men and it paid untold dividends in reducing Spartan morale and the Spartan reputation for military supremacy. The wily Spartan diplomat Antalcidas, who had so brilliantly negotiated the end to the last war, secured the king's peace and advised against Sparta's bullying tactics, now taunted Agesilaus that in this new war he was doing nothing but offering free tuition and target practice to the Thebans.

But then, in 375 BC, something happened which changed Thebes' mindset. At a place called Tegyra, in central Boeotia, smack bang in the middle of the dancing-floor of Ares, a small contingent of Theban troops was marching back to Thebes (Map 2). These men had no intelligence to suggest that a Spartan force was anywhere nearby. Yet suddenly they came face to face with just that. Both sides, it seems, were equally surprised by the encounter. Both sides had equally little choice but to engage. The Theban troops, 300 in number, set off at a run against the Spartans. The Spartans, trusting in their vastly superior numbers and fighting strength against these 300 Thebans, stood their ground. And then the most surprising thing happened. The Thebans not only broke through the Spartan ranks, but instead of carrying on running to escape, they courageously turned back to finish them off. At Tegyra, in 375 BC, a small contingent of 300 Thebans decimated a much larger Spartan force. As Plutarch would later comment, in all wars, whether with Greeks or Barbarians, never before had Spartans, in superior numbers, been overpowered by such an inferior force. The power of a small, elite warrior force, a concept so long central to Sparta's own tale of legendary bravery at Thermopylae, had been turned against it, and the carefully honed image of Spartan power had been irreversibly shattered.

The man leading the Thebans that day was none other than Pelopidas, the body-building philanthropist and hero of the rebellion. The 300 Theban troops were also no ordinary rank and file soldiers. They were known as the Sacred Band. This group of men, described in varying sources as 150 homosexual couples who fought better as a unit than anyone else because of the strong bonds between them, became heroes of the city and the elite force of Thebes. This band of partners, Thebes' only permanent military regiment, would not be beaten in battle for the next 37 years. Their victory at Tegyra not only cemented Pelopidas' power at Thebes, but gave birth to the next phase of the Theban project. Perhaps, Thebans began to dream, they could not only hold off the Spartans but also beat them and take their place as the supreme power in Greece. In just a few short years, the countdown to Theban annihilation had become the countdown to the era of Theban supremacy.

At the same time as the Theban fighters had been playing a cat-and-mouse game with the Spartans, the leaders of the city had also been busy re-erecting the Boeotian confederacy. This federation of cities within central Greece had been in existence since the previous century, but, as we have seen, had been forcibly disbanded at Spartan insistence because it didn't comply with the terms of the king's peace which demanded autonomy for all Greek cities. This had been a body blow particularly to Thebes, which led the confederacy. So it's no surprise that Thebes, as part of its project to reject Spartan mastery over Greece, set about reforming the confederacy as soon as possible after its rebellion. With only Athens to rely on – which had proved itself, at best, to be an unreliable ally – Thebes needed strength in numbers, and that meant presenting a united Boeotian front to the Spartans as soon as possible.

This new confederacy, launched in the aftermath of the rebellion of 378 BC, was substantially different to its predecessor. In the past, all the power had been in the hands of the wealthy aristocrats in the different cities who had also provided the main cavalry fighting force. This time, however, there was a very different emphasis. Every citizen member of the confederacy had equal voting rights (regardless of their wealth) and everyone could serve in the army. This not only made the confederacy the largest experiment in democratic federalism the ancient world had ever known (the Athenian empire had never come close in the democratic stakes), but also provided the confederacy with a massive fighting force to call upon. All citizens voted in the confederate assembly, which had the final say, and every citizen was to consider themselves Boeotian first and a citizen of their own town second. In many ways, it was nothing less than the United States of ancient Boeotia.

But there were some down-sides to this daring democratic experiment. The assembly for all citizens was held in Thebes, so if you wanted to speak at it, you had to travel to Thebes – something that was not always possible, given the distance and demands of the agricultural economy (after all, most Boeotians were farmers and needed to work their land). It would always be easier for Thebans to have their say than the citizens of any other city, and so Thebes tended to dictate confederate policy. In addition, each year seven men were chosen as Boeotarchs – leaders of the assembly and generals of the army. These men were given far-reaching powers to decide confederacy policy when out on active military duty, without recourse to the assembly. This made them very effective in the field – they could respond immediately to events – but it also left the system open to abuse.

Despite its faults, given the circumstances in which it was forged – the Theban rebellion, continued guerrilla warfare against Sparta under the shadow of possible intervention from the Persian king – the Boeotian confederacy brought together cities which had often been at one another's throats into a working, and extraordinarily democratic, union. After the democratic revolution in Athens, it was democracy's second triumph of the century. But who knew, as the cat-and-mouse struggle continued, how it would react to being severely tested in all-out war?

Nobody at Thebes was quite ready to find out – even after their success at Tegyra with the 300 men of the Sacred Band. In 375 BC, just as open conflict seemed on the cards, the Persian king did indeed step in once again to reassert the terms of his peace. While no mention was made of the confederacy as being against the rules, the Persian king did insist on the cessation of military action (after all, he still had need of Greek mercenaries for his own campaigns). An uneasy truce was declared, as Sparta, Athens and Thebes returned home to lick their wounds.

But the Theban project was still very much alive. In less than two years, Thebes was actively seeking to enlarge its confederacy, if necessary by force. Towns on the border between Boeotia and the Athenian territory of Attica, which had wavered in their allegiance to either side, found themselves facing a Theban army at their gates. One town, Plataea (Map 2), with a long history of being central to Greek affairs (it was here that the Greeks had collectively beaten the Persian invasion just over a century before and, more recently, it had played a central role in the Peloponnesian war between Athens and Sparta), was taken completely by surprise. Fearing Theban intentions, the citizens had protected themselves within their city walls whenever they knew the Thebans to be on the march. But when the Thebans were at their assembly meetings, which were famed in Greece for being verbose and long-winded occasions, the Plataeans thought they were safe enough to tend their fields and venture outside the city walls. The Thebans, realising their reputation, played it to their advantage. They went to their assembly meeting fully armed and marched out direct from the meeting to attack Plataea. The citizens had no time to respond and their city was decimated until it capitulated to membership of the confederacy. The same story rang out on every Boeotian border. Cities that were wavering in their support, or indeed had been outspoken in their support for the enemy, were taken by force. The Boeotian confederacy was spreading like a virus and reaching ever closer to the borders of Athenian territory, until Athens and Thebes – supposed allies – were locked in conflict over the rights to control individual towns on the border itself.

This aggressive sabre-rattling expansion of the confederacy ruffled feathers, especially at Athens. Ruffled feathers at Athens tended to mean only one thing – a change in policy by the nervous and trigger-happy democratic Athenian assembly. In early 371 BC, Athens was fearful enough of Theban expansionist intentions to open up diplomatic negotiations again with its old enemy Sparta. This created a complex web of international politics. Athens and Thebes were allied against Sparta. Athens had also been in the process of forming its own alliance of cities across the Greek world, of which more in the next chapter, which also boasted Thebes as a member. Yet Athens was now also allied with Thebes' enemy, Sparta. Athens was attempting to cover all eventualities in an increasingly fractious environment. A renewal of the king's peace was called for in 371 BC and all sides sent ambassadors to Sparta.

This round of peace negotiations was to prove pivotal in Greek history, so much so that Xenophon, the Athenian-turned-Spartan-lover and hero of the march of the 10,000 out of Asia, who in his old age wrote a history of this period, recounted the speeches made by each of the Athenian ambassadors at the negotiations word for word – and Xenophon didn't like recounting speeches unless it really mattered. The big players that day were our old friend Agesilaus for the Spartans, a bevy of orators including the wily politician Callistratus for the Athenians, and Epaminondas, the vegetarian philosopher hero of the Theban rebellion, for the Thebans: three powerful men, three powerful cities and three massive egos, locked in 'peace' negotiations for all of Greece.

At the outset, despite the potential for a clash of egos, all seemed eager for peace, and more specifically, for an end to the traditional clause in alliance treaties which stated that if one city was at war, the allied city would have to come to its aid. Such a stipulation, in a world where every city was allied (and in Athens' case, double- and triple-allied) with someone else, meant that a conflict with one city almost automatically became a globalised Greek conflict. Far from acting as a deterrent to military action by creating opposing 'superpower' blocs, the clause was making military action more likely and far more damaging. The three cities, and their three leading ambassadors, were each attempting to step back from what they saw as fast-approaching Greek global all-out war. As a result, a new peace agreement was drawn up which, while echoing the original terms of the king's peace, made it clear that it was up to each city to decide whether or not to take action to support another against attack. In essence, the ambassadors were attempting to fragment international responsibility and, in so doing, prevent domino-effect ancient world war.

This all seems very sensible, and it served the interests of the three main parties well. Thebes was still not sure enough of its strength, particularly with Athens now siding with Sparta, to want a full-scale conflict. Sparta was trying to turn the tide against the rise of Theban supremacy and its own dwindling power. Athens wanted a balance of power in which no one city or alliance was in control of Greece (at least not until Athens was powerful enough to do it itself). All parties duly signed the new peace treaty. Greece, it seemed, had been saved from destruction. As Xenophon records Callistratus saying on behalf of the Athenians: 'We all know that wars keep breaking out, but that in the end we all desire peace. Why should we then wait till we have all been drained by the perils of war, and not rather make peace before it is too late?'

But that same night, Epaminondas realised that the treaty left Thebes in a very bad position. Under the terms of the new peace, if Sparta did attack Thebes (and knowing Sparta's ability to find a flimsy excuse to do so, that was likely), Athens now was not required to come to Thebes' aid. No one was. The new treaty had left Thebes with the most to lose. Epaminondas had been duped.

The following morning, so Xenophon and another ancient historian, Diodorus, recount, Epaminondas demanded a further meeting. He stepped forward to announce that Thebes had signed the treaty the previous day on behalf of Thebes alone. But Thebes now wished to sign the treaty on behalf of the Boeotian confederacy. It was a tactic designed deliberately to incite the wrath of the Spartan king. Agesilaus flew into a rage. How could they go back and re-sign a treaty they had all agreed and sworn to uphold with solemn oaths to the gods? There would be no going back. But, Epaminondas countered, if Sparta had happily signed for its helot slave territories, and Athens had happily signed for parts of its new alliance, why could Thebes not sign on behalf of Boeotia? Agesilaus responded, not in words, but by erasing the name of the Thebans from the treaty. In one morning, the peace which might just have held Greece back from (another) all-out war was in tatters. Epaminondas had deliberately sabotaged the peace as the only way to force a once-and-for-all conflict that would settle the power struggle in Greece. Whether Thebes was ready or not, Epaminondas knew that this was the city's only chance; and king Agesilaus knew also that Thebes had forced upon Sparta one final chance to reassert its glory. The peace, signed around 27 June 371 BC, and from which Thebes was erased the following day, would be completely dead in less than a month. The ambassadors hurried to their respective cities. Waiting for their arrival, expecting them to be carrying a peace treaty, the citizens of Athens, Sparta and Thebes found them instead carrying a very different message: war was coming, unlike anything that century had yet seen.

Pelopidas and Epaminondas agreed on one thing: the time had come not for cat-and-mouse tactics, but for an open head-on collision between the Theban and Spartan armies. They didn't have long to wait. The Spartan army was already moving north, though not under the command of Agesilaus, who had a tendency to talk the talk but then allow others to fight the battles, particularly since he had developed bad gout in his leg. The army instead was under the command of his fellow king, a man called Cleombrotus. The armies met in the plain of Leuctra on the dancing-floor of Ares (Map 2). They were unevenly matched. Sparta had mustered an imposing force: 11,000 men and 1,000 cavalry lined up against 7,000 Theban soldiers and only 700 cavalry. Finally, the Spartans must have thought, they had their chance on the open field of battle.

On the plain at Leuctra, where the two armies formed up against one another, there was a tomb to two maidens who, years previously, had been raped by a group of Spartans. The maidens had subsequently killed themselves because they couldn't live with the shame and torment of having been so violated. In the nights before the battle, Pelopidas was said to have been visited in a dream by these two girls, who instructed him to sacrifice a virgin in their honour to ensure that they, and the plain of Leuctra itself, were on the Theban side in the battle. Pelopidas' dream caused much dissension in the Theban ranks. Should they really sacrifice a virgin maiden? Previous examples in Greek history and myth had not been without problems. Agamemnon had sacrificed his daughter to get the winds needed to sail for Troy and had subsequently been killed by his own wife. On the other hand, Agesilaus had attempted to repeat this sacrifice and been stopped by the Thebans when he set out on his campaign to take the fight to the Persians more than twenty years before, and his campaign had been a complete failure. Was there a connection between the failure of his campaign and the failure to offer the ultimate human sacrifice? Split between the murder of an innocent and losing the support of the gods, the answer thankfully provided itself to the Thebans in the form of a young mare, which was said to have broken free and galloped up to Pelopidas, as if eager to offer her services. They sacrificed the virgin horse over the tomb and prayed that the wronged maidens and Leuctra would be on their side.

Pelopidas was well aware of the role that propaganda would play in this battle. The Thebans couldn't afford to be overawed by Spartan might, especially given their inferior numbers. Stories like that of the sacrifice at the maiden tomb only added grist to his mill of Theban ego-stroking. Seeing nervousness in the ranks, particularly among the few ally soldiers who had joined Thebes that day, Pelopidas made a big play of giving anyone who didn't want to fight in this battle free rein to leave. Pelopidas cried out with passion and fury that only men who really wanted to fight were worthy of standing in the Theban line, and only such men were worthy of the glory that would be won that day.

But even Pelopidas couldn't convince his wife, who, Plutarch later recounts, begged him to stay at home and not fight. Leaving her behind, he took his place in front of his elite force of the Sacred Band. As noon approached, on that fateful day in the summer of 371 BC, the air became heavy with the expectation of fierce battle and bloodshed.

It was only then that Sparta would have realised how daring Pelopidas and Epaminondas really were. There was a traditional order to how Greek armies formed up their troops. Your best troops always went on the right flank, because the left side was thought to be unlucky. In battle between two opposing lines, this meant that the best troops on either side never actually faced one another. Battles as a result normally followed a set pattern: a cavalry charge, an initial advance, a defeat of the weaker part of the line opposite, followed by a wheeling-round action as the remaining strong forces on either side attempted to get back into position to face the other. But Pelopidas and Epaminondas were having none of it. Their battle plan was sheer shock and awe – there was no time for superstition. They stationed their best troops directly opposite the Spartans on the Theban left flank. As Sparta lined up for battle, they came face to face, not with the weaker allied troops, but with Thebes' best.

At noon, after the initial cavalry charge on both sides had failed to make a difference, rather than marching towards the enemy at a decent pace as the Spartans began to do to the tune of the flute, the Thebans screamed and ran at them at full speed. The Theban line was spearheaded by the fearsome Sacred Band. Smashing into the Spartan ranks, this 300-strong contingent of male couples broke through the front ranks and caused disarray in the Spartan battle line. Backing up Pelopidas and his Sacred Band were the Theban infantry, 50 men deep, under Epaminondas. They made straight for the Spartan king and struck him dead. The battle was over in less than an hour, before the allies on either side had even really had a chance to engage.

Leuctra – the battle that heralded the end of Spartan supremacy and the full flowering of Theban power – was a turning point in the history of Greece, and it was won in no small part thanks to the deep cunning and courage of Pelopidas and Epaminondas. Cicero was later to call Epaminondas the first man of Thebes, and the likes of Sir Walter Raleigh thought he was the greatest of the ancient Greeks. There is a statue to Epaminondas in the main street of modern Thebes. The reputations of these two men were unassailable after Leuctra, even though several of their colleagues who had been with them on the first night of the Theban rebellion in 379 BC, and who had also been present at the battle of Leuctra, would complain bitterly that these two got too much of the glory. Such men even put up their own victory trophy at Leuctra with an inscription saying: 'We were just as good as Epaminondas.' Perhaps these two heroes were a little big-headed about their success. Epaminondas, for all his philosophy, was said to cherish a prodigious pride, so great that he was more proud of his victory at Leuctra than Agamemnon had been of his victory at Troy. The day after the battle, Epaminondas dressed in dishevelled clothing with his hair all askew, telling everyone that he had felt pride worthy of the gods the day before and so today was compensating to bring himself back down to a more human level.

If Epaminondas felt superhuman pride, the Spartans suffered super-human humiliation. Requesting permission to retrieve their dead, they were forced by the Thebans to wait until every one of Sparta's allies had collected theirs. The idea was to allow the allies to collect their paltry number of casualties, which would in turn show up even more clearly just how many Spartan dead lay on the battlefield. In the fields of Leuctra, the Spartan reputation for military invincibility finally died. Sparta would never again rise to the heights of power it had enjoyed in the first decades of the new century.

All that remains today at the site of the one-hour battle of Leuctra is the Theban monument erected shortly after their victory, a stone tower roofed with 'Spartan' shields taken in battle (Fig. 7). The inscription that accompanied it underlined the fact that here was a victory won by the Thebans with the spear. Today, the repaired remains of that monument are visible, set in the midst of wild poppies and camomile flowers, surrounded by sprawling barley fields on a peaceful, green Boeotian valley floor. It's easily passed by as you travel on the road from the small modern village of Leuctra to the west coast of Greece. But to stand by that monument is supposedly to stand on the exact spot where the Spartan king was killed, and where the balance of power in ancient Greece changed for good.

CHAPTER 6

❧

The Slippery Fish

Athens was not present at the battle of Leuctra. Having attempted to negotiate a new peace that dispelled the threatening possibility of global ancient war, it must have been more than dismayed to see, twenty days later, Sparta and Thebes in all-out combat. Athens' attempts for 'peace in our time' had, like Chamberlain's so many centuries later, achieved little more than writing on paper (or in this case probably wax tablets). But Athens, taking advantage of the terms of the new peace, even if, in reality, it was already dead, chose not to take part in the battle. Athens fully expected Sparta to crush Thebes. So when Thebes sent messengers racing to Athens after its annihilation of Sparta at Leuctra, expecting that Athens, its old ally, would be pleased at the news and would seize the chance to send troops to capitalise on the situation, Athens did not know what to do. In the end it chose to give the messenger of victory the cold shoulder. No welcome, no message of congratulations, no promise of support, nothing. Thebes' 'old ally' had once again been tested and found wanting.

Perhaps the Thebans should have expected little else. After all, Athens had already performed several diplomatic pirouettes in its relationship with Thebes that decade. From offering support for the Theban rebellion in 379, Athens had turned to support Sparta that same winter and disavowed the generals it had sent to help Thebes, only to turn back to support Thebes after Sphodrias had so suicidally tried to attack Athens in a single night. Athens' support for Thebes had again wavered when it saw the Boeotian confederacy expanding too swiftly, and Athens had squirmed to get out of its military obligations to Thebes in the 371 peace treaty by siding with Sparta. And now, not having supported Thebes on the battlefield, Athens wouldn't even send a message of congratulations. Athens, it seems, was the slippery fish of ancient Greek international relations.

Athens' slippery activities were not only confined to Thebes. In fact, Athens' history of inter-city and international relations during the first decades of the 4th century BC confirms its oily tendencies. It had escaped from its obligations to Sparta at the end of the Peloponnesian war, first by secretly sending support to Persia (which it later publicly denounced), and then by joining the alliance of cities angry at Sparta's brutish control of the Greek world. Athens had taken Persian money and celebrated the fact that an Athenian admiral was commanding the Persian navy. But soon enough Athens was also sending help to the island of Cyprus, which was in conflict with the Persian king, and also starting to rebuild its influence with Greek cities in the northern parts of the Aegean and on the coast of Asia Minor. It was this two-timing of the Persian king that empowered Sparta to convince the king to lose patience with Athens and enforce the king's peace, with Sparta as its policeman.

Athens' early diplomatic manoeuvres in the new century have been described as an attempt to begin the process of rebuilding its cherished empire, won and lost in the previous century. Whether or not these moves were part of a co-ordinated effort to recreate empire, Athens' flip-flop diplomacy in those early years was completely understandable. Every city was trying to find its way within a world working to a completely different set of rules. Athens had to work harder than most to recover from a crushing defeat and political revolution. It's no surprise that it sought to place itself on the upside of every political and military encounter, just as every other city was doing. Athens wasn't so much flip-flopping on these issues as being opportunistic. Opportunism had replaced ideology as the watchword of 4th-century international politics. Blind allegiance simply couldn't be afforded in a world that was changing so fast, and when the stakes were so high.

The imposition of the king's peace put paid to any notions Athens might have had of forming another empire. Athens was allowed control of three small Aegean islands, one of which was Scyros (Map 2) which lay on its most crucial artery – its grain trade route to the Black Sea – but every other city and island in Greece had to remain autonomous. Empire was dead. But what could take its place? The Thebans had provided the answer in the form of their newly restored Boeotian confederacy. The confederacy, though challenged repeatedly by the Spartans, had not been struck down. It seemed that an alliance of free states might just be acceptable to the Persian king.

But Athens had more pressing concerns. In 378 BC, after it had left Thebes high and dry following the Theban rebellion, and subsequently got back into bed with Thebes after the humiliating Sphodrias incident, Athens had been thrown into the war in central Greece which eventually ended with Theban victory at Leuctra. Though this conflict became a game of guerrilla warfare for most of the 370s, Athens realised it was in a pretty poor state to defend itself. It had rebuilt its walls around the city of Athens (just about), but it had little to defend the surrounding countryside that was so vital for its citizens' livelihoods. The territory of Athens, known as Attica, was at risk from Spartan military incursion, as the ill-fated night march of Sphodrias had so clearly proved. The threat to the Athenian homelands required immediate attention. Homeland security was now Athens' number one priority.

If you travel out to the western boundaries of Attica, you come to the steep Aigaeleus ridge. It provides a natural defence against armies approaching from the west (and particularly from Sparta). But there is a gap in this natural fortress wall. It was a gap known to, and feared by, the Athenians as they set about their plans to protect Attica in 378 BC. Travelling today to this area, you can still see the physical remains of their response – a fortified wall built to close the gap in the ridge (Fig. 8). This wall is a mystery to many scholars, for it isn't mentioned in a single ancient text. The only evidence for its existence is its very presence, 2,400 years later, in this remote district of Attica. But careful archaeology has been able to unravel a little of its story. First and foremost, this was not just a wall. It was a stone fortification reinforced by watchtowers and phased barrier walls, with garrison forts housing, one presumes, infantry and cavalry who patrolled and guarded it. Its brute size is testified to by the fact that it has survived the ravages of 2,400 years of weathering, plundering and war.

Yet it's most likely that this wall was constructed in something of a hurry. Athens had only a short space of time, between throwing its lot back in with Thebes and the military campaign season beginning, to secure its borders against the expected Spartan attack. It needed the wall fast – so fast, it's entirely possible that the whole workforce who had only just finished rebuilding the walls of the city, along with every able-bodied citizen of Athens, was sent to build this defensive wall with all speed, perhaps even within the space of a single week. The only man capable of masterminding such a building project was an Athenian called Chabrias. He had been on mercenary service in Egypt (fighting *against* Persia ... another Athenian slippery fish), where he had gained a great deal of experience in fortress-building, a technique which had not been extensively used in Greece since Greek warfare, up to then, had normally consisted of set-piece battles rather than protracted sieges. Chabrias returned to Greece in 379 BC and was elected general in Athens in spring 378 BC, just as the campaigning season was beginning. It's quite possible that his first order was to build the fortress wall and that the existence of this wall was the determining factor in forcing Agesilaus and his Spartan army into Theban territory rather than Athenian, when his troops arrived some weeks later. The defensive wall of Attica had proved its worth. Athens never forgot again the importance of securing its homeland. It instituted a new system of military call-up in which all eighteen- and nineteen-year-olds were sent on a tour of duty, not to foreign lands, but to guard the boundaries of Attica; and it ensured that, as it elected its military generals every year, one general was tasked with the specific responsibility of defending the countryside. Chabrias was given a statue in the Athenian Agora, and, his job done protecting the homeland, he went to war against Sparta on the dancing-floor of Ares.

At the same time as Athens was engaged in securing its homeland, its thoughts were turning to the international stage. Athens' opportunistic tap dance over the last decades had left it alive, but not secure. Its proto-attempts at a second empire had been slapped down by the king's peace. But the Theban example of the Boeotian confederacy had shown that alliances were possible. In 378 BC, the same year that the defensive wall was thrown up at the borders of Attica, the same year as war in central Greece broke out once again, and exactly 100 years since the foetus of the former Athenian empire had been created, the Athenians founded an alliance which has become known as the Second Athenian League.

The foundation charter of this league has survived to this day. Set up in the beating heart of Athens, the Agora, this document on stone proclaimed the mandate of the league, the oaths sworn by its constituents, and the names of its members. The lengths to which Athens went to avoid falling foul of the terms of the king's peace, which demanded that all cities be free and autonomous, is palpable in the language of the charter:

> In order that the Spartans shall permit the Greeks to be free and autonomous … and in order that the peace and friendship sworn by the Greeks and the Persian king as prescribed in the king's peace may be respected and enforced … if any Greek city, which is not under the control of the Persian king, wishes to be an ally of the Athenians and their allies, let it be so, and, as everyone is free and autonomous, let that city choose whatever form of government they wish and let them never be forced to accept a military garrison, or a governor or pay the tax of empire. Moreover, Athenians will never be allowed to own land or property in those cities …

The charter resolutely repeats its commitment to freedom and autonomy. More importantly, it also tries to calm fears among the Greek cities that this was Athens up to its old tricks. The clauses referring to forms of government, military garrisons, governors, the tax of empire and Athenians never owning land or property all speak directly to what were considered to be the worst excesses of Athenian tyrannical empire. Never again, Athens says in this document, will it be so tyrannical a master. Indeed, this time, it was no master at all. After all, everyone in the league, as Athens kept underlining, was free and autonomous.

How real was this claim that Athens had learnt the lessons of empire and was now interested only in a free and autonomous alliance between like-minded free and autonomous cities? The language was certainly encouraging. Gone was the expression 'Athens and the cities over which it rules', now replaced by 'Athens and the allies of Athens'. Language was backed up by structure. The decision-making engine of the new league was composed of two assemblies: the Athenian democratic assembly and an assembly of representatives of all member cities. No decision could be made without agreement in both houses. Every member of the league had a say (as long as they could get to Athens to express it). Athens kept to its word never to introduce the heavy tax of empire, the dreaded *phoros*, which had been so hated in the previous century. But a levy was introduced (known as a *syntaxis* in ancient Greek, which carried a pleasing sense of community togetherness about it) to help with the costs of running the league.

The language and structure of this new league was also backed up by action in the initial years after its birth. Islands across the Aegean sea and free cities on the coast of Asia Minor like Byzantium (modern-day Istanbul) joined the league (Map 2). Closer to home, Thebes also became a member. By 375 BC, just three years after its inception, it had 75 members. Much of this eagerness for membership came from the central focus of the league against Sparta (as immortalised in the first line of its charter quoted above). The Second Athenian League was a defensive pact against Greece's bully policeman. Even the hasty renewal of the king's peace in 375 BC tacitly recognised and accepted its existence and purpose.

But tension between Thebes and Athens spelt trouble for the league. Thebes was a member of the league as an individual city, but it was also head of the Boeotian confederacy. Such duality didn't matter, as long as both the league and the confederacy were anti-Spartan. But as Spartan power began to wane, and Theban power started to grow, the purpose of the league and Thebes' membership of it became increasingly strained. Athens by 371 BC was neutral at best, if not tacitly supporting Sparta against the growing Theban supremacy. Supposed allies, Athens sent no support to Thebes at the battle of Leuctra and shunned its messengers of victory. At the same time as there was growing tension between members of the league, a bigger issue raised its head. If Sparta was no longer a world power, what was the point of the continued existence of the league, whose purpose had been to bring Sparta back into line? The league was at a crucial milestone. In the previous century, an alliance which had started out as anti-Persian had, after an official peace with Persia, not been disbanded but converted into the Athenian empire. Despite all its protestations and conciliatory language, Athens was now faced with a similar opportunity. What would this slipperiest of diplomatic fish choose to do with it?

To understand Athens' choices following the battle of Leuctra in 371 BC, we have to take a much wider view of the ancient world, what the ancient geographer Strabo would later call *megale Hellas* – greater Greece (Map 3). While central Greece was locked in a battle for military supremacy on the dancing-floor of Ares, there was a great deal else going on in the wider world around them – places, peoples and events in which the central Greek cities had a crucially important, and continually growing, vested interest that would help determine their policies at home and abroad.

By far the most important of these interests was the pursuit of natural resources, in particular food. Central to the Greek diet was grain, and Greece, though a bountiful country in many ways, could not be relied upon to supply the grain needed by the major Greek cities each year. In particular this was a problem for Athens, since it was one of the largest cities located in one of the drier parts of Greece and could rarely, if ever, hope to be self-sufficient. As a result, its search for, and quest to keep control of, good grain-growing areas was a fundamental tenet of Athenian foreign policy. The king's peace, signed for the first time back in 386 BC, had allowed Athens to keep control of three small islands in the north Aegean sea, as we've seen. There was little strategic value in these islands except for the fact that they lay on the trading route to Athens' main source of food: the rich and fertile soil around the Black Sea. Colonised by the Greeks well over a century before, the Black Sea had slowly become a food pump for Greece and particularly Athens. By the end of the previous century, it had been upgraded to a vital artery for the city of Athens, and any cessation in its flow caused major upheaval in the city. It was by blocking the imports of grain to Athens that Sparta had brought Athens to its knees at the end of the Peloponnesian war, and it was through threatening the narrowest point of this artery – the area now known as the Dardanelles, the Sea of Marmara and the Bosporus, the narrow channels and small sea leading up from the Aegean, past Istanbul, into the Black Sea itself (Map 3) – that the Persian king had forced Athens to sign the king's peace in 386 BC. This route, and protection of this route, was vital to Athens' survival. It's no wonder that Athens had sought out Byzantium (Istanbul), the city that controlled entry to the Black Sea from this narrow corridor, as an early member of its Second Athenian League.

The Black Sea, however, was a very different place from mainland Greece. Here, the Greek colonies existed shoulder-to-shoulder with an exotic range of other cultures and worlds. This was the borderland of the ancient Greek world – the frontier region. Surrounding the Greek colonies on the south and east was the northern tip of the Persian empire, on the west the Odrysian Thracians, and to the north the Royal Scythians (Map 3). It was a world where cultural norms were constantly in flux, where systems of government varied enormously, where the exchange of high-value merchandise (perhaps as protection money) was unending, where territorial boundaries were constantly being fought over and where ethnic and civic identity became a melting pot. It was this difficult and unstable world that Athens had to keep in step with if it was to maintain its vital supply of food. That meant dealing with whomever could guarantee what Athens needed – even if they were some pretty unsavoury characters. Opportunism was again the watchword of the day.

One such colony was Panticapaion on the northern coast of the Black Sea (Map 3). It was ruled by a man called Leucon, who had invaded land belonging to a series of local tribes to the north in order to expand Panticapaion's territory. To the Greeks he called himself *archon* (chief magistrate) of the Bosporus and Theodosia. But to the natives he was the all-powerful king of the Sindians, Toretae, Dandarii and Psessi. Athens, as was becoming the norm in this century, had few qualms about dealing with kings – however they described themselves. Leucon was on great terms with Athens – the city even got the privilege of always being the first to have its ships filled up with grain, and they were exempted from the city's grain tax. By the middle of the 4th century BC, Leucon would be supplying over half of Athens' annual import of grain. A similar arrangement was struck with another colony on the south side of the Black Sea, Heracleia Pontice. This city too had fallen prey to the power of a single individual, a man called Clearchus. Invited back out of exile to take control for a limited period and put the colony back on its feet, he had installed himself and his family as monarchs in perpetuity. Once again, Athens had little difficulty in doing, or indeed little choice about doing, business with this strongman.

But Athens' interest didn't stop at grain. The other natural resource that Athenians, and Greeks all over, were fixated on was precious metals. Athens had discovered silver mines in its own backyard in Attica during the previous century, and during the 4th century would be exploiting them at a higher rate than ever before. But it needed more, and the north coast of the Aegean sea was rich in deposits of not just silver, but a whole host of precious metals. With silver and gold, Athens could pay for its grain and everything else it needed. Yet here, Athens had a problem. The northern coast was controlled by the different kingdoms of Thrace (Map 3). Athens, particularly in this period, had few if any secure inroads into this most profitable of territories. As a result, Athens would spend much of the century attempting to secure its influence here. Unlike many other areas of the Greek world in which Athenian interest would change with the opportunistic wind, Athens' desperation for a piece of the north Aegean pie would be unswerving. This area of Greece would be Athens' Vietnam. The city's dogged determination in, and belief in the necessity of, fighting here would in future bring Athens into conflict with the most mighty of states in northern Greece, Macedon, and play a major role in Athens' misfortunes.

Athens' search for grain and other natural resources also took it to the opposite end of the Aegean, to the coast of Africa. Egypt was out, as it was increasingly under the dominion of the Persian king. Instead, the area of modern-day Libya was the home for another of the most powerful cities of 4th-century *megale Hellas*: Cyrene (Map 3). Cyrene had seen the opposite political trajectory to the colonies around the Black Sea. Begun as a monarchy in the previous century, it had converted into a democracy with an assembly of 10,000. Throughout the 4th century, this city would become richer and richer on the back of its trade. Extremely complex and ornate architecture was constructed, marking this city out, despite its location on the margins of Greek world, as a central player in the ancient economy. The city would offer rich dedications at the far-away international sanctuary of Delphi and would proudly display in its own city, inscribed in stone, the list of major Greek cities which it had supplied with considerable amounts of grain during the harsh agricultural seasons of the 320s BC. Cyrene was a cosmopolitan international trading success and its citizens travelled all over the ancient world. Yet its future, isolated as it was on the north coast of Africa, sandwiched between Egypt and the still-powerful Carthaginian empire, was uncertain. Its wealth and success only made it a more obvious target, and by the end of the century it would be in the hands of Egypt as the Greek world began to fragment.

As Athenians tried to work out how to react to the Theban victory at the battle of Leuctra in 371 BC, and specifically what to do with the Second Athenian League which it had been carefully building for the last seven years, the global stage must have been front and centre in their minds. Athens' interests, and its survival, in this new century were tied more closely than ever before to places, peoples and events at the very edges of the Greek world. The Black Sea held the key to Athens' ability to feed itself. The north Aegean coast was an untapped resource of wealth. The north African coast was an increasingly important grain and trading centre. Events in the Persian empire, and particularly on the coast of Asia Minor, had already that century repeatedly proved to be crucial to Athenian interests and development. Sicily and the western Greek world, particularly important trading places like Massalia, modern-day Marseilles in France, and the native Etrurian population of central Italy, were all increasingly part of a global economy in which it was vital that Athens had a role. To maintain its interests, its lifelines and its status, Athens had no choice but to seek, in any way it could, to consolidate and increase its power in these far-flung parts of the Greek world and to continue to fight for its ability to travel safely to and from them.

That need to maintain and increase its presence on the international stage was also driven home by the growth of new powers in central Greece, which were themselves all looking for a share in the territory and wealth of the wider Greek world. The first of these was of course Thebes, which, now the most powerful city in mainland Greece, was seeking to break free from the Second Athenian League and create its own sphere of influence (it would soon start building its own navy to rival Athens'). But the second of these new powers was perhaps more immediately threatening to Athens. North of Boeotia lay the territory of Thessaly (Map 2). This was a vast expanse of land, traditionally broken up between competing ethnic groups and cities. Fruitless infighting between these cities had rendered Thessaly impotent on the international stage for long periods of time. But by 375 BC, one man, Jason, from the city of Pherae, had managed not only to repel the Spartans who had attempted to invade posing as policemen of the king's peace, but, more impressively, had managed to force most cities in Thessaly to accept his leadership. He became *tagos*, the Thessalian term for ultimate leader, of Thessaly. In 375, this had been good news for Athens since Thessaly and Athens were on good terms, united by their dislike of Sparta. Jason's combined army of Thessalians and mercenaries – over 20,000 strong – was a potent force stopping Spartan ambitions to push north. But being on good terms with Jason also gave Athens good relations with the third power of northern Greece, Macedon – and through Macedon, land access to the rich and fertile lands of the north Aegean coast.

By 371, however, Athens, along with many cities in mainland Greece, began to suspect that Jason's ambitions didn't stop at simply restraining Sparta. Like Thebes, he too was bent on supremacy in Greece. When Athens refused to acknowledge the messenger of Theban victory or to send troops to back up the Theban success at Leuctra, it was Jason of Pherae who answered the call and sent troops streaming down into the dancing-floor of Ares. Such a massing of troops headed off a continuation of the conflict. Athens tried to capitalise on the situation by calling another emergency peace conference (the second one in the same year). Sparta had to attend but Thebes refused a deal.

Looking around them, the Athenians must have been very worried about the turn of events in the immediate aftermath of the battle of Leuctra in 371. Thebes was now dominant, and at that very moment refusing peace and mounting a military campaign into the Peloponnese to attack Sparta itself. Cities in the Peloponnese, so long under the thumb of Sparta, were taking the opportunity provided by the Theban victory to revolt. Some of these cities were even beginning to form themselves into their own confederacies based on the Theban model. In central Greece, the cities of Sicyon and Argos were consumed by civil war. Jason of Pherae, leader of the whole of Thessaly, was stand-ing on the dancing-floor of Ares surrounded by a vast army, now on good terms with Thebes. Jason looked set to expand his power base and neither Thebes nor Thessaly now cared much for Athens. Athens' interests in the wider Greek world, its access to the Black Sea, to the north Aegean coast, to north Africa, were all under threat. The Second Athenian League was beginning to falter, and any diplomatic move that Athens made had to, officially at least, conform to the terms of the king's peace.

There were no new members of the Second Athenian League after 371 BC. Its 'nursery tea time atmosphere', as one scholar described it, had become superfluous to the fast-changing, hard-hitting political and military climate of the Greek world. Athens' slippery fish diplomacy, which had kept it on the upside of most issues and allowed it to gather influence within the Persian king's framework of international rela-tions, had now left it beached on the shore, alone, isolated and vulner-able. Athens needed a new strategy, and fast.

CHAPTER 7

~∞~

The Clash of Philosopher
and Tyrant

While Athens was desperately searching for an appropriate response to the fast-changing nature of international relations in the years after 371 BC, the city was also aware of new events in Sicily unfolding at a similar pace. Dionysius I, *strategos autokrator*, supreme commander, of Syracuse and a good swathe of Sicily for the past 30 or more years, was finally nearing the end of his life. Just four years after the battle of Leuctra, in the middle of conducting a complex diplomatic tap dance of his own as he was courted by both Athens and Sparta for his allegiance, Dionysius died. The strong man of Sicily was no more. Who would take his place?

Despite Athens' attempts to woo Dionysius (they even tried to offer him Athenian citizenship to sweeten the deal), it was also Athens, or rather particular people and institutions in Athens, that were responsible for Dionysius' savage tyrannical reputation. Many years before, in 388 BC, the same year in which Dionysius had been lambasted as a tyrant and a suppressor of Greek freedom at the Olympic games by the Athenian orator Lysias and his tent attacked by an angry mob, another Athenian, the philosopher Plato, had sailed to meet Dionysius in Sicily with a much more open mind. A disciple of Socrates (the great thinker who had been tried, convicted and executed by the Athenian democracy in the early days after its restoration), Plato was interested in whether political and military leaders could be influenced for the better by philosophical discussion. Dionysius seemed like a perfect test case. As Plato sailed into the port at Syracuse, he planned, through intense and difficult discussion, to make this strong man a more perfect and just leader as an example for all of Greece.

Dionysius had been encouraged into this meeting by one of his own advisers, a man called Dion who was a fervent admirer of Plato. Dion ensured that Plato was present during a leisure hour of the great ruler, and the conversation soon steered towards human virtue and manliness – two of the qualities Dionysius believed himself to have in abundance. However, Dionysius had misjudged Plato. Used to being surrounded by fawning advisers and men over whom he had the power of life and death, Dionysius was not prepared for a man like Plato who had come to Sicily under the impression that he was able to speak his mind. Soon enough, the leisure hour had become an hour of aggressive discussion and then outright argument as the great ruler became increasingly angry with the philosopher. Plato had the temerity to question whether absolute rulers were always just. Bristling at the implied slur, Dionysius asked him why he had bothered to come to Sicily. Plato replied that he had come to find a virtuous man, but refrained from adding that he had found one in Dionysius. The *strategos autokrator* exploded and left orders for Plato to be sent home. The meeting of great philosopher and powerful tyrant, which had sought to give concrete reality to the idea of just rule by one man in the Greek world, was over before it had really begun. The meeting had become a clash of beliefs, personalities and egos – and it had gone resoundingly Dionysius' way.

Dionysius was so incensed by Plato's audacious responses that he not only sent him home, but sent him home on a Spartan ship. He put the Athenian Plato on a vessel captained and crewed by men from a city with which Athens was at war. In fact, the Spartan ship that Plato was bundled on to had come to Syracuse specifically to ask for Syracusan help in the war against Athens. But this insult was not sufficient. Dionysius also secretly bribed the Spartan captain to either kill Plato on the way home or at the very least sell him into slavery. The great tyrant, it seems, was intent on crushing this upstart philosopher. Plato was sold into slavery on the island of Aegina, just off the coast of the Athenian territory of Attica (Map 2). Aegina was a hotbed for everyone who disliked Athens, and there were many who were willing and happy to see the famous man of words reduced to slavery by the might of the Sicilian tyrant.

In acting so abruptly with Plato, Dionysius had made a crucial error in judgement. For Plato was not a lone bearded philosopher trawling the globe – he was a respected man within Athens with powerful friends and a devoted following. Plato escaped the fate of slavery on Aegina and returned to Athens, his pride severely dented. The following year, he founded a philosophical school in Athens, his Academy, to act as a centre for his teaching and for the pursuit of the values he so admired. This was no hippy commune. Plato's Academy became a crucial arena in the political battlefield of Athens, its members well-connected and influential men not just from Athens but from all over Greece. Dionysius had tried to sell into slavery a man who, not many years later, held one of the most powerful positions in Athens. The clash of philosopher and tyrant had begun afresh.

Philosophers don't fight with swords, but words. The Academy, with its collection of vehemently pro-democratic, anti-authoritarian supporters in Athens, seems to have been primarily responsible for the smear campaign that has blighted Dionysius I to this day. Within years, Dionysius was fighting a losing battle to protect his reputation as a strong, manly and virtuous ruler. The Academy let it be known that his strongman appearance was actually motivated by an uncontrollable lust for power, which was, according to the Academy, the archetypal moral fault of the tyrant. Accompanying that lust for power was its darker flipside – a constant fear and suspicion of everyone. Athenian comedy later in the century would pick up and run with this aspect of Dionysius' character, and particularly his constant fear of assassination. Between the philosophical debate chamber and the comic stage, Dionysius was delivered a mortal body blow to his reputation. His wife, they said, had to be naked every night when he came to bed because Dionysius was afraid that even she might be hiding a knife under her nightdress. His bed, they said, was set in the middle of a moat with only a single bridge to it, which could be drawn up, so that no one could approach him while he slept without making a noise. Everyone meeting him, they said, had to submit to the indignity of being strip-searched because he was so paranoid. And worst of all, they said, he had red hair and freckles.

Against all the odds, this was the man to whom Athens, following the diplomatic catastrophe of Theban victory at the battle of Leuctra in 371 BC, attempted to turn to salvage their international standing. The factions within the democracy at Athens, who were keen to work with this strong man, ensured that he was offered citizenship and that a treaty was signed guaranteeing his support for Athens. The deal was sweetened since Dionysius miraculously won one of Athens' dramatic contests with his own literary creation in the same year. Given the degree to which Dionysius prided himself on his dramatic and poetical ability (he did, after all, have the writing desk of the great tragedian Aeschylus and considered himself enough of an aficionado of Greek myth to interfere with the choices in sculptural portrayal of the gods at the newly embellished sanctuary of the healing god Asclepius at Epidaurus), this was a serious diplomatic plus point in Athens' favour. But the Academy had done its work too well. Dionysius was never fully welcomed into the bosom of Athenian politics or policy because of the Academy-sponsored public perception of his vile character, and the city's flirtation with him, not least because of Dionysius' own death in the spring of 367 BC, was short. The second round of the clash between philosopher and tyrant had been a resounding win for philosophy.

Dionysius I was replaced by his son, Dionysius II. Dionysius the son was a very different man from his father. Softened by the luxuriousness of his upbringing, weakened by a career to date that had required him to accomplish nothing of any note, he stood resolutely in his father's iron shadow, which had, by contrast, been forged in the heat of battle during the Peloponnesian war crisis that had enveloped Greece at the end of the previous century. Dionysius II's only claim to fame, according to the later biographer Plutarch, was to have engaged in a drinking bout for 90 consecutive days.

This was not all the son's fault. The father, after all, as Plato's Academy was only too willing to underline, had been so paranoid about his own life that he didn't trust his own wife. Why should he trust his son either? In order to render him impotent, the father had purposely denied the boy access to education and training which would have prepared him to lead. He was, according to Plutarch, on his accession to the position of *strategos autokrator* and tyrant of Syracuse, 'stunted and deformed in his character from his lack of education'.

The intellectual power behind this rather limp figurehead was Dion, the man who had served Dionysius the father for a good part of his rule and who had been instrumental in inviting Plato to Syracuse some twenty years before. Somehow Dion had managed to survive the taint of association with Plato and continue to serve his master (it might have had something to do with the fact that he was the brother of one of Dionysius' wives). But with the changeover of power came a new opportunity to stamp the philosophical mark on Syracuse's rulers – and where better to start than on a man who had been lacking the education he needed for this very role?

Dion was not the kind of man who engaged in 90-day drinking bouts. He was, after all, a follower of Plato, a man who advocated the importance of measured response, justice, wisdom and good sense. Dion was a man who always demanded more of people, who stood aloof from fellow mortals, who was never satisfied with everyone's efforts and who, like Plato and Socrates, made it his business to point out to other people their own character flaws. He must have been a brilliant individual, but constantly racked by his own high intellectual standards – an inspiration to work with, but also just a real killjoy. Plutarch thought so, calling him 'an unpleasant and irksome work colleague'. In short, he was just the sort of man to very quickly get on the wrong side of the new ruler of Syracuse.

The new tyrant's other advisers didn't like Dion any better, and were swift in their attempts to poison the ruler against him. But for all his own character flaws, Dion was an important asset in the Syracusan camp. He alone had kept up a positive dialogue with Plato's Academy and with Athens, and he alone could help restore the reputation of the Syracusan rulers and do something to abate the steady stream of character assassination emerging from Athens. Dion and Plato were practically pen pals, and so it's no surprise that in the year 366 BC, when Plato was in his sixties, Dion's invitation for Plato to return to Syracuse was accepted. On the horizon appeared the possibility of an entente between the philosopher and the tyrant, a new dawn of relations between Athens and Syracuse, and most importantly, the possibility of creating a leader schooled in and guided by the highest philosophical standards. Plato had the opportunity to secure for Athens a strong ally that it had lost with the death of Dionysius the father the year before. In the fast-changing, opportunistic, giddy and complex world of Greece at this time, such a possibility was very welcome indeed.

Plato was convinced to go, not perhaps so much because he wanted to school the new ruler or help Athens in its foreign policy nightmare, but because, according to Plutarch, he was still secretly so ashamed of his failure to have any impact on the father twenty years before. He thus felt duty-bound to try again with the son, if only for the sake of his own reputation. Dionysius the son was also persuaded into the meeting – most likely because, while Plato's teachings didn't sound like they would fit with 90-day drinking bouts, Plato's visit did offer him the opportunity to accomplish something his father had fundamentally failed at. It was most probably thanks to this need to outdo his father that Dionysius ensured that Plato was given the royal welcome. Having been thrown off the island 22 years earlier and bundled aboard an enemy ship taking him to death or slavery, Plato returned to be welcomed onto Syracusan soil by nothing less than the royal chariot.

To begin with, the meeting of these two most opposite of characters, mediated by the irksome and difficult, if brilliant, Dion, was a great success. Dionysius the son was eager to paper over his reputation for stupidity and so was keen to make Syracuse a new intellectual capital in the Greek world. Philosophy was the new booze and philosophical symposia replaced the more typical wine-laden orgies. According to Plutarch, the palace was said to be filled with the business of knowledge, and everywhere one went there was a light sandy dust in the air, thanks to the multitude of mathematicians and philosophers who used loose sand to trace out their ideas on the palace floors.

This utopian image could not last for long. The advisers of the new ruler, who had long been opposed to Dion and his philosophy, detested the new flavour of the regime and were jealous of Dion's influence. What did a powerful ruler, they whispered into Dionysius' ear, need philosophy for? People were beginning to talk about Plato's influence, they continued, and through Plato, about Athens' influence on Syracuse. Most crucially of all, they urgently hissed, this soft approach was beginning to make Dionysius look very weak compared to his iron-man father.

Dionysius the son, so keen to better his father, could not help but be swayed by the arguments. Dion was exiled. Plato was imprisoned. The entente between philosopher and tyrant had once again turned sour. Like lovers driven mad with jealousy, Dionysius promised Plato he would release him if only Plato would agree that he didn't respect Dion any more and that instead he had the most profound respect and admiration for Dionysius. Before Plato had to decide who was his best playground friend, war was once again looming and Dionysius was forced to let Plato go. On his departure, Dionysius begged Plato not to smear his reputation like he had done his father's, not to say anything evil about him to the Greeks, and not to start a revolution against him in Syracuse. As Plato sailed away back to Athens, this time in his own ship, he could feel fairly confident that the third clash between philosopher and tyrant had been his for the taking. Returning to Athens, where the exiled Dion had been welcomed into his Academy, Plato, despite his advanced years, had a new goal: to turn the irksome Dion into the kind of leader he had envisaged all his life. The tyrant Dionysius II had not heard the last of the philosopher Plato.

CHAPTER 8

~~~

The Implosion of Greece

While our attentions have been turned to the globalised and inter-connected nature of the wider Greek world, and particularly to the fate of philosophers in Sicily, events back in central mainland Greece now demand our consideration once again. The era of Theban supremacy had begun following the battle of Leuctra in 371 BC, announced not least by their victory monument at the battlefield and by their dedication of a huge treasure house at the international sanctuary of Delphi to celebrate their new-found success (Figs 6 and 7). Sparta was on the back foot and Athens' foreign policy was not providing the cover or security it needed. Jason from the city of Pherae, now supreme leader of all Thessaly, was hovering in central Greece with a large army. Civil war had broken out in several mainland Greek cities as factions supporting or opposing Thebes sought to gain political control, and the great Persian empire across the Aegean sea was, as ever, watching events with predatory interest.

In 370 BC, just as Jason, the leader of Thessaly, looked to be tightening his stranglehold on central Greece after presiding over the important athletic games held at Delphi, not far from the dancing-floor of Ares, he was assassinated. Assassinated by his own cousin who took his place: Alexander, the new supreme leader of Thessaly.

At the same time as blood was being spilt among the Thessalians, the Thebans were taking advantage of their new-found dominance in Greece to expand their circle of influence. The two heroes of Thebes

– Pelopidas, the body-building philanthropist and leader of the elite Sacred Band, and Epaminondas, the vegetarian philosopher and mastermind of Leuctra – were on the warpath. But neither could know then that Leuctra was the last large set-piece battle these two heroes would ever fight in side by side.

As Jason of Pherae was being assassinated to the north, Epaminondas and Pelopidas decided to press home their advantage by taking the fight south to the gates of Sparta itself. The whole southern part of Greece, the Peloponnese, which had been kept under strict control by Sparta, was now starting to come apart at the seams. Cities, scenting Spartan blood in the water, were taking the opportunity to rebel, declare their freedom and form their own alliances. Inspired by the example of the Thebans and their Boeotian confederacy, a new Arcadian confederacy was born in the central Peloponnese not long after Leuctra. As the political formula of federalism spread on the southern winds, the political power map of Greece was being redrawn.

These newly empowered cities and confederacies were given courage and support by the imposing presence of Pelopidas, Epaminondas and their troops in the Peloponnese itself. The city of Mantinea, which had been decimated and reduced to a series of leaky shacks by Sparta (ironically with Theban help) years earlier, now slowly rebuilt itself with Theban support (Map 2). The Mantinea that emerged, like a butterfly from a grub, was bigger and stronger than ever before. It was one of the great architectural triumphs of the century. A new walled fortress city in the Peloponnese, a visible testament to the fall of Sparta, stood out imposingly over the landscape.

As well as creating, however, Pelopidas and Epaminondas also destroyed. As they marched further and further south into the belly of the Peloponnese in the winter of 370 BC, they ravaged the land as they went. Rarely, if ever, had such an extensive military machine been in motion during the harsh winter months. As the last months of 370 turned into the cold beginning of 369 BC, the Theban army, seemingly unstoppable, continued its march south until it came to the gates of Sparta itself. As the Theban army lined up against the stockade of Sparta, none wept more than the Spartan king Agesilaus. He was the man who had been thrust into the kingship, had taken Sparta to war in Asia Minor and central Greece, hijacked the king's peace, bullied central Greece, forced a puppet government on Thebes, failed to contain the Theban uprising, lost his temper at the peace negotiations of 371 BC, struck Thebes out of the peace treaty and thus precipitated the great showdown between Thebes and Sparta at Leuctra. As the Theban forces gathered at the gates of Sparta, Agesilaus knew that he had been largely responsible for the coming of this day. Plutarch later wrote that Agesilaus was 'tortured by the thought of his reputation in history – since he had been the man who had taken control of the city when she was at her best and now led her to her worst. He was responsible for making the city's proud boast, which he had often himself repeated, null and void: that a Spartan woman would never see the smoke of an enemy's fires.'

Spartan women – for the first time in the history of Sparta – now saw the smoke of the enemy's fires at very close range indeed. They faced the harrowing realisation that war was no longer to be conducted at arm's length but that violence could now strike even at the heart of the most protected community. And yet, for all Thebes' might, the city of Sparta did not fall that winter. Sparta held its city wall and was spared the final – even though perhaps deserved – humiliation. But there was still much more damage that Pelopidas and Epaminondas could inflict. As we have seen, Sparta had long depended on the population of Greeks surrounding the city, which it had enslaved centuries before. These slaves, the helots, from the area of Messenia, were eager for the chance to rebel against their masters, and the Theban army provided just the necessary cover to do so. Pelopidas and Epaminondas, though they did not take the city of Sparta that winter, changed its way of life irrevocably. Messenia was freed – Sparta lost its helot slaves – and in an incredibly short space of time, a new walled city of Messene was created to rival the newly-built fortress city of Mantinea. You can still visit the city of Messene today and marvel at the sheer size of its fortified walls. They tower over you – the work not of men, but of heroes and gods.

Sparta, in its entire history, never had a more disastrous winter than that of 370–369 BC. By the end, it had lost its pride, its slaves – and almost its own city. Within years it was hemmed in by several new fortress cities creating a solid chain around Sparta, preventing it from ever marching north to central Greece again. Sparta was boxed in and isolated in the southern tip of Greece. Its access to the dancing-floor of Ares was clamped shut. It was, for the first time not out of choice, isolated and alone.

The campaign that winter, by contrast, had been the most successful ever for Thebes. Which makes it all the more extraordinary that Pelopidas and Epaminondas, returning to Thebes, were immediately put on trial for their success. The case against them was a technicality. By campaigning through the winter of 370–369 BC, they hadn't returned to Thebes at the end of 370 to be re-elected as generals for the following year. In the midst of their success in the southern Peloponnese, they should, according to their accuser, have stopped, come home, been officially re-elected and subsequently returned. Their accuser was none other than one of their original fellow leaders from the Theban rebellion of 379 BC, who had become irritated at how much Pelopidas and Epaminondas were hogging the limelight. The case was serious enough, despite it being a technicality, to be brought to court in Thebes. Pelopidas, for all his body-building, was said to have broken down in tears like a baby and pointed the finger at Epaminondas, saying that Epaminondas had forced him not to return home. According to Plutarch, Epaminondas, in contrast, the vegetarian philosopher with a reputation for arrogance, looked the judges straight in the eye. He admitted that he had broken the rules, asking for the maximum punishment of death and a tombstone that listed his achievements for Thebes: laying waste to Sparta and the Peloponnese, freeing the helots, building Messene, rebuilding Mantinea, and helping to organise the Arcadian confederacy, not to mention giving the Greeks back their freedom.

The judges in the courtroom started to laugh at the idiocy of the case and left the room without even bothering to vote for an acquittal. Epaminondas, it seemed, could do whatever he liked.

What Epaminondas wanted to do was fight – but not any more with Pelopidas at his side. Whether or not Pelopidas' weakling betrayal of Epaminondas in court had anything to do with it, the fact remains that Pelopidas and Epaminondas never went on campaign together again after the winter of 370–369 BC. Instead, they each created their own spheres of influence: Pelopidas to the north and Epaminondas to the south. Having been acquitted in the spring of 369 BC, Epaminondas invaded the south again in the summer of that year. Yet the balance of power in Greece, in the short break between the successful winter campaign, his court appearance and his return to the south, had changed again. So frightened was it by Thebes' demonstration of its military might that past winter, Athens, struggling to find a new foreign policy, had fallen into bed with the one city that would return its approaches: its old arch-enemy, the equally struggling and isolated city of Sparta. When Epaminondas returned in summer 369 BC, he found a combined Athenian and Spartan army ready to head him off. That year he did not make it so far south, and his campfires were not able to besmirch the view of Spartan women safe inside their city walls.

Pelopidas to the north had an altogether more difficult job. Jason, the previous leader of Thessaly, with whom Thebes had been on good terms, had been assassinated and replaced by his cousin Alexander in 370 BC. Yet some cities in Thessaly had taken the opportunity presented by the crisis in succession to revolt against this new tendency to bring all of Thessaly under a single leader. Thessaly split into two camps, one headed by the city of Pherae (where Jason and Alexander were from) and one headed by the city of Larissa further to the north, near the border with Macedonia. Larissa's options were limited, and so the city turned to Macedon for help against the military might of Pherae. The Macedonian king, who had also come to the throne in 370 BC, was only too happy to oblige, sending in troops to protect them. The question which Pelopidas had to face as he marched north later in 369 BC was which side to support: Jason's blood-stained successor, Alexander, or the rebellious city of Larissa with its Macedonian backer? The answer, for the moment at least, was Alexander. Marching north, he forced the newly-crowned Macedonian king out of Thessaly and even managed to agree a treaty that officially made Macedon a Theban ally. As a guarantee of the peace, Pelopidas demanded hostages from the Macedonian king. Thus it was that, late in 369 BC, a certain young Macedonian noble called Philip was escorted along with a group of other high-value hostages to Thebes. There, Philip was accommodated within the house of one of Thebes' up-and-coming generals, a man called Pammenes, who was in turn close friends with none other than the great Epaminondas. For the next three years, this young man lived with the Theban general and had the opportunity to study and hero-worship Epaminondas at close hand. No one could know that, at the heart of Thebes, listening to its political, military and religious debates, drinking in this exposure to the customs and values of central Greece and establishing relationships with people who mattered, was a young man who would, in 30 years' time, rule over them all: king Philip of Macedon, father to Alexander the Great.

The irony of the situation was that while Thebes kept Philip safe as a hostage in central Greece, Macedon, like Thessaly, was in the grip of a vicious power struggle which could well have seen Philip struck dead. The Macedonian king who had agreed the treaty with the Thebans and become their ally was, by the beginning of the following year, assassinated by another man who would be king. This killing, it was whispered in central Greece, had been even more underhand than that which had ended Jason's life. The new pretender to the Macedonian throne, a man called Ptolemy, had achieved the assassination only with the help of the previous king's own mother, who was also Ptolemy's lover. Like a scene out of Greek tragedy in which family relations have gone obscenely awry, one can imagine the shaking of heads in cities like Thebes and Athens: those barbarian northerners – what sick news would come next?

Thebes had a decision to make – or rather Pelopidas had a decision to make. Did he continue to support Alexander of Pherae, the Thessalian, and avenge the late Macedonian king with whom he had been on good treaty terms, or not? Marching north again in early 368 BC, Pelopidas decided to take on the might of Macedon and its new ruler. He had men, battle-hardened, and many mercenaries. But the new Macedonian king, Ptolemy, thanks to the bountifully fertile and rich lands of Macedon, had cash – and mercenaries follow cash, not causes. Ptolemy liberally bribed Pelopidas' men as they marched towards him so that, by the time the two armies came face to face, Pelopidas was left embarrassingly short of troops and over-exposed. He had little choice but to negotiate a truce and return home to Thebes. The magic was wearing off this Theban hero's crown.

Pelopidas did not just return home. He actually agreed to switch sides. By the winter of the same year, 368 BC, Pelopidas and the might of the Theban army was again marching out north, this time not to attack Macedon, but to turn on their old ally Alexander of Pherae. Once again, the balance of power had lurched suddenly. Alexander was a brutal, cruel man – not even Plato attempted to reform him. He was the kind of man who buried people alive, who would dress his enemies up in bear skins and then set his hunting dogs on them to tear them limb from limb. He had even turned the spear with which he had slain his uncle, Jason, into an object of a religious cult. This was the kind of man who, once Thebes' ally, was now Pelopidas' enemy. Pelopidas, embarrassed into having to attack Alexander following his failure against the new Macedonian king earlier that year, was ill-prepared for the venture against such a man. Soon enough, Pelopidas himself had been captured by this sadistic ruler. Imprisoned in Pherae, Pelopidas faced up to the prospect not only of a violent and cruel death, but the death of his reputation as a heroic and successful Theban general. From the hero of the Theban rebellion and the battlefield of Leuctra, he was now a lone man in a prison cell waiting for his execution. Plutarch later recounts how he welcomed this fate with unnervingly good cheer. Sending a message to

Alexander, Pelopidas asked the Thessalian to hurry up and start tortur-
ing him. Alexander, mystified at someone eager to experience such pain,
asked why he was in such a hurry to die. 'Because,' Pelopidas is supposed
to have replied, 'my death will hasten your own, since it will make you
even more hated by the gods than you are now.'

While waiting for his fate, Pelopidas didn't waste any time in giving the gods a helping hand to assure his future revenge on Alexander.
He took the opportunity to 'befriend' Alexander's wife (although why
he was allowed to even meet her is a mystery) and 'installed in her the
courage' (Plutarch draws a veil over how he managed to do so) later to
murder her own sadistic husband. A few years later, Alexander's wife
would stand over her husband's body, having masterminded the plot
for his slaughter, as a sword was run through him by one of his own
brothers. Pelopidas, while waiting for his own death, had managed to
sign, in the most unusual way, his executioner's death warrant.

Though the speed of events in Greece had, if anything, intensified in
the first years of the 360s BC, it was unclear what had been achieved.
Sparta, ringed in by newly built fortress cities, was now in alliance with
Athens, which prevented Thebes from causing further damage in the
Peloponnese. Thessaly, once Thebes' ally, was now its enemy and had
captured one of Thebes' most illustrious heroes. Macedon, with its
grisly accession record, was an unreliable friend. Back in Thebes, the
enemies of Pelopidas and Epaminondas, who believed they were still
getting too big a share of the limelight, had once again attempted to
hamper the heroes in their quest for Theban supremacy. Epaminondas
had been forced to stand trial for a second time on the technicality
of having allowed a Spartan force to pass by without decimating it,
because, it was alleged, he was a friend of the Spartan commander. This
time the charge seems to have had some weight to it and Epaminondas,
the great hero, was demoted from Boeotian general to ordinary rank-
and-file solider. How the mighty had fallen as Epaminondas, the architect of power in mainland Greece over the previous decade, was forced
to slip back into the ranks. Thebes, by the end of 368 BC, was without

both of its most talented generals, and without them its future looked a little more uncertain.

That uncertainty, that sense that all the cities of Greece were being caught up in a diplomatic and military tornado in which none of them had an exit strategy or even a definable set of goals except to avoid annihilation, drove many of them to seek a way to halt this process. In 368 BC a peace conference was called at the international sanctuary of Delphi by none other than the king of Persia himself. Picking this spot was a powerful statement about the intentions of the conference. Previous peace conferences had been held in the city that happened at the time to be the strongest in Greece (like the ones in Sparta in 386 and 371 BC). This conference belonged to no one city, but was held in neutral territory – the sanctuary of Delphi, the home of the gods – an ancient version of modern-day Switzerland. Not only was it neutral territory, but the sanctuary had an extremely powerful and imposing religious presence in cities and states across the Greek – and indeed entire known – world. A call to a peace conference from Delphi could not be ignored. Geographically, Delphi sat near the dancing-floor of Ares in the belly of mainland Greece. Mythically, Delphi was known as the *omphalos* – the belly button – of the entire ancient world. In 368 BC, the call went out from the Persian king for Greek cities and states to return to the neutral, powerful, physical and mythical centre of the Greek world. The ace card had been played to prevent Greece from speeding ever faster into an inevitable crash of twisted weapons, bodies and dreams. If this didn't work, nothing would.

The peace conference, despite the best efforts of Delphi, its governing body and the king of Persia who was keen to see peace in the region (if only for his own profit), was a disaster. Sparta, as diplomatically blunt as usual, demanded the return of its helot slaves. It also demanded that Thebes be forced to give up its Boeotian confederacy. The demands were outrageous, given Sparta's current position of weakness. Thebes simply walked out of the conference. The cities of Greece, it seemed increasingly clear, were unable to resolve their differences. In a world where the code of behaviour bound every man and city actively to do good to their friends and harm to their enemies, none of them had sufficient power to impose their will irreversibly on the others, and none could settle within agreed spheres of influence and keep to their boundaries. The cities of Greece seemed strapped into a model of politics and international relations which would inevitably end in a sickening self-implosion. Now that the chance of agreed peace was dead, there was only one way forward. As had happened so many times already that century, they all turned to the Persian king. Whoever could gain his support would have the authority and muscle to enforce their will on Greece. Thebes' tantrum walk-out had embarrassed the Persian king enough for him to be willing to return his support to Sparta. But instead of sending a force sufficient to deliver a killer blow, the Persian king sent a paltry offering of 2,000 mercenaries. Not enough for a decisive victory – in fact, only enough really to ensure the continuation of this increasingly bitter struggle.

Thebes as a result was thrown from this peace conference into an even more frenzied round of military and diplomatic activity in a desperate attempt to shore up its ebbing supremacy. Thessaly, having imprisoned Thebes' leader, was now in alliance with Athens and in turn with Sparta. The whole of Greece was once again allied against Thebes, whose first move was to try to free its beloved general imprisoned in Thessaly. Yet the first force it sent north to take on Alexander of Thessaly embarrassingly failed to free Pelopidas from his clutches. Standing in the rank-and-file was the demoted Epaminondas, who had watched the generals he was now forced to obey make a hash of the campaign. Within months, Thebes was obliged, in order to save face against Thessaly, to eat its own words of censure and reinstate Epaminondas as general to lead another campaign to free his one-time bosom buddy.

Epaminondas could be a general of lightning action, as his speed marches and city-building campaigns in the Peloponnese in 369 BC had proved. But this time, he also proved himself a master strategist with the ability to move more slowly and carefully. Knowing that his force was no match for the brute machine of Alexander of Thessaly in open battle, he approached slowly, allowing fear of his name to wreak havoc in the Thessalian lines. Even Alexander wasn't immune to this carefully orchestrated war of psychological attrition. Plutarch later commented that, on hearing that Epaminondas was approaching like a lion stalking its prey, Alexander 'though a bird of prey himself, now huddled himself in a ball like a slave, his wings drooped'. Alexander offered peace and the return of Pelopidas. Epaminondas had mind-gamed his way to victory.

A newly released Pelopidas was returned to Thebes and almost immediately sent on a diplomatic mission to Persia. Everyone was sailing the Aegean sea to get their ambassador into the Persian court in order to win the ear of the Persian king. Pelopidas, never known for his philosophy or intellectual conversation, was nevertheless an expert at putting others at their ease. With consummate skill, he quickly trumped the other Greek cities' ambassadors and persuaded the king to do another U-turn in policy. Persia now supported Thebes, who would attempt to bring a peace to Greece. Sparta would not regain its helots and Athens would be forced to keep its growing fleet off the seas. But once again, this so-called 'peace of Pelopidas' was doomed to failure. Its terms were extremely disadvantageous to Sparta and Athens, who would not accept them unless absolutely forced to – and the only thing that would force them to do so would be a massive Persian invasion force, which the Persian king refused to send. In fact, he sent no immediate military back-up for the peace treaty terms. Pelopidas could only return to Greece, announce the terms and tell everyone to agree. No wonder Athens and Sparta rejected it out of hand. The implosion of Greece was still well on course.

The rejection of the never-acceptable-nor-enforceable peace of Pelopidas ignited an even faster chain of military events in Greece. Epaminondas immediately launched a new campaign against the Peloponnese. He forced major cities at the entrance to the Peloponnese, the narrowest point of Greece called the Isthmus (the area around the

Corinth canal which you can still sail through today (Map 2)), to submit to Theban rule. Progressing further south, he promised support to
the fledgling Arcadian confederacy formed in 369 BC, and helped in
the construction of another new walled city to act as its capital. This
city was called simply Megalopolis – the 'great city'. Sparta was now
hemmed in by a strengthened chain of newly built and heavily fortified glorified watchtower cities. Within a year, Epaminondas had forced
Sparta to accept once and for all the independence of Messene, the area
from which for centuries Sparta had cultivated its slave helot population. Thebes' supremacy seemed once again assured.

Yet Thebes' contentment was short-lived. Events were moving too
fast in too many parts of Greece for its hold on power to be permanent. At the same time as Epaminondas was having his success in the
Peloponnese to the south, Athens was locking horns with Macedon and
Thessaly over the rights to cities on the north Aegean coast, that fertile
and wealthy land from which Athens belligerently and pig-headedly
always wanted a piece of the pie. Athenian naval and military expeditions were constantly being sent north, as Macedon, Thessaly, Athens,
Thrace and even Persia jumped in and out of alliance with one another
and with the three prized cities being fought over – Olynthus and
Amphipolis to the west and the Chersonese (the modern-day Gallipoli)
peninsula to the east (Maps 2 and 3). At the same time, the Macedonian
throne was again thrown into crisis by another assassination and disputed accession to power. At the same time again, the Persian king's
position was unsettled by the beginnings of a revolt against him. The
revolt centred around the cities on the coast of Asia Minor and so, just
as with the revolt led by Cyrus at the beginning of the century, Greek
soldiers were dragged in to fight as mercenaries, and Greek cities were
also forced to take sides and choose whether or not to support the
rebellion in some way. In the middle of the 360s BC, it must have felt
like the whole of the ancient world was on fire, with many cities fighting
on an increasing number of fronts, trying to keep up with, and make
decisions about, fast-changing events in a world where, despite the fact

that battles could be won in an hour and alliances could change in even less, news and instructions could spread only as fast as the horse could gallop and the boat could sail. The Greek world was spiralling out of control.

364 BC saw Thebes more active and frenetic than ever before. Pelopidas, fresh back from his embassy to Persia, was now leading another invasion north against his old adversary and former captor Alexander of Thessaly. His mission, supposedly to aid certain Thessalian towns against the force of Thessalian tyranny, was in reality all about personal revenge. Unlike Epaminondas, who had skirted around Alexander, avoiding direct contact and allowing psychological warfare to do its work, Pelopidas joined in open battle with Alexander on the plains near his home town of Pherae. Pelopidas was left with few men because bad omens of misfortune had preceded the battle, discouraging the main bulk of the Theban army from fighting. He was left only with the brave and the reckless. His strategy matched the mindset of his men. The battle was furious and Pelopidas had only one target: Alexander himself. Throwing himself forward in a win-or-lose-all move, he went in for the kill, only to be hacked down by Alexander's bodyguards. Despite the fact that the Thebans eventually won the battle, Pelopidas, the hero of the Theban rebellion and one of the architects of Theban greatness, was dead.

Plutarch recounts the reaction of his men. 'It is said that the warriors, on hearing of Pelopidas' death, did not bother to take off their armour, un-tack their horses or even bandage their wounds, but came, the sweat of battle still dripping off them, immediately to see the body. Acting as if the corpse could still sense the world around it, they heaped the spoils of victory in front of Pelopidas. They sheared their horses' manes, cut short their own hair, and, going to their tents, refused to light the fires or cook any food, as if they had been entirely defeated that day instead of being victorious over their enemy. From the city of Thebes soon came the magistrates and priests bearing gifts. Taking up the body to carry it home, they were even begged by the most revered of the Thessalians to allow Thessaly the honour of burying such a hero.'

There have been bigger and more ornate funerals for despots and monarchs, Plutarch continued. But there has been no funeral where more people, from so many different cities, have so spontaneously and willingly sought to show one man so much honour. In death, Pelopidas, it seems, had done what he could never achieve in life: he had brought the cities of Greece into agreement.

But that agreement wouldn't last long. In the same year as Pelopidas was killed fighting in Thessaly, Epaminondas, fresh back from his latest charge into the Peloponnese, was setting sail in Thebes' newly constructed navy (built with Persian money), taking advantage of Athens' increasingly precarious position on the north Aegean coast, around the Black Sea and on the coast of Asia Minor, to worry at Athenian interests in the region. His target was the cities, which still technically were allied to Athens as part of the Second Athenian League. The fleet was welcomed at key cities like Byzantium (modern-day Istanbul), Chios and Rhodes (Map 2). But none was willing to openly commit against Athens. The winds of change were blowing around the Aegean much too fast for any of these cities to overtly and completely throw their lot in with just one of the powers thirsting for supremacy.

At the same time as Epaminondas was sailing the Aegean seas, the attention of Thebes was refocused closer to home. The Boeotian city of Orchomenus, which had traditionally been an arch-enemy of Thebes, was once again stirring up resentment against the city. The Thebans, on edge with so much at stake in the power game of the Greek world, lashed out in response. They struck Orchomenus, killed its soldiers, put all the men to death and sold its women and children into slavery. The city was razed to the ground. Thebes was becoming desperate and violent in its attempt to hold on to the precarious reins of power. But its actions served only to swell the ranks of those keen to see it fall. The clouds of a decisive battle for the leadership of Greece were once again beginning to gather. Less than ten years after the battle of Leuctra, which was supposed to have settled the question of supremacy in Greece for good, the cities of Greece were once again gunning for a showdown.

By 363 BC it was clear where that showdown would take place. The Arcadian confederacy in the Peloponnese, newly born and supported in its infancy by the Thebans, had run into trouble. Overreaching, the confederacy had run into conflict with the city of Elis, which ran the international sanctuary of Olympia and its prestigious Olympic games. The Arcadians had taken to the battlefield for ownership of the sanctuary and the battle had raged within the sacred precinct itself. So much had it consumed the sanctuary that, centuries later, the skeletal body of an archer from the battle would be found still lying in the eaves of one of Olympia's temples where he had dropped dead. But the problem was not so much the battle for the sanctuary as the means by which the Arcadians financed it. They used the precious metal dedications, marble offerings and gold and silver, left there for the gods over the previous centuries within the sacred precinct, to pay for mercenary soldiers. This was a sacrilegious step too far – like stripping and selling the contents of the Vatican to finance its military occupation. The city of Mantinea, one of the newly formed fortress cities that Thebes had helped to reconstruct earlier in the decade, now took Arcadia to task over its misuse of the sanctuary and its contents. The local conflict soon spiralled into a national crisis. Thebes would support Arcadia and the confederacy. Sparta and Athens would support Mantinea. The new battle for the leadership of Greece would take place not on the dancing-floor of Ares, but in the very region Thebes had attempted to build up over the last decade to contain Spartan ambition and thus ensure peace.

Epaminondas, in July 362 BC, lined up his troops at Mantinea (Map 2). He brought with him his remaining allies from central Greece (including the recently subdued Alexander of Thessaly). Lining up against him were the cities of Mantinea, Sparta (still under the by now old Agesilaus) and Athens. Epaminondas had approximately 30,000 troops under his command, his enemies 22,000. It was one of the largest battle counts the ancient world had ever seen. Epaminondas, the

Theban hero, placed himself at the head of his troops. He instructed his cavalry to kick up a cloud of dust so that the enemy wouldn't be able to detect his troop arrangement and tactics. But trusting in the strategy that had brought him victory at Leuctra nine years before, he stationed himself and his Thebans on the unlucky left wing. Facing up against his old enemy the Spartans, he led his troops into battle to decide the fate of Greece.

Xenophon, the Athenian who had gone off as the rich young adventurer to fight for the Persian Cyrus and subsequently led the 10,000 Greeks out of Asia, the man who had moved to Sparta and put his children into the Spartan education system, the man whose home was not more than 60 kilometres from the battlefield at Mantinea, ended the history of Greece that he wrote in his old age with his account of this battle. But not because this battle delivered on its promise to be the final decider of power relations in Greece – in fact, quite the opposite. Xenophon ends his narrative in despair: 'There was more confusion and disorder in Greece after the battle than before. This is where I will put down my pen. Perhaps someone else will write about what happened next.'

Epaminondas was dead, killed in action, perhaps even by Xenophon's own son. Both sides had managed to hold (different parts of) their battle lines. Neither was sure who had actually won the battle. In the confusion, both sides erected monuments in an attempt to claim the victory. Both sides went home with little resolved. Human life had been wasted on a massive scale as Greece had spun out of control and self-imploded in a pointless clash of arms at Mantinea. On Epaminondas' tombstone, he was credited with helping all Greece to win freedom and independence. In 362 BC, as the dazed and battle-weary Greeks returned to their homes, freedom and independence seemed bitter prizes which, instead of bringing peace, had brought about a depressing round of endless war. Xenophon, now an old and bitter man, had put down his pen in disgust at what Greece had done to itself.

CHAPTER 9

❦

The Cow's Bladder, the Love Curse and the Caricature

What kind of impact did these political and military events have on the landscape, society, cities and lives of the ancient Greeks? It will come as no surprise, given the fact that Greece seemed to exist within an almost perpetual state of war in the first 40 years of the 4th century BC, that one of the more remarkable surviving pieces of literature from this period is about that very subject. It's a frank and straightforward text dealing with every aspect of preparation for, and engagement in, the art of war – and more specifically, siege warfare – written by a man called Aeneas in the mid-4th century. With this handbook, anyone had the potential to become a tactical military commander, to learn how to conduct sieges, and to undermine their enemy's psychological state. Every citizen living in the cities of Greece now had a ready set of notes to hand on how to survive being under siege, including crucial pieces of knowledge like how to prevent sabotage to crossbows and how to smuggle arms into the city. By far my favourite, however, is how to send a secret message. You can choose between sewing a message into the sole of a shoe, hiding a message in a wound dressing, or, best of all, writing your message on an inflated cow's bladder, which, deflated, can be inserted and hidden within a flask of oil.

Aeneas the Tactician, as the author has become known, opens our eyes to a world in which the art of war had been developing at a tumultuous pace. Traditional campaign seasons were no longer binding, guerrilla skirmishes were now as popular as set-piece battles, mercenary soldiers were as valuable as citizen troops, if not more so, traditional enemies could find themselves fighting on the same side, cities were maintaining permanent armies rather than forming them only at times of need, city-sieges were now commonplace, and the development of military technology had taken off. Warfare had been taken out of the distant plain and made to menace even the most impregnable of cities like Sparta. It reached into everyone's psyche. Aeneas gives us a gateway into the cruel inventiveness of the human mind as the different cities of Greece struggled to react to the changing world around them and fought for their own survival and supremacy. It's a manual produced by one man, but also, in essence, the product of a new, unnerving way of life.

But it would be wrong to think that the only thing to grow out of this heady atmosphere of animosity was a manual on how better to butcher people. The fascinating fact is that, if you look a little above the parapet of war, the 4th century BC becomes a treasure trove of creativity, diversity, construction and discovery, as individuals and cities respond to, cope with, and escape from the realities of the world around them. Cities preparing for constant warfare, which now menaced their own front gates on a regular basis, built grand city walls, for example the rebuilding of Athens' walls; there was the creation of new fortified cities in the Peloponnese during the period of Theban supremacy (Mantinea, Megalopolis, Messene) and earlier at Syracuse in Sicily under the military-industrial complex of the warlord Dionysius I. The first decades of the century created a wealth of impressive cityscapes which towered over their inhabitants and which transformed the landscape around them. These new cities, particularly in the Peloponnese, helped redraw the political map of Greece by making new political alliances, confederacies and independent states into a physical, touchable, concrete reality and, in doing so, transformed the perception of different civic and ethnic identities within that world (Map 2).

The tense, fast-changing environment of the 4th century produced not only city walls. Sculptors were also increasingly called in to make visual the dreams of powerful individuals, to translate euphoria at military success or the achievement of peace into marble and bronze works of art, to push the boundaries of what was artistically and physically possible as one city tried to rival another. The result was a century of extraordinary artistic creation: from the expensive rival monuments to military and athletic victory which stood facing off against one another at the international sanctuaries of Delphi and Olympia (Figs 5 and 6); to the touching statue of a female figure of peace, Eirene, holding the infant god of wealth, Ploutus, in her arms, set up in Athens to mark the slim hopes of peace glimpsed in the mid-370s (Fig. 9); to the arrogantly elaborate funerary monuments for individuals in many cities across *megale Hellas*, best exemplified by the Greco-Persian creation of the Mausoleum (Fig. 11); to the display of the taboo-breaking first fully naked female statue of the goddess of love and sex, Aphrodite, at Cnidus on the coast of Asia Minor (Fig. 10). Artistic creation in the 4th century reacted to, personified, articulated and soared above the realities of the world in which it existed.

The 4th century BC was also filled with creativity on the theatrical stage. Greece, or rather in fact Athens, is credited with making tragedy an art-form in the 5th century, producing playwrights whose names have echoed through the ages: Aeschylus, Sophocles and Euripides. For the 4th century, however, the theatrical stage seems at first sight to have gone dark. Who can name off-hand a 4th-century tragedian of worth? Yet such an initially unfavourable impression hides a very different reality. Greek cities were falling over themselves to build theatres in the 4th century. From the theatre of Dionysus at the foot of the Acropolis in Athens, which was finally built in stone instead of temporary wood in the 4th century (Map 1), to the spectacular stone theatre at Epidaurus, which still hosts performances to this day, to a theatre for 20,000 spectators at the newly formed capital of the Arcadian confederacy at Megalopolis, to the Sicilian city of Segesta – by the end of the 4th century, nearly every major city and sanctuary in Greece and the wider Greek world had a theatre.

What was put on in them? So little has survived, but we can glimpse enough to know that the 4th century was incredibly productive. There was a palpable thirst for restagings of the great 5th-century tragedies. But there was also a huge amount of new material. One 4th-century playwright, Astydamas the younger, who seems to have been a relative of the great tragedian Aeschylus, may well have produced something in the order of 240 plays during his lifetime. Civic festivals to celebrate tragedy and comedy were springing up not just in Athens, but for the first time were being exported across Greece and even to southern Italy and Sicily. Actors and playwrights were superstars. They formed trade unions and had fan clubs. Today, famous actors are often recruited as UN goodwill ambassadors, but in the 4th century BC, actors had enough pull even to be sent on diplomatic missions to represent particular cities in international negotiations. In 348 BC, Athens would send a delegation to bargain with the all-powerful king Philip of Macedon which included their most famous actor, a man who preferred to be known by his stage name: Neoptolemus (the son of the god-like Achilles).

This marked rise of interest, and investment, in theatre across the Greek world underlines the popularity of drama in ancient society. But more than that, it emphasises the importance of what drama offered: the creation of a space in which live political, social, cultural and religious issues could be discussed and thought about at a safe distance. The stage was as important as the political assembly in helping people to reflect upon their changing world. Aristophanes, the comic playwright whose career spanned the 5th and 4th centuries BC, was particularly adept at responding to the mood of the people. In 395 BC, as beleaguered Athens was being drawn into fresh conflict with Sparta, his play *Ecclesiazusae* (*Women at the Assembly*) was written and performed at Athens. Its plot is simple. The men are making a hash of running the city's affairs. The women of Athens plot to take over because they are much better at running home affairs. Having seized power, the women lay out a plan for a proto-communist state. Everyone will be equal and have equal access to everything – including sexual partners. So, the argument goes, if you are a man who wants to bed a pretty girl, you first have to pleasure an ugly one (and the same for the women with handsome and ugly men), so that everyone gets a fair bite at the cherry, as it were. The plan of course falls to pieces, but the play aptly represents the sheer frustration felt at the ongoing political upheaval in Greece at the beginning of the century. In 388 BC, just eight years after his *Women at the Assembly*, Aristophanes chose to update and restage one of his old plays, *Wealth*. By this time, Athens was once again feeling the economic squeeze and was about to be forced into accepting the terms of the Persian king's peace. The play responds to that mood by creating an idyllic world in which wealth is equally shared and everyone has everything they need.

But the building of new cities and city walls, the fashioning of unparalleled varieties of elaborate and intricate sculpture and the creation of grand theatres and sardonic comedies were not by any means the most impressive or perhaps the most important cultural achievements of the Greek world during the 4th century. If you visit Greece today, what will strike and impress you most are not the city walls and fortifications, the sweeping theatres, or even the sumptuous sculptures housed in Greece's many museums, but the religious sanctuaries and temples that dominate the landscape. From the more famous, like the Parthenon in Athens, to those off the beaten track, like the oracular sanctuary of Dodona in north-western Greece, these religious sanctuaries and their temples stand as the best testament to the most crucial aspect of life in ancient Greece: the power of the gods.

The many gods of the Greek world were everywhere and in everything (even going to the theatre was part of a religious festival). The gods were all-powerful, and so it was critical that mere mortals did everything they could to keep them on side. Part of that business of

keeping the gods on side was the building of altars and temples to worship, honour and bribe them with sacrifices (the Greek gods appreci-
ated nothing more, it was said, than the fine fragrant smoke drifting up
to Mount Olympus from pieces of burning bone wrapped in animal
fat placed on the altar). Greek religion had no central book of rules
and moral stories – no equivalent of the Bible or the Koran – nor did
it have any defined creeds of belief as many religions do. Instead, Greek
religion was made up of a series of prescribed actions and rituals which,
together, gave a rhythm and sense to the harsh realities of life. Religion
fed into, and bound together, every aspect of social, cultural, political
and military life, and yet at the same time it was an extremely flexible
system which could incorporate new gods and places of worship as it
went. But most important of all, it was omnipresent. The Greeks would
have had trouble understanding the question, 'Are you a believer?' For
them, there was no option. The gods existed and ruled over the world.
That was simply how it was.

The ancient Greek world in the 4th century BC saw a rush of temple-
building to honour the gods, which rivals pretty much anything seen in
previous centuries. It was not a rush centred on one city, like Athens had
been the centre of a building spree in the previous century. This time, a
great proportion of the whole ancient world was busy temple-building.
This may at first surprise us, given the turbulence of that world and the
dangers and difficulties, particularly economic difficulties, in commit-
ting to a large, costly project such as building a temple (about the most
costly single project ever undertaken in the ancient world). The citizens
of Plataea in central Greece, for example, thought it safe to come out of
the city to tend their fields only when the Thebans were gassing away
in their long-winded assembly meetings. When would they find time to
safely build a temple? Yet the rush of temple-building during this period
could equally be understood as a dramatic response to that same uncertainty and turbulence. In times of crisis, Greeks turned to their gods
for help in an attempt to understand why those gods had allowed such
things to happen. In a world that was imploding on itself, perhaps the

only answer was to redouble the efforts where the gods were concerned in order to secure a more peaceful future.

One of the most interesting things about this spree of temple-building is how it both reflects and supersedes the military tenor of the time. At the turn of the new century, as Sparta was careering around the coast of Asia Minor and in central Greece trying to take over the remnants of the Athenian empire and establish itself as the new supreme power in Greece, a temple was on the verge of completion in the highlands of the central Peloponnese. Visiting this temple today involves a lengthy drive up winding roads and around precipitous corners until you seem to be touching the clouds. The air there is cold and dry as it whips around you. Goats, the only local inhabitants, clamber skilfully up and down the rock face and across your path. There, at a place called Bassae, standing on a pinnacle of rock, is a colonnaded temple piercing the skyline. It's an extraordinary sight: an intricate piece of human creation in a world dominated by the blunt power of nature. Today, still standing after more than 2,000 years of being battered by the winds, it's covered by a white aero-dome for its own protection. It looks as if some kind of spaceship has landed in the middle of the sleepy Peloponnese.

The temple of Apollo at Bassae is composed of an innovative and playful mix of different architectural styles, designed perhaps by the same architect who masterminded the Parthenon in Athens. Its architectural sculpture, a continuous, finely-sculpted storyboard of warfare which ran around the walls of the inner sanctum, is stunning in its vivacious energy and intricate detail (it can be seen today in the British Museum in London). The question becomes – what is a temple like this doing in a place like that? A wonder of human ingenuity and skill, it sits in the middle of nowhere. The clue is in the descriptive epithet given to the god whom the temple celebrated: Apollo *epikourios* – Apollo 'the mercenary'. Long ago, this route over and through the mountainous region of Arcadia resounded with the sound of marching feet as soldiers travelled from and towards Sparta. Through the 4th century, as we have seen, those soldiers would continue to pass that way and back again with increasing frequency as war spread like wildfire through the Peloponnese. The temple to Apollo the mercenary seems to have been built in recognition of the needs of the men who passed through there, as a place to which they could turn for guidance and pray for their safe return. Standing lonely on the mountain-tops today, the temple of Bassae stands as a reminder of the many who would not return.

The temple at Bassae echoes the military mood of the end of the 5th century and the early decades of the 4th century BC and the concerns of the many men who spent much of that time at war. Back in central Greece, we can see another temple that, though seemingly above the rigours of war, also played its part in this military power game. On the much-disputed border between the territories of Thebes and Athens, there sits the settlement of Oropus. Not far from the settlement is a wooded cleft valley with a stream running through the bottom of it. It's a place simultaneously full of eerie silence and echoing noise as the streaming water finds its way through the valley floor, the sound deadened by the thick forest around it. The air is full of expectation and other-worldliness. In the middle of the 4th century, as tensions continued between the major cities of Greece and as the might of Macedon began to be felt the length and breadth of the country, a temple was built in this sacred place to celebrate the mysterious oracle Amphiaraus and his cult of healing. The calm and peace of the site today belies its political and military importance. By building a sanctuary, the city constructing it could lay claim to ownership of the territory around it. This sanctuary lay in something like the ancient equivalent of Kashmir – an area of land whose ownership was hotly disputed between Athens and Thebes. The sanctuary became, just like the city of Oropus nearby, a pawn in the game of control between these two cities and changed hands several times in the first 60 years of the 4th century.

But it's also crucial to realise that not all the temples constructed in the 4th century became part of this campaign of military aggression. One of the consequences of continued warfare in the Greek world had been the increase in popularity of a relatively new god: Asclepius – the god of healing. His acme came in the 4th century when a massive new sanctuary was laid out in which to worship and commune with the god at a place called Epidaurus (the sanctuary incorporated the big theatre that you can still see plays in today). Epidaurus was not far from the Isthmus, the narrow central crossing point which connected the Peloponnese to the rest of the Greek mainland (Map 2). Here, in this central location, a sanctuary was constructed, not just for one city to control, but open to all who wanted to come.

Surviving to this day are the records, inscribed on stone, detailing the phases of the entire construction project. Ambassadors were sent out across Greece to promote the cult and collect funds for its construction. Contracts with builders were agreed, permissions signed, snag lists checked off, financial guarantees made – these documents provide a precious spy-hole through which to observe how the Greeks pushed through such massive community projects. Overwhelmingly, the impression comes through that the authorities at Epidaurus were picky, demanding, non-delegating micro-managers. They oversaw the minutiae of the construction process, even taking interest in the cost of repairing particular types of ropes used to help make a wagon-cart able to withstand a heavy load of stone.

But what is really fascinating is not so much the costs of the project as where the workers came from. Each city did not have its own supply of workers and craftsmen. Instead, when a city wanted to build something, it put the call out to craftsmen from all over the Greek world, who would gather in the city for as long as there was work to be done. Like a swarm of birds migrating around the Mediterranean, these craftsmen – builders, stonemasons, marble and metal specialists, sculptors, architects – were an incredibly international bunch. For over four years at Epidaurus, around 200 specialists from all over ancient Greece were at work. As the cities of the Greek world continued to make war against one another, the ironic result of the increasing need for sanctuaries of healing was that the sanctuary at Epidaurus itself became the highly visible outcome, not of military struggle, but of international architectural and artistic collaboration. Nor was it simply evidence for collaboration between artists and architects. Even rulers from as far distant as Sicily were involved. Dionysius I of Syracuse, for example, was in communication with the sculptors at Epidaurus over whether or not to represent the god Asclepius with facial hair.

Another such highly visible example of international collaboration at a time of international war was at the great oracular sanctuary at Delphi. Situated again in central mainland Greece, this sanctuary was the mythical centre of the ancient world. It had played its part many times in the politics and war of Greece (Fig. 5), most recently in hosting the abortive peace conference of 368 BC. Its main temple, dedicated to Apollo, had been rebuilt several times over the previous centuries. But in the late 370s Delphi was once again struck by a massive earthquake that destroyed the temple. The sanctuary was too important to leave in ruins. But Delphi was a neutral international sanctuary. So whose responsibility was it to pay for the rebuilding of the temple? As with many such negotiations in modern-day international bodies like the UN and EU, with which Delphi has often been compared, it was decided that the burden should be shared. Every city which gave money to help with the rebuilding of the temple at Delphi was listed on a series of donor plaques set up within the sanctuary for all to see. Visiting Delphi, the viewer was confronted not with a picture of Greek cities at each other's throats, but of them standing side by side in a communal effort to rebuild a temple in a place which had, for hundreds of years, acted as a central meeting point for the Greek world.

Looking at temples offers a fantastic insight into the religious and political values, aspirations and motives of cities, sanctuaries and groups of people. But we can also look at evidence for particular kinds of religious practices going on around these temples to understand how individual people acted and reacted in their everyday lives to the turbulent climate that surrounded them. In the 4th century BC, at a remote site in north-western Greece, an oracle of the father of the gods, Zeus himself, was gaining in popularity at a place called Dodona (Map 2).

The sanctuary had long been a simple affair centred on a sacred tree. But in the 4th century, demand for the oracle, and investment in the sanctuary, seems to have taken off. From the point of view of modern scholarship, the best thing about this sanctuary is the way in which the questions posed to the oracle were recorded. In many oracular sanctuaries, questions would be spoken out loud or written on papyrus – methods of transmission which leave few archaeological footprints over thousands of years. But at Dodona the questions were written on small pieces of metal, folded over and buried at the site. The result, over 2,000 years later, is a direct insight into the concerns and worries of the everyday men and women of ancient Greece. One questioner asks whether he should live with his half-sister; another if he should marry another woman; a troubled homeowner asks if Thorpion really did steal the silver; a concerned father asks how his daughter can best preserve her virginity. Despite the constant warfare and the brutal rollercoaster of international affairs going on around them, it's a rare privilege for us to be able to witness at close hand people's attempts to understand and cope with the problems of day-to-day life, a life that echoes with many of the same sorts of concerns that face us today.

The 4th century also offers us plentiful evidence for the increase in popularity of a different form of religious interaction between individuals and the divine: the curse. Calling upon the strength of the gods of the earth and the underworld, as well as the spirits of the dead, individuals could try to control the world around them by 'binding' people with a curse to their demands or, worse, to a particular grisly fate. These curses have survived to us today because, just like the oracular questions at Dodona, they were written on small folded pieces of metal and buried in graves or sanctuaries of the underworld to gain the power of the divine and so infect their intended victim. They cover a wide range of issues encountered in the business of daily life, including success and failure in the law courts, the theatre and commerce. In the territory of Athens, one person railed against other people's success, cursing them thus: 'All these men, I bind to unemployment, obscurity, bad health, failure and death – not just to them but to all their wives and children too.' But by far the biggest growth area for curses was not war or business, but the prickly matter of love. Examples abound of those who, smitten and subsequently rebuked in love, turn to the gods for their revenge. 'I bind [curse] Aristokydes and any woman who strips for him. Do not let him ever marry anyone else', curses one female jilted lover. Another is harsher (this time a man): 'I bind her hands, her mind, her spirit, her head, her heart and her tongue.' Another woman, seemingly gazumped by a new lover, is harsher still: 'I turn Euboula away from Aeneas, from his face, his eyes, his mouth, his breasts, his spirit [this could also be his penis – the Greek word has multiple meanings], from his stomach … from his arse, and from his whole body.'

These curses do more, however, than provide a magazine-style problem page of the ancient world for nosy 21st-century eyes. Combined with the Dodona evidence for the increasing use of oracles by individuals desperate to learn the best course of action for the future (one could also point to the greater use in this period of more dangerous procedures through which to learn the future, like attempts to consult the spirits and bodies of the dead), they underline an increasing sense of uncertainty about life among individual people, and an increasingly aggressive set of attempts to regain some kind of control over it. By the end of the century, curse-sellers could make a good living by wandering the streets of Greece offering their wares. This sense of uncertainty was not, however, simply motivated by the constant war and the political and economic change going on around the people living in the different cities of ancient Greece. It was also motivated by a sense of the changing nature of the most basic tenet of that world: belief in the gods themselves.

Earlier in this chapter, I argued that Greeks would not have understood the question 'Do you believe?' since there was little alternative – the world was as it was. But that monopoly came under threat in the 4th century BC. The threat came not, as one might expect and as we often fear today, from the globalisation of the ancient world and the resultant mixing of cultures, customs and belief systems. The Greek gods were, after all, infinitely flexible, as the introduction of the god of healing Asclepius to the godly line-up had proved. In the later part of the century also, Athens would happily be making space available in its city for the worship of foreign gods like Isis and Bendis by traders and resident immigrants from Egypt and further afield. Nor was the problem the increasing use of 'shadowy' underworld religious practices like curses, often referred to, wrongly, as Greek 'magic'. The problem was not the flexible boundaries of whom or what one worshipped. The problem rested in a more basic rejection of the power of the gods and questioning of the way in which they should be worshipped, if at all.

The origins of these movements are hard to trace but were for certain entangled with the growth of philosophy, and particularly the growth of intellectual scepticism, which led some to challenge even the existence of divine power. New forms and practices of worship gathered strength in the 4th century. One group, known as the Pythagoreans – who probably counted Epaminondas, the great general of Thebes, among their number – believed in the transmutation of souls between animal and human form. As a result, they didn't believe in animal sacrifice and were practising vegetarians. The problem here was not that they worshipped different gods, but that they differed on how to worship them. Refusing to partake in animal sacrifice meant that Pythagoreans wouldn't take part in the big civic rituals, at which animal sacrifice was hugely important. These people, because of their beliefs, cut themselves out of the social fabric of civic society and reinforced this message by often withdrawing to live in their own separate communities. Another such splinter-faction were the Orphics, who, like the Pythagoreans, were also vegetarians. But in some ways they went further. They imagined the relationships of the gods and their respective roles in the world in a significantly different way to the norm, practised different burial rites, and even seem to have created a central creed of belief and a bible-like collection of religious writings. By the end of the 4th century BC, the Greek world was filled not just with different gods but with increasingly distinct camps of religious belief, which had profound, divisive social and political implications for their civic community and identity. Religion had always been the thing that brought Greeks together. Now, that was not as certain as it had been.

The problems caused by this diversity of religious belief were exacerbated by the growth of scepticism and scientific investigation in the 4th century BC – most clearly in the field of medicine. One 4th-century medical writer would challenge the labelling of a particular illness as the 'sacred disease' (modern-day epilepsy), arguing that the illness had nothing to do with the will of the gods – it had a human cause. Such a rejection of the role of the gods – and by extension, their role in healing – was felt even at the new and popular healing sanctuary at Epidaurus. By the end of the century, the sanctuary was taking its competition so seriously that it inscribed its success stories on public stone plaques to advertise that the godly healthcare system worked just fine. A woman, the plaques pronounced, who had been mysteriously pregnant for a full five years, was miraculously made to give birth by the god. A man with paralysis in his hand was given back full use of his fingers. The blind were given back their sight, the dumb their voice, the bald their hair – and the sanctuary even advertised that a cup, broken in fragments, was miraculously repaired by the god.

An investigation into the religious practices of the Greeks in the 4th century thus underlines some of the tensions felt in the Greek world as a whole at this time. New developments in religious practice and belief shook the foundations of individual and civic communities, but also provided new ways in which those individuals could feel more in control of their lives and the world around them. New religious building both reflected the increasing military tenor of the ancient world and loudly articulated that temple-building could still be something which brought the Greeks closer together. Similarly, the spread of theatre and drama, particularly comedy, both underlined a common bond between cities spread across the Greek world and gave them a space in which to reflect upon the difficult conditions they faced and the ingrained differences between them. Sculpture and architecture immortalised the intense conflict in which Greece had embroiled itself, but also inspired that world by creatively pushing forwards the boundary of the possible.

In such an uncertain world, it's not surprising that a search for something certain became something of an obsession. The 4th century BC was *the* century for serious investigations, across a wide range of fields such as philosophy, drama, science and art, into the systems and creatures of the natural world as well as the nature of human knowledge and interaction, love, wisdom, law, purity, political activity and the soul. Philosophers like Plato, Aristotle and Epicurus, proto-medics like Empedocles and Praxagoras, comic playwrights like Aristophanes and Menander, artists like Lysippus and Praxiteles, took people from every part of the ancient world on an absorbing journey into the very heart of what humanity, society and nature were really about. Such a journey inevitably at times came into conflict with more traditional thinking, as with the question of healing through divine or human means. The 4th century was a time of brutal military and geo-political upheaval, but it was also, in part as a result of this, a time of intense self-reflection and progressive (if sometimes confrontational) discovery. It's no accident that the same century that produced Aeneas and his manual of siege warfare also produced, among many other great thinkers, a man called Theophrastus, who wrote both an enquiry into the nature of plants and a brilliantly observed caricature sketch of different flawed types of human personality and how to recognise them. The Greek world was in the grip of tumultuous change and, in this new era of reflection and investigation, everyone could not but become more aware both of themselves and the world in which they lived.

CHAPTER 10

━◦◦━

Ten Years That Changed the Ancient World: 362–352 BC

A debilitating stalemate had come to mainland Greece in the immediate aftermath of the battle of Mantinea in 362 BC. It was difficult for anyone to imagine what might come next. Most of the men who had had experience of the last great conflict of Greek cities against Greek cities – the Peloponnesian war at the end of the previous century – were dead. Most of the great revolutionary leaders of the early part of the 4th century BC – men like Pelopidas and Epaminondas of Thebes – were also dead. Thebes, which had so relied on the genius of these individuals to lead its quest for supremacy, had now lost its way Sparta was alive, but exhausted and demoralised. Athens was frustratingly unable to hold on to any semblance of supremacy in the wider Greek world and was still locked in conflict to maintain its vital arteries to food and natural resources across the Aegean. An exhausted Greece shuffled towards a peace table in the immediate aftermath of Mantinea. The result was a common peace – in ancient Greek, a *koine eirene*. The use of such hopeful words summed up the bitter need for what they promised. But the cities of Greece had been here too many times before to believe fully in its terms. How many peaces had been signed and either ripped up or ignored immediately afterwards, in the past 40 years? This one looked no more promising: just a way of giving each city some breathing time before they launched into another round of horn-locking and head-ramming. Sparta didn't even sign it. As Greece eased towards the end of another decade of almost constant conflict, the same pattern seemed to be repeating itself once again. Sparta was isolated. Thebes tried vainly to gather allies against Sparta. Athens equivocated. The Persian king was nowhere to be seen.

But something *was* happening. Outside of the mainland cities of Greece, in the wider Greek world, a set of circumstances was coming into alignment like the sun, moon and earth during an eclipse. Against this backdrop something extraordinary would happen, and within a decade the ancient world would be changed forever. But no one at the time could have known just how dramatic that change would be, or even that it was just over the horizon.

The driving force behind these celestial circumstances was instability – the sort that had plagued the wider Greek world, just like central Greece, for most of the current decade. In Sicily, the clash between philosopher and tyrant was still very much alive. Dionysius II, the stupid, drunken successor to his father, the warlord Dionysius I, was still in charge. At the last count, he had exiled his philosophical, brilliant, yet annoyingly critical adviser Dion, and sent Plato packing back to Athens, begging him not to perform a character assassination on him like Plato had managed to orchestrate for his father. But Plato, sitting in his Academy back in Athens, with Dion now resident, had other plans. Dion was to become his new protégé. Dion would be the first true philosopher-ruler.

The most critical part of this training, Plato realised, was to smooth off Dion's rough edges. He was frankly too annoying, too critical, too intellectually aloof for anyone to ever vote for him, let alone support him as their leader. He needed to be humanised. He needed an image make-over. Plato sent him to spend time with carefully chosen people in the Academy, across Athens, and in the different cities of central Greece, who could be counted on to give him some of the necessary magic: sweet-tempered people who would round off his pompous aloofness and give him the 'common touch'. Plato was creating a popular sensation.

Dionysius II had no such luck. He had exiled Dion, pretending to the people of Syracuse all the while that he would be recalled one day. The mystique of the banished hero is a powerful aphrodisiac to people held tight under the thumb of a tyrant. Dion's value started to climb in Syracuse without either Dion or Plato lifting a finger. Dion – the aloof intellectual with little skill at courting the people – was, before Dionysius' very eyes, morphing into a swashbuckling hero who had the women of Syracuse in particular in a swoon. Plutarch, the later biographer, recounts how the women of Syracuse would put on mourning dress for his absence as they went about the city, and send him care packages to help him through his exile. Love letters and small forget-me-nots made their way to Athens and to the Academy, to this most unlikely of pin-ups. Dion had gone from zero to hero in no time at all.

It wasn't long, of course, before Dionysius lost patience. His pretence that Dion was merely temporarily exiled started to slip. Dion's possessions and property in Syracuse were attacked and confiscated. Dionysius' mood wasn't improved by reports coming from central Greece about how well Dion had reacted to Plato's make-over. He was being welcomed across Greece as the must-have guest. Even Sparta liked him so much that they intended to make him an honorary Spartan citizen. Dionysius responded with cringeworthy ineffectiveness. He tried to establish a new Academy in the heart of Syracuse to outwit the greatest wit of them all: the philosopher Plato himself. Dionysius went round Syracuse trying to recite lines of philosophy that he had learnt off by heart to make himself look brilliant – and got most of them wrong. The rising tide of mirth directed against this butcher dressed in a philosopher's beard finally proved too much. Dionysius called Plato back to Syracuse for one final meeting. He promised that Dion would be reinstated in Syracuse only if Plato came to visit. Now in real old age, Plato, ever the optimist, went back to Syracuse. This was the rematch between philosophy and tyranny.

Dionysius offered Plato the most impressive of gifts – the right to come into the tyrant's presence without being strip-searched. Lucky Plato. But the tyrannical wolf was still no philosophical lamb, and the meeting was little more than an ambush. Plato's life was threatened and an urgent plea to the nearby city of Tarentum on the coast of Italy fortunately provided a ship in which Plato could sail away to safety. The parting words between Plato and Dionysius, according to Plutarch, summed up their clash. 'I suppose you are going to tell everyone about me?' Dionysius is supposed to have snarled. 'I very much hope I and the Academy have better things to talk about than you', Plato tartly replied before getting on his ship.

Plato washed his hands of the tyrants of Syracuse. But he had created someone who would not. Dion, now with his character smoothed and his admirers waiting for him, plotted the downfall of Dionysius. The final straw was Dionysius forcing Dion's wife, who all this time had been stuck in Syracuse (and must have been quite bemused at her husband's new-found pin-up status), to take a new husband. The invasion of Syracuse was initiated by Dion gathering troops as he went. It was said that a man loyal to Dionysius tried to warn him of the impending arrival of Dion but that his letters were stolen from the messenger's bag by a wolf while he slept. On such quirks of fortune did the fate of Syracuse rest.

By sheer chance – and thanks to the wolf's hunger – Dion found the city of Syracuse largely undefended, due to the fact that Dionysius was out on campaign elsewhere. Moving effortlessly to the centre of the city, and no doubt avoiding a gaggle of screaming female fans as he went, Dion declared that Syracuse was free from the tyrant. They loved him for it. But no man can stand up to the crushing weight of expectation created by a reputation crafted from afar. Dion soon found himself under renewed attack not only from Dionysius, who came back home to find his city taken over and subsequently made repeated attempts to win it back, but also from the very people who had welcomed him. Wounded in battle, Dion's new mask of cheeriness and approachability

1. An ancient portrait bust of Alexander the Great.

2. The Pnyx hill in the centre of Athens (with the Acropolis and Parthenon in the background) where the democratic assembly of the Athenians met, as it remains today (below).

3. The public graveyard of Athens, the Cerameicus, as it can be visited today, with the ancient grave markers for fallen heroes of the city.

4. The landscape of the ancient city of Sparta, overlooked by the Taygetus mountains (below).

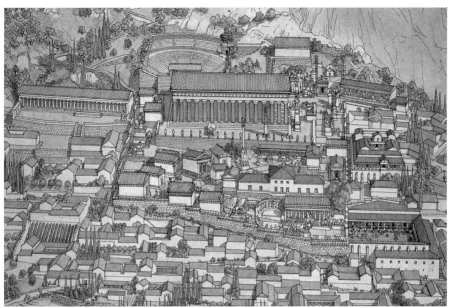

5. A reconstruction of the ancient international sanctuary of Delphi, nestled in the Parnassian mountains.

6. A reconstruction of the ancient international sanctuary of Olympia, on the plains of the Peloponnese.

7. The Theban victory monument located on the battlefield at Leuctra.

8. The remains as they can be seen today of the defensive wall built by the Athenians to protect Attica against Spartan invasion.

9. A Roman copy of the statue of Eirene and Ploutus sculpted in Athens in the 4th century BC.

10. A Roman copy of the Aphrodite of Cnidus, the first-ever fully naked female statue in Greek art.

11. A recreation of Mausolus' funeral Mausoleum, one of the seven wonders of the ancient world.

From J. Stevenson, *A Restoration of the Mausoleum at Halicarnassus*, 1909

12. The law for the protection of democracy set up in Athens in 338 BC, as it survives today, with the young personification of democracy crowning the old man of the people (below).

American School of Classical Studies, Athens: Agora Excavations

13. The lion set up by King Philip of Macedon sitting over the murdered bodies of the Theban Sacred Band at the battlefield of Chaeronea.

14. The temple and oracle of the god Ammon at the Siwah oasis in the Egyptian desert.

15. The remains of the great
Persian capital of Persepolis.

16. The *Tyrannicides* statue
group, which was returned to
Athens by Alexander the Great.

began to slip and be replaced by his old aloof intellectual rigour and criticism. Opponents in the city protested that they had replaced a stupid drunk with a watchful and sober master – and they weren't sure which they preferred. Dionysius, losing hope, sailed off into the sunset for an easy life of exile, but even then the people of Syracuse didn't settle with their new leader. Like the British rejection of Winston Churchill in the election immediately following victory in the Second World War, the citizens of Syracuse now moved to throw out Dion and his merce-naries. Plutarch later commented that 'the people, trying to stand on their own two feet after being ill for so long infected with tyranny, tried to overreach in demonstrating their independence, and made a griev-ous error.'

Dion was driven out of the city that had welcomed him with adoring arms. But the Syracusan people soon found themselves in trouble again from Dionysius, who was encouraged by the rejection of Dion to have one more attempt at regaining power. Dion, sighing his masterfully philosophical sigh, with all the intellectual aloofness that must have so irritated the people of Syracuse, is supposed to have said to his troops: 'Stupid Syracusans, the most foolish and ill-fated of people – they don't deserve your help but if you do want to fight for them, then let us do so once again.'

The showdown in the very streets of Syracuse between the forces of Dion and Dionysius was a bloody struggle to the death. Dionysius was consumed with a passion to turn the city into a living tomb. Dion and his men were forced to fight from street to street in thick smoke as the city burned around them. Their hard-won victory and the final exile of the tyrant Dionysius was celebrated most by the women of Syracuse, who had fallen in love (once again) with their hero. But Dion, like the philosopher he was, attached little importance to women throwing themselves at him. His eyes were fixed firmly on the judgement of the Academy in Athens and of his philosophical counterparts. So it must have been with great surprise and sadness that Dion found one of his old friends at the Academy now working to undermine him. The man, a certain Callippus, had been a close companion during Dion's days at the Academy but now sought to turn the people against him. The women of Syracuse, sensing that their hero was in danger, gathered together to force Callippus to swear that he would do Dion no harm. Callippus, a philosopher but clearly not a believer in oaths, waited until the very day that was sacrosanct to the god under whose auspices he had sworn his oath to murder Dion. This man, this philosopher-ruler, this saviour of Syracuse, was killed by hired assassins while begging for his life, locked and cornered in his dining room. It was the sad end of a man who had wanted little, it seems, but to be the kind of leader that the Greek world could only dream of.

At the other side of the Aegean, on the coast of Asia Minor, a similar competition for power between individuals had been gathering pace. From the mid-360s BC onwards, there had been a series of rebellions by powerful local governors against the might of the Persian king himself. The latest, in 362 BC, the same year as the battle of Mantinea in central Greece, was by a man called Mausolus. He governed an area on the southern part of the coast called Caria, centred around his soon-to-be-completed new capital, Halicarnassus (modern-day Bodrum in Turkey (Map 2)). Mausolus was a man of expensive taste with a liking for grandiose design. Soon enough, Halicarnassus would be furnished not just with a palace for him to live in, but a funeral monument ready for his death that became one of the seven wonders of the ancient world – a monument whose style still bears his name: the Mausoleum (Fig. 11). But unlike mausoleums today, often of limited size, this Mausoleum was on a scale almost unimaginable. Finished by Mausolus' wife Artemisia, who ruled Halicarnassus after his death (how different is this to the limited political power of women in mainland Greece at the time), the Mausoleum towered over the community, focusing everyone's attention on one individual. Even in death, Mausolus was assured of not being forgotten.

Mausolus' attempts to join the rebellion against the Persian king quickly fell flat, as a key rebellion ally had turned tail and fled back to join the king. But the region remained fundamentally unstable, not least because the Persian king died in 359. His new, inexperienced successor came to the throne in the midst of a power crisis and while Persia was still at war with Egypt. The new king slowly came to grips with his kingdom, but in the meantime the coastal area of Asia Minor was a playground for powerful individuals to set up their own mini-kingdoms and independent dynasties. In the early 350s BC, this coast-line of the Aegean, which housed a potent mix of Greek cities, Persian subjects and governors, independent cities and mini-dynasties, was a powder keg waiting to explode. It didn't have to wait long. The coastline had long been of interest to Athens, which had made efforts to recruit islands off the coast, and cities on the coast, to join its league back in the 370s. In the 360s those islands and cities had been plagued by ambas-sadors from both Thebes and Athens, each tempting them to either split from the league or remain within it as the league hovered between anti-Spartan alliance and Athenian proto-empire. In the run-up to the battle of Mantinea, Athens became anxious to protect its assets, particularly from the Persians who were at that time very pro-Theban, and from the increasingly provocative Thracians. Athens sent its fleet to be sta-tioned off the coast of Asia Minor to make the Persians and Thracians think twice. By the late 360s, Athens was fighting both of these powers for control of cities on the Chersonese peninsula at the entrance to the Black Sea (Map 2). The admiral in charge was a man called Timotheus, a pupil from the school of our political commentator Isocrates, and the son of the famous Athenian admiral Conon who had commanded the Persian navy against Sparta at the beginning of the century. The son returned to fight the enemy his father had served.

In 358 BC, Mausolus, having shied away from rebellion against the Persian king, now stepped forward as the would-be protector of the Asia Minor coast, uniting many cities in an alliance against Athens. Just four years after the crippling battle of Mantinea, Athens was at war across the other side of the Aegean with this charismatic dynast. Returning to its old tricks of empire, Athens was soon attacking islands and cities on the coast and sending in garrisons where it could. But Mausolus was a worthy and powerful opponent. He managed to repel the Athenian navy and force Athens to agree terms in 355. Athens, despite giving assurances that it welcomed peace, was having none of it, and went back in more brutally than ever before. Athens once again attacked the city of Sestos on the Chersonese peninsula and resettled it with its own people in 353. When Mausolus finally died in the same year and was laid to rest in his magnificent Mausoleum, Athens also began the process of reclaiming the island of Samos for itself in a similar manner. Many of the islands and cities along the coast looked around for someone who could help them. Who could they turn to?

At the same time as Athens was engaged on the coast of Asia Minor, it was still also locked in a fierce battle with both the Macedonians and the Thracians for its prized foothold in, and share of the huge wealth of natural resources of, the north Aegean coast. In the 360s, that war had concentrated over the ownership of the town of Amphipolis to the west, as well as, as we have seen, the Chersonese peninsula to the east (Map 2). Timotheus, the son of the admiral Conon and pupil of Isocrates, who was sent to fight Mausolus in Asia Minor, had gone there direct from fighting for Amphipolis (via fighting at the Chersonese peninsula) and would, after taking on Mausolus, be forced into sailing up and down the coastline to and from the Chersonese peninsula, quelling mini-rebellions as they sprang up. By the early 350s, Athens was in a very difficult position. Its continued struggle for Amphipolis and the Chersonese peninsula was still far from a resounding success. Its attempts to retain its league and foothold in Asia Minor had been thwarted by Mausolus, who had spearheaded the rebellion against Athens. Athens' major league allies – including even the precious Byzantium (Istanbul), which guarded the route to the grain-producing Black Sea – rebelled. Athens had been forced into its old tactics of making allies (independent of the league) and enforcing on them old empire-like terms. The era of autonomy and freedom guaranteed by the former Persian king was dead. The Greek world had broken loose and there were seemingly no rules to how the game should be played. It was every city for itself.

By the mid-350s BC, central Greece was in stumbling deadlock, the coast of Asia Minor was alight, the north Aegean coast was in uproar and Sicily was in the grips of a power crisis. Unlike the succession of supreme powers that had each, in their turn, attempted to impose their supremacy over Greece and the Greek world in the first half of the 4th century, mediated by the threatening presence of the Persian king, now everything was simultaneously in flux and no one, it seemed, had a secure enough power base and powerful enough forces to take advantage of it. Isocrates, our political pamphleteer who had become increasingly well-known for his commentaries on the state of Greece throughout the first half of the century, now acutely summed up Athens' predicament in two new political pamphlets. The first, published in 357 BC, argued that Athenians should not act as selfish individuals but pull together for the safety of the city. The second, published in 355, was simply called *On the Peace* – a work filled with despondency and disenchantment about the state of the world and how Athens had fallen from grace. It's a window into the black hole that the Greek world had found itself in, and a call for the radical shake-up that was needed to emerge from it. 'Make peace', Isocrates beseeched Athens, 'with all mankind.'

It was against this backdrop, when the Greek world was at its weakest, when central Greece, Sicily, the north Aegean and the coast of Asia Minor were in the grip of war, when no single Greek city or Asia Minor dynast had the power or influence to exert leadership or gain supremacy, when Isocrates was calling for a completely new approach to the problems at hand and beginning to write furiously to powerful individuals across the ancient world who might step forward to unite Greece, that a new player stepped boldly into the light. That player was Macedon and its leader was king Philip II, father of Alexander the Great.

How come it was at this moment that Macedon became a power to take so seriously? Macedon, the area above Thessaly on the northern borders of Greece, was rich in natural resources and fertile lands, a place keen to play a larger role in central Greek politics, but plagued, just like Thessaly, by an unstable succession of kings with a propensity to murder one another (back in the 390s it had had five kings in six years). Thebes, marching north in the 360s, had come into contact and fought both against and with the kings of Macedon. It was Thebes that had been responsible for exacting hostages from the Macedonian king in 369 and it was Thebes that had brought one of those hostages, the young Philip, into contact with central mainland Greek politics, warfare and diplomacy. It was Thebes that had most probably saved Philip's life – keeping him safe from the violent accession tussle in Macedon – and when he was finally released back home, he probably had more experience, knowledge and personal friendships across central Greece than any other Macedonian.

Philip returned to Macedon to find his homeland once again plagued by instability. Another Macedonian king (who had assassinated his predecessor) was himself assassinated in 365 by the man who subsequently took his place. This new king found the going very tough indeed. Macedon was rich in resources but it was internally divided, consumed by dynastic turmoil and with no proper standing army. It was a rich cherry for the picking. To the north and west it was surrounded by vicious tribal neighbours who had warfare in their blood and who were keen to grab as much of Macedon as they could. To the south was Thessaly, in similar dynastic turmoil, but with similar greedy eyes focused on Macedonian flesh. To the east were the cities of the north Aegean coast, over which Macedon was constantly in conflict with Athens and with the powerful king of Thrace.

When this new Macedonian king died in battle fighting the invading tribes from the west just five years after he came to the throne, power passed to Philip. In 360 BC, just as central Greece was descending into further pointless conflict and as every arena of the Greek world was in turmoil, Philip set an equally weak, disorientated and lightweight Macedon on a very different course. His first moves were of lightning speed and ferocious brutality. He was the first king for at least ten years not to have come to the throne through assassination. But while previous kings had held their nerve to dig the knife into their predecessors, it seems that they were unwilling to cut down their current competition, who, unchecked, often later became their executioners. Philip was taking no such chances. Assuming the throne through legitimate succession, he took to striking down any who were, or could be, a threat. Soon enough, Macedon had only one man alive powerful enough to lead it.

Having dealt with Macedon's internal succession dilemma, Philip turned to the next most pressing problem, the threat from outside Macedon and particularly the invading western tribe, the Illyrians, who had been responsible for killing his predecessor (Map 2). They were still in the full flood of invasion. Here Philip proved his consummate skill as a military general, beating the Illyrians back to their own borders. But instead of simply continuing the war, which he knew he did not have the military strength to do, Philip now turned on his charm. Beating them back to his borders, he followed up the military offensive with lavish gifts to dissuade the Illyrians from invading again. The whole point of invasion for the Illyrians was to grab a piece of the rich Macedonian pie. If Philip was going to hand a good amount of it over at no cost to them, why should they bother to invade? Philip's combination of force and consummate diplomacy neutralised the immediate threat to Macedon from the west and gave him time to turn his attentions elsewhere.

This policy of creating breathing space for Macedon was replicated on its eastern borders. Macedon actually made a peace with Athens over the disputed town of Amphipolis on the north Aegean coast and removed the Macedonian garrison of soldiers from the city. All this may have seemed like a policy of retrenchment and isolationism. But it was in fact vital cover for Philip's next move: the establishment of strong relationships with the rest of the Greek world and the complete overhaul of Macedon itself.

Macedon had, for as long as anyone could remember, been divided into two mini-kingdoms. Philip made them, for the first time, one united entity. Partly that union was created through marriage. Philip had six wives in total. But unlike another famous king with six wives – Henry VIII, who would take another bride only after he had divorced or chopped off the head of the last – Philip collected them as he went, like the Persian king across the Aegean. Each marriage was an intensely important diplomatic union, not just between the divided entities of Macedon, but also with the bellicose tribes that surrounded Macedon to the west and south. Philip was soon connected by marriage to Illyria, Epirus and Thessaly. By vows of marriage (backed up by the threat of the sword), Philip united Macedon and permanently neutralised a good deal of the threat to its borders.

Marriage was not the only type of relationship he cultivated. He had been a hostage in Thebes for several years and in that time had met, and made good friends with, many important Thebans, Athenians and men from other Greek cities. These relationships he cultivated assiduously. Friendship was an important business in ancient Greece. Friends didn't just like to hang out with one another. They did things for one another. They had obligations to one another. They were bound to one another. Philip, having made friends with up-and-coming young men in the early 360s while at Thebes, now, at the dawn of the 350s, had friendships with some of the most powerful adults in Greece. Philip had a voice in many cities, a friend obligated to help their friend the king of Macedon. In a world that had been plagued by the vagaries and slippery-fish diplomacy of democratic assemblies, shifting alliances and opportunistic allegiance, Philip had a solid and dependable connection to important individuals who influenced policy in cities across Greece. Sometimes, of course, such friendships needed a little coaxing, and Philip was a dab hand at creating just the right sort of impression. Often friendship could be best expressed, or rather secured, with an expensive gift. But occasionally something a little different was required. One fragment from an almost-lost ancient historian has survived through the millennia to us today, telling us how Philip won over his neighbouring Thessalians. 'Knowing that the Thessalians were licentious and wanton in their mode of life, Philip organised parties for them and tried to amuse them in every way, dancing and rioting and submitting to every kind of licentiousness ... and so won over most Thessalians by parties rather than presents.'

But Philip's attention was only half focused on securing his, and by extension Macedon's, relationships with the rest of the ancient world. His attention was also resolutely focused on internal reform of Macedon itself. That reform was divided into two main areas. The first aimed to create a stable and workable system of government focused on the king. In this, there was no better model to turn to in the ancient world than that of the greatest king of them all – the Persian king, whose empire Macedon would come to take over in the next 30 years. The Persian king always attempted to ensure that all nobles could best serve their own interests by serving the king as best they could. The entire Persian court was based on a system of patronage that flowed from the king downwards; the result being that, on balance, everyone had more to gain from continuing within this system and by doing the king's bidding than by trying to kill him and take over for themselves. Such a system not only strengthened the power of the monarchy, but created a system of government through which the monarch could govern his realm quickly and efficiently. Macedon was now equipped by Philip with such a system, instituting official titles (and heavy pay packets) for men who served the king: the king's bodyguard, the king's royal pages, the king's royal secretary, the king's royal archivist and so on. Such titles and jobs were accompanied by promises to the Macedonian nobles that they would be richly rewarded for their loyalty with tracts of land captured in future campaigns. Philip soon stood at the head of a highly organised system of government, which, for the first time in Macedon, had everyone gunning in the same direction.

But Macedon still needed bullets for that gun. It still needed an army strong enough to capture the tracts of land to give to nobles, and to back up when needed Philip's diplomacy of wine, women, song and lavish gifts. This was the second plank of Philip's internal reform programme. Armies had normally relied on the aristocracy, who could afford to keep a horse and heavy armour to fight as cavalrymen. Increasingly, however, as Philip had seen at first hand while in Thebes, highly trained groups of foot soldiers, like Thebes' infamous Sacred Band, could provide a lightning strike at the heart of an opposing army with just as much, if not more, success than a cavalry charge. It was with this kind of lightning charge in mind that Philip reformed the Macedonian phalanx: infantry soldiers, densely packed with less armour for faster manoeuvrability. To compensate for their lack of armoured protection, he gave them an entirely new kind of weapon: the pike, known as the *sarissa*, some 18 feet (5.5 metres) long. For anyone who has ever engaged in the bizarre activity of punting, imagine taking an extra-long punt pole and charging with it levelled at elbow height at your enemy. It was a tough weapon to manoeuvre, but, with practice, it was a devastating implement of death. A densely packed phalanx of men, each armed with a 5.5-metre-long razor-sharp implement, would make contact with an enemy before they could do much to fight back. It was like a hedgehog with impossibly long spines rolling down the hill and engaging in battle – a sharp, bristling organism of death. Philip ensured that his men were vigorously trained on all terrains and in all weathers – an idea almost unheard of in a world where most campaigning was still done in spring and summer and most soldiers had day jobs elsewhere. Macedon was creating a permanent, highly trained force on a scale never even imagined in mainland Greece. Thebes' Sacred Band, its only permanent force, was 300 men. By 358 BC, just two years after Philip took control of Macedon, he could call on 10,000 warriors.

Philip also ensured that men were promoted within the infantry based on skill rather than simply due to their birth – a seemingly sensible notion but one still infinitely rare in a world resolutely organised by class. At the same time as giving a mobile meritocracy to the poorer soldiers of Macedon, he also reorganised his aristocratic cavalry to create an elite bodyguard for himself and a larger, lighter-armed cavalry squadron which could support the fast infantry advances. For the first time, the cavalry and infantry were trained not simply to act in waves, one after the other, but to work together. And for anyone who was good enough to be in the cavalry but couldn't afford it, Philip ensured that they were supplied with enough land to be able to make the grade. Philip's far-sightedness didn't stop at the advantages of meritocracy; it also extended to the merits of technology. He was one of the first to create a corps of engineers, whose sole job it was to support his advancing army and create new weapons of mass destruction for them to use. It was this corps that would eventually perfect the siege engine and the torsion catapult that Philip's son, Alexander, would use to such devastating effect in the years to come.

It's difficult to overestimate the importance of the changes instituted in Philip's first years of power and the degree to which they changed the future of Greece. In a world in which the cities of Greece were in stalemate and the wider Greek world threateningly unstable, as old empires were falling and even the power of the Persian king seemed to be on the wane, Macedon bucked the trend. The new Macedon fashioned under Philip was unlike anything the Greeks had seen before. Macedon was incredibly rich in resources and in men. It occupied an increasingly important geographical position at the western corner of the Aegean sea, the linchpin between central mainland Greece and the north Aegean coast (Map 2). It wasn't a single city-state, but a vast region populated by a single ethnic community. It was a community united not only by political ideology, but by blood. It was a community united by blood under the leadership of one man, who had proved himself to be the most canny of political, diplomatic and military operators. Within three years of Philip coming to power, Macedon had shattered the shackles which had long kept it from realising its potential. With a new, highly trained and viciously effective army, easy access to the Aegean sea, a single chain of command and a secure relationship with every one of its borders, Macedon was, almost out of nowhere, the new power of the Aegean. In fact, within a world so divided by stalemate, factions and instability, it was the only power in the Aegean that had the potential to do anything about it. The beast had been woken and now was the perfect time for it to flex its muscles.

In 357 BC, the beast of Macedon made its first move, taking back Amphipolis on the north Aegean coast (having earlier removed its garrison to placate Athens while Philip was occupied with internal reform). Continuing along the north Aegean coastline, Philip gobbled up the gold and silver mines as he went. The tussle between Athens, Macedon and Thrace for undisputed control of the north Aegean coast continued for the next nine years, resulting in whole cities being obliterated and entire populations sold into slavery, and costing Philip one of his eyes – forever blinded in the heat of battle.

Yet while this crucial tussle for power was ongoing, Philip was clearly also busy elsewhere. It's said that on a single day in the summer of 356, while he was in the middle of securing a victory against the town of Potidea in northern Greece, three pieces of important news were delivered to him. First, that his generals had won an important victory against the (once again belligerent) Illyrians to the west. The second was that his wife, Olympias, had given birth to a healthy son – the boy who would be Alexander the Great – which meant that Philip now had a legitimate heir. The third was that his horses had been victorious at the Olympic games. It was perhaps this third victory that impressed the rest of Greece most of all. This king, this ruler of men, had now won a victory at the most important athletic competition known to the ancient world. The hero-cult of the individual ruler had been born.

Not everyone was pleased to see him win. In fact, there was serious concern over whether he should compete at all. The one rule at the ancient Olympics was that you had to be Greek to compete. In days gone by, this had been fairly uncontroversial. Despite the fact that the concept of Greece as a single nation had never existed thus far in the ancient world, most cities agreed on who was and who was not 'Greek'. But Macedon had always presented something of a difficult case. In the previous century, a Macedonian king had initially been refused entry to the games on the basis that he wasn't Greek. In this new century with its more globalised existence, in which Greeks were interacting with an increasing number of kingdoms, tribes and races at the boundaries of the known world, as individual and communal identity became more diversified and international thanks to constant trade and population movement, the question of where one drew the 'Greek' line had become even more difficult to answer. Partly motivated by the desperate desire to prevent Philip from gaining even more celebrity status, and partly by a real uncertainty over whether this territory of Macedon, so unlike the city-states of central Greece, was really 'Greek', there was renewed disquiet about Philip's entry to the Olympics. But such discussion, and his subsequent success in the games, only added to his star status. Athens couldn't have been more unhappy. At the same time as Isocrates was beseeching a beleaguered Athens to pull itself together, to make peace or face destruction, Philip was winning prizes, having sons and exponentially increasing his power. It must have felt like the Greek world was on a see-saw that had just dramatically tipped in the other direction.

But the year 356 BC also saw a much more serious clash over another of the prestigious international sanctuaries, Delphi. While the Greek world's eyes were trained on Philip's stunning victory at the Olympic games in the Peloponnese, back in central Greece, tensions were boiling over in a tussle between local communities around the sanctuary of Delphi. Following a dispute over the use of land sacred to the gods, the small city of Phocis had moved in to occupy the great sanctuary. Just as the Arcadians had fought for, occupied and used the wonderful riches of Olympia in the 360s and been admonished for it, this occupation of a neutral international sanctuary (and the decimation of its riches to pay for mercenary troops) brought condemnation from Delphi's governing body. But more seriously, just as the Arcadian occupation of Olympia had set off a chain of events leading to the implosion of Greece at the battle of Mantinea in 362, so the Phocian occupation of Delphi was to lead inexorably towards another great clash.

The problem, once again, was the complex, intertwined nature of inter-city and international alliances. The local city of Phocis had taken over Delphi, tacitly supported by Athens and Sparta. Thebes opposed them (how little had changed from previous decades in this century). But Athens, Sparta, Phocis and Thebes were also linked to supporting different factions within Thessaly (again, how little had changed). This time, however, the difference was that certain factions within Thessaly were linked to Philip of Macedon and his newly galvanised Macedonian state. Within three years, this local conflict exploded in a country-wide sacred war. Philip duly supported his friends in Thessaly. Athens, already wary of Macedon thanks to its continued tussles in the north Aegean, responded with new alliances with any king and tribe sur-rounding Macedon who would answer its call. After an initial surprise defeat, Philip unleashed the full fighting force of Macedon. The infantry with their 5.5-metre-long *sarissas* were sent marching south. In 352 BC, acting like the vengeful arm of the wronged god Apollo, whose sanctu-ary at Delphi he claimed he was acting to free, Philip annihilated the Phocian force, crucified their general, and forced 3,000 of their merce-nary soldiers to commit suicide by jumping off a high cliff to be dashed against the rocks by the angry sea below. Taking control of the whole of Thessaly, Philip was now leader of by far the largest and most powerful Greek states in the entire ancient world. Occupying the north-western corner of the Aegean, his influence now extended like the arms of an octopus to the south and the east, wrapping around the Aegean sea itself. Acting to free Delphi, Macedon was now fully engaged in a sacred war that brought it into direct conflict with the cities of central Greece. In the ten years since the battle of Mantinea, the power balance of the Greek world had changed beyond all recognition.

CHAPTER 11

❧

Survival Strategies

Nowhere can we see better the plentiful array of survival strategies adopted to ride out the constantly unpredictable waves of diplomatic, military, social and economic turmoil of the 4th century BC than at Athens. Athens was, after all, at the heart of much of that turmoil in the first half of the century, and the second half of the century was shaping up to place Athens in just as much trouble. The city had been through a full cycle of suffering, recovery, expectation, success and a return to failure and suffering. It had begun the century by losing its empire and its democracy. Surviving revolution and a radical reinstatement of democracy, Athens had attempted to negotiate its way, with oiled opportunism, through the political minefield of this new world. Keeping its eye firmly on its grain routes to the Black Sea and north Africa, it had attempted to work within the new world order and establish itself a new empire of sorts. But events had moved too fast, and its obstinate desire for a piece of the fertile north Aegean coast, alongside constant meddling in Asia Minor, had brought it into head-on conflict with Persia and Macedon. What was it like to be inside Athens during this time? How did the Athenian society, economy and democracy respond to the events echoing around them?

If you spoke to an Athenian businessman in the 350s BC, just as the beast of Macedon was advancing south towards Delphi, his response would be that the Athenian economy was in real trouble. Athenians relied on several different sources for their income. The first, of course, came from working the land that they owned in the territory of Attica that surrounded Athens. The second, increasingly important source of income was from manufacturing. Athens was host to a myriad of different manufacturers ranging from one-man-bands to early forms of 'just-in-time' factories. In the beating religious, economic and political heart of the city, the Agora, which you can still wander round today in Athens, over 170 different types of goods and services could be purchased, ranging from exquisite metalwork to the cheapest of vegetables. Businesses were valued not just in terms of the goods they produced, but also for the number of slaves they owned. Demosthenes, the political orator whose name, reputation and opinions would dominate Athens' history for the next 40 years, owed much of his family's wealth to his father's factories. His dad, as Demosthenes proudly recalled in one of his law court speeches, had one factory making furniture that employed twenty slaves and another, making knives, which had 33 slaves. The frank admission, and easily calculable economic value, of slave ownership reveals a basic, if unpalatable, fact about Athens. The shining, often honoured originator of democracy was a society based irrevocably on the sweat and toil of a massive slave population.

The most important, and perhaps the most problematic, source of income for Athenians was, however, trade. Perhaps half the resident population of Athens was involved in trade in one way or another. Such a dependence on trade had originated out of a need to supplement natural resources and foodstuffs to ensure that Athens was self-sufficient. By the middle of the 4th century, this had grown into a complex and international trade market spanning the entire ancient world. Athens had always been renowned for sailing the seas, and its traders were perhaps more active than any other. The port of Piraeus, connected to the city of Athens and cocooned behind protective fortification walls, was the heart and life-blood of Athens' economy (Map 1). It was through this port that men, money and goods flowed into the city. But Athens was not only importing essentials. It was also a massive exporter of high-end goods that were sought after across the ancient world. Most of the exquisitely painted drinking-party tableware sets we find buried in tombs in central Italy today were made in Athens. Athens even seems to have made goods specifically for export – creating special styles and designs that appealed to foreign tastes. In the 4th century, Athens was exporting particular types of goods made specifically for sale in the north Aegean on the island of Thasos, for colonies in southern Italy, and even as far away as Carthage on the coast of north Africa (Maps 2 and 3). In return, they were receiving specialist goods from those cities: Thasos, for example, was renowned for its wine and exported its luxury product to be poured down the throats of rich Athenians.

Athens was, of course, not the only Greek city heavily engaged in trade. The 4th century had seen a massive expansion and globalisation of the trade network. Within the remote hills and mountains of the central Peloponnese, as armies had marched back and forth, traders had followed. Slowly a network of usable roads had been constructed to enable wagons and trade to move more freely. The connection of central Greece to the very edges of the known world in places like the Black Sea had necessitated the development of regular import and export runs by entire fleets across the Aegean and beyond. Armies marching to new locations on the north Aegean coast and in Asia Minor had created new captive markets for the sale of goods and services, and people wishing to make a fast buck had followed the armies wherever they went. Cities sitting on the edge of the Greek world had moved fast to create roles for themselves as gateway communities to the barbarian populations that lay beyond. The colony of Massalia, modern-day Marseille in France (Map 3), had made its fortune by becoming the gateway importer of wine, which it then sold on to the native Gauls and Celts across ancient France. The French, now as then, loved their wine. Massalia made a fortune on the back of wine imports and soon moved to not just import, but produce its own wine, which came in specially-shaped amphora jugs unique to Massalia as a sign of quality (the label on the bottle mattered even then). Yet perhaps the effect of all this wine flowing through the city necessitated a rather odd and unique political constitution.

Massalia, technically something akin to a democracy, was governed in reality by a small group of nouveau riche traders. They ensured strict rules to maintain order. Women weren't allowed to drink wine. Porn was forbidden. Foreigners had to leave all their weapons with the police on entering the city, and execution, the ultimate punishment, was to be carried out with a sword kept especially rusty for the occasion.

This era of constant trade ploughing the waters of the Mediterranean created both opportunities and problems. One of the worst problems was pirates. Piracy was an endemic problem in the Mediterranean, as anyone was within their rights, if they had the might, to grab ships – even Athenian ambassadors on official state business had been known to make a small side trip, having spotted a valuable cargo en route. The island of Melos offered a safe port to pirates keen to offload and sell their contraband (Map 2). The city of Zankle in Sicily was famed for breeding the most ferocious of pirates, and the island of Aegina, just off the coast of Athens, was the black market in which to sell stolen goods (it was the island on which Plato had been sold into slavery when thrown out of Sicily by Dionysius I). Few did anything to curb the threat. Admirals of different fleets in fact quite liked having pirates around. Fear of pirates was a useful bargaining tool in forcing small cities and islands to agree to alliances with bigger cities (whose fleets could offer protection against their worst excesses). Equally, admirals would often get a little money on the side by operating their own private protection rackets and would even, in some cases, employ pirates to rough up a particular city or island before descending with the main fleet to take it over.

If piracy was one of the disadvantages in an era of international trade, one of the bonuses was the creation of the business of banking. Coinage was by the 4th century BC fully in use across the Greek world. Indeed, it was so much in use that when one Athenian commander found himself stuck in the middle of nowhere with his army needing to get supplies, his attempts to barter for goods with the locals were refused; they demanded coinage as the only acceptable form of payment. Stuck for petty cash, the general was forced to mint his own coinage on the spot to pay for enough food to feed his troops. But in a similar bind to most of Europe before the introduction of the single currency, every Greek city minted its own coinage, which had value, most often, only within the city boundaries. That meant that, whenever a trader came to a new city, he had to find a way of exchanging money from his previous port for the coinage of the new. Entrepreneurship ensured that this need was soon filled. Money-changers set up their tables in the ports of cities around the Aegean to enable traders to exchange coinage, and they also came to act as depositories for traders' cash surpluses while they were in a particular city. Soon enough, these money-changers began to offer maritime loans to provide insurance to traders against loss of cargo through shipwreck or pirates; and before long, loans could be obtained from them for buying land or businesses, and to finance international trading or even military expeditions. The ancestor of the modern-day bank had been born in Greece. The ancient Greek for table is *trapeza*, and it's no coincidence that the modern Greek word for bank is exactly the same. The money-changing tables of ancient Greece are the ancestors of its present-day banking community.

It will come as no surprise that many of these money-changers were resident foreigners living permanently in the different cities – men who could perceive the needs of foreign traders because they themselves worked in the business. Athens in the 4th century had a huge resident immigrant population, perhaps 10,000 strong, who became their own class of citizen: the metic. Denied voting rights, they were, however, an extremely important cog in the Athenian economy and became over time enormously wealthy. One of the first great banking dynasties, the family of Pasion, whose sordid inter-family squabbles would be the reality soap opera on the front page of Athenian gossip columns for the next twenty years, were themselves nouveau riche metics.

If this was how individuals and businesses made their money, how did cities? In part they made their money through military expeditions and the subsequent gathering of plunder. But increasingly they came to rely, as modern governments do today, on claiming a slice of individual and business profits in the form of tax. Back in the 380s, Athens had ordered a Domesday Book-like recording of all land values in its territories and imposed taxes on the land as a result. There was a tax on sales in the market-place, a tax on moving goods through ports, on businesses, on specific forms of employment such as prostitution (though it was illegal for citizens to be prostitutes, there was a sophisticated series of agreements governing the rights and responsibilities of prostitutes: aggrieved 'service providers' were happy to complain to the highest authority in Athens about being ripped off whenever the need arose). There was a special tax on metic resident foreigners living and working in Athens. Rich citizens in Athens were also forced to perform public services for the city, like paying for the cost of a theatrical production or fitting out a trireme warship. Tax-collecting was even a business in itself – the city of Athens would put up for tender the contracts to collect tax, and demand a certain amount; any surplus collected by the people who won the contract could be kept as profit.

By the 350s BC, the Athenian economy was inextricably bound up in, and dependent on, a globalised economy based on trade. This not only provided livelihoods for individuals and encouraged increasing numbers of both citizens and foreigners to relocate away from the agricultural fields to successful business centres like Athens, but also provided a large amount of the tax revenue taken by different Greek cities – much of which, as we have already seen in a previous chapter, was pumped into public works: theatres, sanctuaries and fortification walls. The system worked just fine – until it crashed.

While there had been crashes before in this developing global economy – particularly associated with the recurrent tides of war in ancient Greece, such as after the battle of Leuctra in 371, and also with the occurrence of bad harvests and subsequent grain shortages in 386 and 362 BC – the economic crash in the 350s, especially for Athens, was on a scale not previously experienced. The catalyst for the decline, of course, was war. Athens had been exhausted by the constant clashes in central Greece leading up to the battle of Mantinea. Its debilitating involvement on the north Aegean coast and in Asia Minor through the early 350s continued to put strain on its resources as it attempted to fight a two-front war on different sides of the Aegean. Its new league, which had provided some income, was now in open rebellion. Macedon and Thrace were sapping its strength in the north, Mausolus in Asia Minor. More grain shortages followed in 357 and 355 BC. Isocrates was pleading for Athens to make peace to avoid destruction. Athens' trade routes across the Aegean, its vital arteries to unlimited supplies of natural resources in the Black Sea and north Africa, came under increasing threat. The result was a credit crunch of the kind we are all too familiar with today. Athens' place in the international trading network suddenly looked shaky. There was a crisis of confidence. Trade in and out of Athens, previously a torrent, reduced to a trickle. More critically, silver production was at its lowest level ever. The Athenian state, in 355 BC as Philip of Macedon was swooping down through central Greece, was on the brink of ruin.

This was, as our own governments constantly remind us today, not a credit crunch restricted to one city, but a global problem. Athens, however, because of its excessive exposure to the wider world, felt it very hard indeed. The response can be seen both in the gloomy prognosis for the future in Isocrates' *On the Peace* which we saw in the last chapter, and also in a raft of economic literature, written throughout the first half of the 4th century, which was now given renewed attention as Athenians looked for a way to deal with the crisis. Our old friend Xenophon, hero of the 10,000's march out of Asia, Athenian-turned-Spartan, narrator of Greece's implosion down to the battle of Mantinea, had also written a tract of economic advice for Athens, his *Oikonomikos*. The word originates from the ancient Greek for the home, the *oikos*. *Oikonomikos* translates literally as the 'affairs of the home', but it's also where we get our word 'economics': the first half of the 4th century bore witness to the birth of the concept of economics and economic theory, which would again be taken up by the philosopher Aristotle at the end of the century. Xenophon's economic policy advice was clear from the very etymology of his title: forget the international stage and global trade – back to basics is the way forward. Everyone should look after their own homes and become individually self-sufficient. The concept of 'economics', it seems, was born out of an impassioned plea to return to the homestead and to the good old days of agricultural self-sufficiency.

Yet in the midst of the crisis in the 350s, Xenophon himself seems to have written a new piece which offered very contradictory advice to his previous work. This new text, the *Poroi*, was a complex analysis of the relationship between prosperity, employment, consumption and expenditure, which preached a very modern way to extricate Athens from its financial crisis: spend. Money, however, shouldn't be spent on the ordinary citizen but on the people whom it was most critical to attract to Athens to get its economy flowing again: rich foreigners. As we've seen, Athens was already a hotbed of immigration and resident foreigners, who made up a large percentage of the banking population among many other trades. But if Athens was to survive, Xenophon now argued, it had to attract more. What could Athens, cash-strapped as it was, have to offer? The answer was its reputation. Athens, more than any other Greek city, had been in the previous century at the centre of a golden age. Such a reputation surrounded it like a halo. Only Athens had had a great empire, only Athens had buildings as exquisite as the Parthenon, only Athens could claim to have been, and still be, a major centre for high culture like philosophy and drama. To be a citizen of Athens was to wear a badge of honour that even the most grudging had to acknowledge. Its reputation had a tangible, concrete, economic value. Athens could barter its reputation for money – and in so doing, save itself.

Xenophon's advice, which was echoed constantly by the orator Demosthenes over the next twenty years, was brutally clear and practical. Give rich foreigners first-row seats in the theatre, give them breaks from paying extra taxes, and make it easier for them to become full Athenian citizens. Reward good service to Athens with the ultimate honour of citizenship, and Athens could pawn itself out of trouble. Athens followed this advice to the letter. In the following decade, for example, Athens granted asylum and citizenship to a certain rich king

Arybbas from north-western Greece, and even invited him for a state dinner at public expense. It was no accident that the trickle of public honours for living individuals, which were unheard of in the previous century and had only begun at the dawn of the current one, increased to a torrent in the 350s and 340s BC. Athens cried out across the ancient world: 'Give us your riches and we will make your name immortal as a citizen of the greatest city in the world.'

But the economy wasn't the only internal problem that Athens had to grapple with in the 4th century. Our last sighting of the Athenian democratic constitution was in the immediate aftermath of the restoration of democracy, in which the democratic citizen body was swearing an oath to hunt down and kill anyone who tried to overthrow the system. The beginning of the century also saw a revision and republishing of the laws of the city, and a new era of power for the rule of law, supplemented by shiny new law courts built in among the market-trading and politics within the heart of the Agora. The next 40 years down to the 350s saw, if anything, a gathering emphasis on the importance of law and the need to keep control of an ever-expanding and increasingly international city population. The first priority was to ensure the machinery of democracy. The assembly, the brain of the democracy, in which all decisions of the city had to be made, required a minimum number of attendees for its decisions to have legal weight. With the instability that plagued the century, that majority was sometimes hard to find. From late in the previous century, hard cash had been handed out to compensate people for giving up their time to attend the assembly for the democracy; in the late 4th century, the rate of pay would be increased dramatically to ensure attendance levels.

It was not only at assembly time that Athens was keen to ensure its population did its duty. With its growing international economy and population, Athens also instigated a new swathe of bureaucracy – officials whose duty it was to oversee the heart and lungs of the city, and, perhaps most importantly, to make sure that its stomach was fed. Officials were chosen to guarantee the upkeep of standards in the city, to ensure the quality of goods on sale in the marketplace, to maintain honest standards of business, to keep a check on the price of grain, and to oversee the grain supply. Yet, at the same time as Athens increased its official bureaucracy, it seems to have tackled the problem of policing in a very different way. In the previous century, policing in Athens had been undertaken by a band of foreign soldiers – Scythians. These men, with their unmistakable bow and arrow, foreign dress and pointy hats, were as close as Athens came to a permanent police force. Yet in the 4th century, the cost of maintaining a force large enough to keep control of Athens' expanding population seems to have been too much. The Scythians melted away and were replaced by a two-part enforcement system. On the one hand, a series of public slaves were employed in positions akin to our modern chiefs of police, to spearhead important investigations and to act as a point of contact on safety issues for the citizenry. But the bulk of day-to-day policing, it seems, was left instead to the citizens themselves: citizens kept each other in check in a massive version of Neighbourhood Watch. Such a system worked only thanks to a very traditional and powerful code of what was and what was not acceptable behaviour, supplemented by occasional examples of vigilante justice. Ancient Athens, it seems, was policed by a system of self-regulation, a system which we also rely on more and more in the UK today, at least for minor crimes, as police resources are stretched increasingly thinly.

Yet at the same time as the city was keen to demand that every citizen did their duty, it was also keen to ensure that no one elected to office had the opportunity to mislead the city. During the decades of war and instability that swirled around it, Athens actually made huge leaps towards a professional system of checks and balances to prevent what it feared most: the overthrow of its beloved democracy. Every official, when they came to the end of their term of office, had to submit to an official inspection of both their work and their finances (no chance for fraudulent expenses to be claimed by public servants in ancient Athens). Severe fines were instituted for any found wanting. An official archive was also created for the first time in which anyone could check laws, policy documents and public accounts. And any citizen could bring a charge against any other citizen if they believed their actions in the democratic assembly to be illegal. We are used today to a democratic system in which we elect representatives, expect others to keep tabs on them, and are not surprised when they are found wanting – there is, as newspapers keep telling us, a failure of trust in politics. But in ancient Athens, every citizen was called upon to be an active member of the democracy; nearly every citizen would serve in at least one, if not more, official capacities during their lifetime; and people were furiously active in keeping checks on their fellow democrats. One man was acquitted of acting illegally in the democratic assembly a staggering 75 times. Even the cleverest and most Teflon-coated of modern political operators would have found it hard to escape judgement in ancient Athens.

It's a curious fact that fans of Athenian democracy nearly always refer to its heyday as occurring in the 'glorious' 5th century BC. To some extent its successes (and indeed 'birth') in the 5th century are undeniable – Athens grew to control a huge empire and built wonders of the world like the Parthenon. But that's not the whole story. Not only does a good part of our hard evidence for the internal workings of democracy come from the middle 4th century (which we have conveniently, if shoddily, often used to talk about the nature of the democracy 100 years earlier in the 'glorious' 5th century), but it was also in this period that an active philosophical debate about the nature of democracy really started to take off. While the 5th century is often referred to as the 'golden age', it was in fact now, in the midst of the economic, military and diplomatic instability of the mid-4th century, that democracy as a system had its most introspective, and some might say finest, hour.

Nowhere is that clearer than in the law courts of Athens. The rise of the rule of law was the engine room of the success of democracy in this period – ten court rooms working flat-out up to 225 days a year in the mid-4th century. It was, however, a very different world to the legal system of today. There was no city-wide state prosecution service that brought cases on behalf of the public. As with policing, it was a case of do-it-yourself. A crime would be tried only if a citizen brought it to court. Lawyers didn't exist. Instead, the person bringing the case had to speak for himself. The written law was less than half the case: the key element was convincing the jury. People bringing prosecutions spoke in front of huge juries – sometimes 500 people – who were fellow citizens, paid for their services like those attending the assembly, and picked using a randomiser machine akin to those used in modern-day lotteries, so that it was impossible to predict which juror would hear which case and thus bribe them in advance. The range of types of prosecution that could be brought was enormous: prosecutions, counter-prosecutions, diversionary prosecutions, subsequent prosecutions, public and private prosecutions. Athens was humming with litigation in the 4th century and it was through this antagonistic – if not entirely just, and certainly amateurish – process that Athens navigated a course of internal social stability within an uncertain world.

But the law courts also highlighted, perhaps more clearly than anywhere else, the sore point of the Athenian system. It will not have escaped your attention that Athens, up to this point in the story, has been notably lacking in interesting individuals who were responsible for spearheading Athenian political and military endeavours: no Agesilaus of Sparta, no Pelopidas or Epaminondas of Thebes, no Dionysius I and II of Syracuse, no Philip of Macedon. To be sure, Athens housed people who commented on and engaged with these individuals: Plato, Isocrates, Lysias. To be sure, philosophers and political commentators like Plato and Isocrates had called for Athens to find its own energetic leaders. To be sure, there were individuals who played important roles on Athens' behalf – its revolutionary heroes like Thrasyboulus, its military generals like Timotheus and Conon, its philosophers, its actors – but all did so on behalf of the city and its assembly, to whom they were beholden. No Athenian walked away from a trial for breaking the bounds of his officehood like Epaminondas did at Thebes, for example (even the hero Thrasyboulus was censured by the city of Athens). More often than not, in fact, individuals got burnt by the democratic assembly as it changed its mind and left them to fend for themselves (remember Athens changing its mind about supporting the Theban rebellion and punishing the generals whom the city had itself sent to support Thebes).

Athens' democratic ideology left little space for individuals to assert their power, especially after the powerful reinstatement of democracy at the beginning of the century, which mandated every citizen to kill anyone who looked like they were taking over. Yet it could not but rely on individuals to carry out particular duties on behalf of the city; and, particularly in an era when warfare was a permanent feature and powerful individuals were coming to power across the Greek world, it could not but negotiate, and do business, with such individuals on a regular basis. The sore point of Athens was this constant tension between the individual and the collective and the power balance between them.

The law courts made this tension visible because, though no lawyers were allowed, a citizen could ask a professional to write their speech for them, although the citizen always had to stand and deliver it. Hence arose a gathering of important rhetoricians whose skills made them extremely desirable to both defendants and prosecutors in a system that relied so heavily on persuading a jury, rather than on the written word of the law. So what, you may ask? An individual – whoever wrote the speech – was still being judged by the collective. The problem, or rather the concern, was that a professional speechwriter could craft a speech so skilfully that it could convince a juror even if the truth of the matter was otherwise. A skilled individual could hoodwink the collective. The result was a constant tension in the law courts between putting forward your best case and not appearing to be too skilled at it. Nearly every law-court speech surviving to us today starts with a different version of the immortal line: 'Unaccustomed as I am to public speaking ...'

These professional speechwriters not only wrote speeches for others. They would often be in court defending or prosecuting on their own behalf. Their notoriety in the public sphere, the public awe for their wisdom and skill – even if tinged with suspicion – and their sheer ability to persuade their fellow citizens, made them extremely influential people in every part of the democracy. Lysias, the orator who had survived the tyrant takeover and reinstatement of the democracy at the beginning of the century, not only brought some of those tyrants to court himself, but was also chosen, as we saw in an earlier chapter, to deliver the funeral oration on behalf of the city in one of the first wars of the new century. By the middle of the 4th century, this collection of powerful orators, who sat at the point of tension within the Athenian system, had grown enormously and wielded massive political power. These individuals would come the closest that anyone ever did in Athens to replicating the power and authority of the individual stars we have seen in other cities and states of Greece.

That power was accompanied by a not-so-subtle shift in political, economic and philosophical thinking. Since the beginning of the century, Athens had been forced to interact with powerful individuals in cities and states around the ancient world, and had been at the centre of the debate over whether or not such powerful individual leaders were a good thing (remember how Plato had targeted and subsequently slimed Dionysius I of Syracuse). But in the 350s, that debate about individuals outside Athens turned to focus on the promise of powerful individuals within Athens. We saw earlier in this chapter how responses to the economic downturn had focused either on a return to individual isolationist economics or alternatively on attracting rich individual foreigners to the city. The individual orators in the law courts were now at the zenith of their influence. And even the philosophers promoted a more individual message. Plato, in one of his final works called *The Statesman*, ridiculed democracy and gave a blank cheque to a man of extraordinary wisdom, a utopian ruler who would rule in conjunction with the rule of law. Thus it was that as the 350s drew to a close, even Athens – which had so far, unlike many other cities and states in Greece, kept the power of the individual at bay within its boundaries, even if it was forced to engage with many such individuals in the wider Greek world – started to falter. In the next 30 years, Athenian policy towards the powerful individual rulers across the ancient world would be framed and dominated by a handful of its own individual citizens who would decide Athens' future, and ultimately its survival.

CHAPTER 12

≈≈

Saviour or Tyrant?

No one individual did more to shape Athens' future in the coming decades than Demosthenes. Born in 384 BC, in the direct aftermath of the king's peace which had redrawn the map of international relations in the ancient world, Demosthenes had grown up in difficult circumstances. The original Athenian rich-kid, his family was extremely wealthy (his father, as we saw in the previous chapter, had two slave factories making different kinds of goods). Demosthenes was paying for plays to be put on in Athens all by himself from the age of five. Yet tragedy struck just two years later when both his parents died, leaving him an orphan. His life became even more difficult as the guardians left by his father to protect him actually squandered the majority of his inheritance. Demosthenes grew up knowing that if he did not retrieve it, he would face a life of poverty. But he was no muscleman who could force his opponents' hands. In fact he was a lean and sickly-looking child who played little sport – certainly not the image of every ancient Athenian girl's pin-up. His nickname at school summed up his early reputation: *batalos*, which translates as 'effeminate flute player', or more insultingly, 'pussy'.

Yet this uninspiring child was addicted to watching the business of the law courts and the assembly in Athens. It was said that he decided to become an orator while listening to the impassioned debates in the assembly about the direction of Athenian foreign policy in the late 360s. Yet his plan to become an orator was not, initially at least, aimed at directing Athenian policy. Instead, he had personal revenge in mind. He got that revenge by the only way open to an impoverished weakling at the time: through the law courts. The explosion of the rule of law and the power of the courts in 4th-century Athens provided Demosthenes with all the muscle he needed, if only he could speak well enough to convince the jury. That he did, and just as the sickly boy turned into a man, he won his first victory against his old guardians and recovered what was left of his stolen inheritance.

Demosthenes enjoys an astonishing reputation as an orator and a statesman in the modern world. There are few orators and politicians in modern history who have not made some reference to him as an inspiration in their own lives. Yet, as always, there is a more complicated story to tell of the man behind the myth. His oratorical skill was not a natural talent but instead the result of constant effort and practice. Demosthenes was often shouted down in his early days as a law court speechwriter and speaker because he was too long-winded and because his voice, just like his body, was weak and indistinct. It didn't help that few Athenians could really identify with him. He was a 'water drinker' – teetotal – and that didn't sit well in a society centred around the wine jug.

To counter these problems, Demosthenes did everything he could – particularly to improve the quality of his voice. He had a subterranean study in which he would practise every day to make his voice more resonant. He tried to make himself understood while he filled his mouth with pebbles so as to improve his enunciation. He recited his speeches while running up and down flights of stairs and he talked in front of a mirror for hours on end to see and adjust his facial expressions. He was addicted, like his friends in the theatre from whom he took much advice, not so much to what he was saying but to the importance of getting the tone and look of it right. He seems to have understood the fundamental importance not of what you said, but how you said it. Such a belief, however, put him directly at the sore point of Athenian society. In a world that didn't like professional speechwriters because they had the rhetorical power to make the weaker argument appear the stronger, here was a man who was giving every effort to making that fear come true.

Demosthenes was always a man of hard work. Though surrounded by other orators in Athens who could, off the cuff, speak words of winged eloquence, he was a man who had to prepare. He rarely spoke on the spur of the moment, but only when he had had a chance to think through and prepare his answers, so much so that his opponents always teased him that his answers on any matter smelt of the lamp-grease from the oil-lamp wick by which they had been written the night before. He was not a man who could always make up his mind in an emergency or who could respond eloquently in real-time negotiations during foreign trips. Yet, occasionally, just occasionally, he would speak out spontaneously, and when he did so, it was always on a subject about which he knew a great deal and about which he was crazily passionate.

Such a man as Demosthenes was difficult to place in Athens in the 350s. He was a natural in the law courts where he could prepare his speeches and convince his juries. It was here that, after winning back a portion of his inheritance, he began to make his name. But what use could a man like Demosthenes, who didn't like speaking off the cuff, be in a place like the political assembly? What use could he be in a world environment in which the economic, political and military situation was constantly shifting, the issues at stake constantly changing, and Athenian foreign policy constantly tap-dancing its way around the world? What Demosthenes needed was a single issue, an issue on which he could be an expert and on which he could prepare his remarks or be knowledgeable enough if necessary to speak off the cuff. He needed one policy, one target, one figure, one enemy, one man against whom he could direct himself. The Greek world had seen fit to deliver just such a man at just the time when Demosthenes was beginning his public career: king Philip of Macedon.

Demosthenes found his cause soon after the balance of power in the Greek world had changed irreversibly in the ten years between the battle of Mantinea in 362 and Philip's successful pursuit of sacred war into central Greece in 352 BC. He was perhaps the first to understand the threat that Philip posed to Athens, and certainly the first to speak out so publicly about it. In 351, he accused Athens of acting like an ill-bred fencer who, instead of defending himself, leaves his guard open, welcoming the attack of his opponent. Two years later, as Philip continued to menace Athenian interests in the north Aegean, Demosthenes accused the Athenians of behaving like impudent young men who borrow money at stupidly high interest rates, only to realise that they have a debt they cannot pay and are living on borrowed time until the bailiffs arrive. Demosthenes had a single message, one keynote, which he would hold to throughout his career: Philip is the enemy and Athens must do everything it can to stop him.

Demosthenes was not the only voice in Athens at this time. Athens was full of talented and vociferous men who, with the increased importance of the law courts, had a stage on which to put forward their views and, equally importantly, battle with their colleagues and opponents over policy. Many of these men were students of the great philosophers and political commentators of the century like Plato and Isocrates. Between them, this crop of orators offer us an intricate picture of the dilemmas and decisions that faced Athens and the wider Greek world, and the intrigue surrounding each twist and turn of Athenian policy.

There was no more important grudge match in Athens during the next twenty years than that between Demosthenes and another Athenian orator called Aeschines. Like Demosthenes, Aeschines had been born at the beginning of the new century. But unlike Demosthenes, he had been born into poverty as a schoolmaster's son. His training, it appears, had been not in the law courts but on the stage as an actor. But, again unlike Demosthenes, he also had an aptitude for physical activity and had actually fought in the great implosion of central Greece at the battle of Mantinea in 362 BC. Rising from the status of actor-turned-solider to orator and ambassador, Aeschines had come face to face with Philip in an early embassy to the new Macedonian sovereign. It was probably at this time that he became a trusted friend of Philip – one of those friends whom Philip cultivated so assiduously in cities all around Greece – men who were obligated to do favours for, and support, one another. Aeschines was Philip's man in Athens. And Demosthenes hated him for it.

The antagonism between these two men in Athens was, throughout their lives, downright dirty. Demosthenes would accuse Aeschines of having a whore for a mother (in the absence of much hard evidence in Athenian law courts, reputation and ancestry were everything), and Aeschines would accuse Demosthenes of having a barbarian Scythian woman from the remote Black Sea as his. Demosthenes would accuse Aeschines of taking Philip's money to speak his cause. Aeschines would accuse Demosthenes of taking Persian gold to speak theirs. Demosthenes would go after all of Aeschines' friends and colleagues with prosecutions for treason and anything else he could make stick. Aeschines would retaliate with counter-prosecutions of religious impurity, sexual misconduct and political tyranny.

These slurs were more than just an attempt to stain personal honour. Attacks like these on your opponent's reputation in the law courts were a sure-fire way to have their opinion discounted in the political assembly. They were also a way of casting suspicion over an individual's fundamental loyalty to the city. In the final analysis, men like Demosthenes asked Aeschines: Who would you stand with – your friend Philip or your city? Where does your loyalty lie? In a city where Athenians had sworn to kill anyone who worked against their democracy, Aeschines' answer had serious implications for his future life expectancy. The battle between Demosthenes and Aeschines was no simple, if abusive, rhetorical flourish – it was deadly and real. It polarised Athenian political opinion and debate. It divided Athens into two distinct camps: Demosthenes or Aeschines, pro- or anti-Philip. You had to be in one or the other. The rest was no man's land.

In Demosthenes' camp was an orator called Hyperides, who was another pupil of Isocrates, our political commentator *par excellence* of the period. An excellent public servant, albeit notoriously self-indulgent in his private life, he was an active member of the anti-Philip party in Athens, although he would later fall out with Demosthenes, a dispute resolved only just before the end of both their lives. On Aeschines' side was a man called Dinarchus, whom scholars have called a 'small beer' version of Demosthenes, and a man called Demades. Demades was a very different kettle of fish from Demosthenes. He was a rich dilettante with a natural gift for oratory. While Demosthenes would be slaving away late into the night perfecting each phrase of his speech, Demades would turn up at the assembly (no doubt with a hangover), listen to Demosthenes' polished words and then stand to give some off-the-cuff remark which had the citizen body begging for more. The social commentator and philosopher Theophrastus, who would write a perfectly observed set of social caricatures (his *Characters*) near the end of the century, later commented that Demosthenes was worthy of the city, but Demades too good for it. How Demades got this reputation isn't quite clear. The man had no single policy he stuck to. Unlike Demosthenes, he would change his opinions following the way of the winds. That put him on Aeschines' pro-Philip side for much of the next twenty years. He was also shameless. When speaking about the amazing party trick of one poet who was paid vast sums to recite verse, he is supposed to have claimed: 'You think it impressive that this man be paid a talent of money to recite, I tell you I am paid ten times as much by the Macedonian king just to keep quiet.'

These men framed Athenian debate and policy, in part by trying to convince the Athenian assembly of the sense of their own view, but also in large measure by destroying the reputations of the other side and thus winning by default. At stake was nothing less than the policy of Athens, the future of Athens, the future of Greece, and their own lives. Most of these men, in playing their part in the brutal dawn of a new world order, wouldn't survive to the end of the century. Hyperides and Demades would be executed. Aeschines and Demosthenes would be exiled and Demosthenes himself would commit suicide. Few men survived a long time in the front row of Athenian politics. Athens, for all its glory and shining white marble, could be a very unpleasant place in which to live.

One man who survived longer than most was the Athenian general Phocion. The son of a pestle-maker, he was another pupil of the philosopher Plato. He was a military man of ultimate self-discipline – he supposedly even refused to wear shoes or a warm cloak when out on campaign. He went around Athens brooding and sullen, never smiling or paying court to anyone, a little like the heart-throb Dion of Syracuse. Phocion's 'forbidding brows' were famous across the city of Athens. A consummate military strategist, he was elected general a staggering 45 times during his life, and was involved in almost every military campaign from the 370s onwards. Plutarch later recounted how different he was to most orators in Athens in his day. Whereas others would try to court the people's goodwill and go with the way of the winds, or else stick resolutely to one policy, Phocion judged each situation on its merits, wouldn't hesitate to stand up and oppose the people if he thought them wrong, and never did anything to court their favour. He called the shots as he saw them, with Athens' best interests at heart, even when the assembly was baiting him with taunts of cowardice for not being willing to go to war. Such strength and irreproachable service to his city won him the respect of the assembly. In times of crisis, the Athenian assembly would always call for his words of counsel as its soberest and most sensible adviser. Already at the heart of Athenian politics for the past 30 years, Phocion would be at its centre for another 40. But now, in an attempt to steer a middle course through troubled waters, even Phocion was beginning to lose his grip, not only thanks to the tumultuous events in the wider Greek world but also due to the bitter atmosphere of deadly animosity within Athens itself. Even Phocion, this most able and sensible of men, wouldn't meet with a natural death.

While Athens was divided into pro- and anti-Philip factions, events were moving on in the Greek world, giving more weight and attraction to the idea of a single powerful leader. Over in Sicily, which seems to have acted as some sort of petri dish for experiments in political government for mainland Greece through much of the century, the latest stage of experimentation with single rule was taking place. Plato had tried to reform Dionysius I and failed. He had been invited back to reform Dionysius II and failed. He had schooled a new philosophical leader, Dion, smoothed out his edges, and sent him back to take over Syracuse. This Dion had done, with the help of a powerful female fan club, and seen off Dionysius II. But the people had turned on Dion several times, eventually leading to his assassination by another member of Plato's select Academy.

This new leader, Callippus, was no match for Dion or for Syracuse or Sicily. Within a year he too was dead and Syracuse had descended into the same sort of internal fragmentation and fratricide to which Macedon had been prey for much of the first part of the century. By the time Philip was taking over central Greece, Sicily was a depopulated shambles, exhausted by civic strife. Any sense of law or community had been lost as rival chieftains battled with one another for a flimsy hold on a pathetic amount of local power. Syracuse, transformed under a series of individual powerful leaders into one of the most prestigious cities of Greece, having lost that leadership, was now falling into rack and ruin. Carthage, that old enemy from the coast of north Africa, sensed its opportunity to invade and push back the Greek frontier. In desperation, Syracuse sent a message to its ancestral mother-city back on the mainland for help. Corinth, with enough of its own battles to contend with, responded with a pathetic force: seven ships, 700 men and one old man as general, a man who had no knowledge of Sicilian history or political affairs. It must have appeared to the desperate Syracusans as a cruel joke. But how could they know that their saviour had just arrived on Sicilian shores?

Plutarch, who later wrote a biography of this old general, records how the officials of Syracuse would remember this man at his funeral: 'He conquered the tyrants, dominated the barbarians, gave new life to the most important of the destroyed cities and gave back to the people of Sicily their laws.' In just eight years, this old man purged the island of mini-tyrants, finally exiled Dionysius II to Corinth where he would live as a tourist attraction, achieved a decisive victory over the Carthaginians, and began a massive programme of revival and extension, by both rebuilding communities and by destroying the most important emblems of the previous tyrannies. The destruction of the tyrant's stronghold in Syracuse was a particular propaganda success. With all the symbolism and importance that would, centuries later, be invested in the destruction of the Berlin Wall, the old general now invited every citizen of Syracuse, on a single day, to bring their crowbars and help to destroy piece by piece this now irrelevant monstrosity of history.

This general didn't take the tyrant's place. He built a constitution, which blended freedom and autonomy with control and regulation. In this man's Sicily, there was no place for tyrant or mercenary, no place for one city to dominate over another, but instead his emphasis was on population growth, economic expansion, reconstruction, independence and peace. His Sicily was a Mecca for those tired of a cruel, violent world. Over the next ten years, while Philip would continue to strengthen his hold over Greece, this man built his community in Sicily. In a reversal of the normal trends of events, this man wasn't assassinated, nor did he die in battle. His work done, he retired from his job to live his last years in quiet contemplation. Plutarch, in perhaps one of the most moving pieces of ancient biography to have survived into our hands today, relates:

[H]aving, by general consensus, performed the best and most heroic deeds of any Greek of his time, and having been the only person to actually achieve all those things which the orators, in their speeches at city assemblies, are constantly encouraging the Greeks to do and be ... having displayed great ability and courage in his encounters with Barbarians and tyrants, as well as justice and temperance in his dealings with Greeks and friends, having set up victory trophies from his battles without causing his fellow citizens grief and having, in less than 8 years, handed over to her people a Sicily purged of her cancerous miseries and illnesses, at last, being frail with age, he began to lose his sight … and became completely blind.

He was buried in the heart of Syracuse, its Agora market place. If you visit the modern city of Syracuse, bustling with traffic and gelato-sellers, take a moment to wonder if, at some point in your day, you haven't walked over the final resting place of one of Sicily's, perhaps Greece's, most honourable leaders. His name was Timoleon, which in Greek means 'honoured by the people', son of Timodemos, 'honoured by the citizen body', both honoured by the ancient people of Sicily.

Greece, it must have seemed in the early 340s BC, was surrounded, not by the instability and fragmentation that had plagued it and the wider Greek world in the 350s, but by examples, and sometimes very encouraging examples, of powerful leaders who could solve the problems seemingly endemic in city-on-city strife. It was also the time in which the less successful of those leaders became a very public lesson to one and all. When Dionysius II was finally exiled to Corinth by the great Timoleon, he was set up as a public example of the kind of leader Greece didn't want. Like some modern-day failing celebrity whose every step into ill-repute and self-abuse is photographed and vilified in the tabloids, Dionysius II became a freak show whom people could visit to watch his fall into ruin. Plutarch later recounts how everyone wanted to see this man 'wasting his time at the fishmongers or sitting in the perfume shop'. They all wanted to see his dignity stripped bare as he 'drank diluted wine from the corner taverns or fought in public with common prostitutes, or tried to teach girls how to sing better, earnestly arguing with them about the choice and melody of their songs'.

But sometimes it was not just the people who were interested in the example set by these celebrity failures, but other leaders as well. King Philip of Macedon was intensely interested in the lessons to be learnt from the political experiments of Sicily. He himself visited Dionysius

II in Corinth to talk to the man about his experiences and particularly those of his father, the great warlord Dionysius I. Over dinner with the fallen star, Philip is supposed to have asked him when his father, whose hours of the day were filled with running Syracuse and fighting across Sicily, found time to compose tragedy. The son, who had never managed to equal his father's success, must now, mired in his own failure, have suffered the final humiliation of being asked not about his own life but about his long-dead dad. He's supposed to have replied simply and sullenly: 'While eating.'

While Philip was talking with the disgraced celebrity leader of Syracuse, more talk was going on in Athens between the pro- and anti-Philip factions. As examples of successful powerful leaders stacked up around the Greek world, as the bitter cost of continued unrest and instability became more and more visible, as the inability of the traditional model of city-on-city power politics to achieve peace became more clear, as Philip descended into central Greece to settle the sacred war over Delphi, there was no more important political argument in Athens. It was time for Athens to decide, once and for all, where it stood. No more slippery-fish diplomacy, no more flip-flop opportunism. This was a hard call.

It was in this environment that Athens had to decide whether Philip was a saviour or a tyrant, an enemy or a friend. It was at this time that Demosthenes, moving on from simply warning about the dangers of Athens' inactivity against Philip, stood up to slander Philip himself. Philip was, Demosthenes screamed at the Athenians, nothing more than a charlatan, a man who had hoodwinked everyone who had had dealings with him and played upon the folly of each person by exploiting their own ignorance. He was, Demosthenes said, the kind of man who took everything of value for himself – the worst kind of man – a tyrant.

It was also in this environment that Isocrates, the political commentator and voice of the conscience of Greece for the past 50 years, now himself just turning 90 (an incredible achievement in a world where life expectancy was much lower), stepped forward once more. Isocrates, besotted with Athens his whole life long, was now beginning to sing a very different tune to Demosthenes. Having witnessed the twists and turns of Greek history through the bitter civil war at the end of the last century, through the internal conflict that had plagued central Greece in the first half of the present century, through the vast cultural, geopolitical and economic changes that had taken place in the wider Greek world, through the brutal swing in the balance of power in the previous ten years, Isocrates now began to believe that Athens was no longer capable of providing what Greece so badly needed. On the lookout for the just and strong leader of his dreams who would unite Greece and restore it to greatness, Isocrates wrote a public letter simply entitled *To Philip*. His advice was simple: 'It is the duty of a man who is high minded, who is a lover of Greece and who has a broader vision than the rest of the world, to use his talents to make war on the barbarians … to deliver them from evil and to make them into cities and fix the boundaries of the Greek world.' Philip was, in Isocrates' failing eyes, the saviour. But whom would Athens believe and follow?

≈≈≈

CHAPTER 13

The Final Showdown

Philip by 352 BC had crucified the offending generals who had had the temerity to take over the international sanctuary of Delphi and squander its divine riches. He stood as leader of the powerful states of Macedon and Thessaly. His initial attempts to go further south, however, into central Greece, were blocked by the combined forces of Athens and Sparta, who held him back at the pass which for centuries had been the crucial bottleneck for would-be invaders of Greece: Thermopylae. This narrow pass, which the infamous 300 (or rather 301) Spartans had defended to the death against the foreign Persians over a century before, now became the pass at which to hold off, not a foreign invader, but a Greek would-be ruler of Greece.

Philip, acting with his usual military acumen and skill, instead of forcing the bottleneck, sought ways to move around it. He continued to bleed Athens dry fighting on the north Aegean coast until he had hacked away sufficiently at Athens' interests and military reserves. Turning his attentions back to the south, he sought a way around the blocked pass at Thermopylae. The answer lay in the long seahorse-shaped island which stretches parallel to the east coast of the Greek mainland: the island of Euboea, long an Athenian territory (Map 2). It was now that Athens got word of revolts on Euboea. It was rumoured that Philip might well be behind the rebellion. Athens was terrified. If it lost Euboea, then Philip could simply move his troops onto the island (at its narrowest point, the channel of water between the island and the mainland is about 40 metres), march down it and back on to the mainland, thereby circumventing the narrow pass at Thermopylae, and push onwards into central Greece. Like water flowing around a dam, the gushing torrents of Philip's marching men would find their way into central Greece and be unstoppable. If Euboea fell, Greece would fall with it.

Athens' belligerent tone suddenly seemed to put it in a very weak position. Philip simultaneously began to menace its arterial grain route to the Black Sea, threatening to cut off food supplies. Yet at the same time, he started to request a peace treaty and an alliance. It was a brilliant tactic of divide and conquer. By requesting peace, rather than simply being the harbinger of destruction, he ruined any chance Demosthenes might have had of uniting Athens and Greece against him. He wants peace, people argued to Demosthenes, who advocated war. Let us give him peace. After all, for decades, peace was what Greece had been searching for. Demosthenes' attempts to gather all of Greece in an alliance against Philip, as a result, met with a lukewarm response. In 346 BC, Demosthenes faced the humiliation of being sent with his arch-rival Aeschines by the city of Athens on an embassy to agree peace with Philip. This peace negotiation would later be torn apart in the law courts of Athens by Demosthenes and Aeschines themselves, each accusing the other of betraying Athens. But for now, it was Philip who was calling the shots. Delaying the negotiations, he used the leverage of his new reputation as 'Philip the peacemaker' to split the remaining allies away from Athens and, by bribing the surviving enemy mercenaries, ensured that his troops could march past Thermopylae and deep into central Greece. While Athens' hands were tied in peace negotiations, while Demosthenes was forced to swallow the bitter pill of allying with Philip, Philip did what Athens had sworn it would never allow him to do on the battlefield: take central Greece. Before Athens really knew what was happening, Philip was at the gates of the sanctuary of Delphi and celebrating its freedom by hosting the sacred games. Within months, he had meted out punishment to those who had abused the sanctuary, been welcomed by the sanctuary's famous oracle of the god

Apollo, and been installed with a permanent seat on Delphi's governing council. Philip was here to stay and Athens could now do very little about it. The city was forced to sign a peace with Philip, give up its claims to the rich resources on the north Aegean coast, and return home humiliated. Demosthenes was devastated. Aeschines stayed on as an honoured guest at Philip's feast to celebrate his victory. Philip 1: Demosthenes 0.

But Demosthenes wasn't to be defeated. While peace with Philip was Athens' only option in 346, Demosthenes never stopped arguing that Philip was Athens' enemy. He took every opportunity he could to undermine the peace and to sour relations between Philip and Athens. He was obsessed because he saw the world as being either in the hands of Philip or of Athens. He believed that on the back of the fate of Athens' freedom and independence lay the freedom of the whole of Greece. What was good for Athens was good for Greece. In a newly globalised and constantly changing world, Demosthenes expounded a very old, blinkered, self-centred, empire-like idea: what is good for the 'centre of the world' (Athens) is good for the world as a whole. But did Demosthenes ever realise that such a rigid way of looking at the world, fashioned in his mind thanks to Athens' imperial past, would put Athens out of touch with the realities of the world around it, and lead ultimately to it losing the freedom and independence it so cherished?

Whether he realised it or not, Demosthenes was soon given very visible evidence that the rest of the Greek world didn't subscribe to the 'what is good for Athens is good for you' mentality. As Philip continued his diplomatic offensive deep in the Peloponnese in southern Greece, Demosthenes went on his own counter-offensive. To prevent the smaller cities of the Peloponnese allying with Philip, Demosthenes charged them 'in the name of freedom and the independence of Greece' not to sign with the Macedonian king. But these cities replied that, the way they saw it, it was Philip who was guaranteeing them freedom and independence from Athens and Sparta. Demosthenes was, quite simply, out of step in the dance of Greece that was being played to Philip's tune. Philip 2: Demosthenes 0.

But Demosthenes was still not to be defeated. While he couldn't convince the rest of Greece to follow him, he could still convince Athens and the Athenian assembly to hold out against the Macedonian. Returning to Athens, he accused Philip of plotting against the whole of Greece and managed to convince the citizens of Athens to send ambassadors to Philip demanding (as if they were in a position to demand anything) a renegotiation of the peace treaty. Philip, while continuing the diplomatic offensive in central and southern Greece, had turned his military attention back to the north. He had used the peace treaty with Athens to push home his advantage on the north Aegean coast and take the fight to the other power in the region: Thrace. Spreading eastwards, the octopus tentacles of Macedon swirled further and further across the land to the very boundaries of the Greek world until they reached around the entire top of the Aegean and down into Asia Minor and the Persian empire. But while the Athenians waited for an official reply to their request for a renegotiation of the peace treaty, Demosthenes managed to convince the Athenians to keep biting at Philip's heels in the north Aegean with small raids and support for the valiant few who fought against him. Philip 2: Demosthenes 1. Philip, increasingly exasperated by Athens (and by Demosthenes), sent the Athenians a stark warning: back off or face the consequences. Demosthenes, with his angry rhetoric, was forcing Athens into an all-out confrontation with the Macedonian king. But did anyone believe Athens could win?

Ever since peace had been declared between Athens and Philip in 346 BC, Athens, it seems, had been in a state of civil unrest. Demosthenes' henchman, the orator Hyperides, tried to prosecute the author of the 346 peace. His intention was, by dishonouring the man, to dishonour the peace by extension and hasten its demise. But this was really a sideshow to the confrontation between the main rivals Demosthenes and Aeschines. In the three years after the peace, the rivalry between these two degenerated into deadly hatred. The fight was over nothing less

than who had failed in their duty to Athens during the 'peace negotiations' that both Demosthenes and Aeschines had been sent on, and
which Philip had used as a delaying tactic to force Athens into a more
vulnerable position. Sensing that the Athenian people were inherently
suspicious of Aeschines' personal friendship with Philip, Demosthenes
went for the jugular and accused Aeschines of treason in the courts.
Aeschines replied with a counter-prosecution against Demosthenes'
co-prosecutor. This counter-prosecution took precedence in the court
diary and bought Aeschines some time. It turned out to be his finest
hour. Aeschines won his case against Demosthenes' co-prosecutor, and
when Demosthenes' original case finally came to trial in 343, Aeschines
was acquitted on all charges. Philip's man in Athens was still secure,
even if somewhat tainted with suspicion. Philip 3: Demosthenes 1.

But it wasn't just unrest caused by the tension between the pro- and
anti-Philip camps that permeated the streets of Athens in those years –
it was also a more deep-seated uneasiness about the safety of the thing
the city held most dear: its democracy. In 346, the same year as the
peace with Philip, Athens undertook a complete revision of its citizenship lists – like a modern-day survey of the nation – to find out who
exactly could legitimately claim Athenian citizenship. Anyone found
wanting was expelled. Athens was boarding up its windows and engaging in almost a siege mentality. As the threat from Philip increased over
the next six years, the city made moves to ensure that its war chest was
in the healthiest possible condition, diverting profits from every other
part of the city, including even those reserved for putting on theatrical
productions and festivals. Just two years later, on the eve of the impending clash that many feared and some hoped would decide the fate of
Athens and of Greece, the city, reacting like a cat on a hot tin roof to
each piece of rumour about civil unrest, enacted a new law which reiter-
ated the punishments to be handed out to anyone attempting to subvert
the democracy. The law-givers set up copies of the new law in different
places around the city to make sure everyone knew about it. One of the
stones inscribed with this law survives to this day. Above the legal text

is an image, an aide-memoire to passers-by to remind them what the law was about (Fig. 12). The seated figure of an old man, representing the people of Athens, sits next to the standing figure of a beautiful young woman, representing democracy, who crowns the old man. But despite the poetry and power of the image, there is sadness in democracy's eyes and a fragility to the old man of the people that suggests the truth of Athens' state of mind. Despite, and in no small part because of, Demosthenes' constant haranguing of the people that it was their destiny to stand up to the Macedonian king, there was real fear in Athens about what might come next.

What came next was a complicated tangle of international events which led to a head-on collision between Philip and Athens. Demosthenes, despite losing face when he lost his court cases against Aeschines, was now busy acting as ambassador for Athens abroad. He had been sent to the far reaches of the Aegean, at the entrance to the Black Sea, to broker a new alliance between Athens and the city of Byzantium. Byzantium had initially been a member of Athens' league, but left in open revolt in the 350s. It had since been courted by all the major players because of its strategic importance at the mouth of the Black Sea, source of the biggest grain supply in the ancient world. Athens, now that Philip was menacing its grain arteries, needed to be sure that Byzantium was again on its side. Successful in his mission, Demosthenes returned to Athens and was then involved in quelling the local revolts on the island of Euboea, which Athens felt was strategically essential to the safety of its own territorial borders. In the following year, 340 BC, Demosthenes was honoured for his services to Athens. Despite his failure to destroy the pro-Philip camp, he was now undisputed top dog in the city. Philip 3: Demosthenes 2.

Yet almost immediately, Philip moved to upset Athens' security. He launched a siege on the very city with which Demosthenes had just concluded an alliance: Byzantium. Athens and Philip were now officially at war. Yet here, perhaps to the surprise of many, Philip failed to take the city, as so many commanders over future centuries would likewise fail to do. The presence of the Athenian fleet, coupled with the strength of Byzantium's defences (not to mention the fact that Philip's trumpeted catapult machines didn't work properly), meant that Philip suffered an unusual and rather embarrassing setback. Isocrates, our political commentator, who had taken a shine to Philip and his potential to lead Greece, wrote to admonish him for taking such risks with his own life. Could it be, just possibly, that Philip was stoppable? Philip 3: Demosthenes 3. The game for Greece was neck-and-neck.

Yet in the following year, 339 BC, another chain of events was set in motion that changed the score sheet once and for all. Delphi, the international sanctuary which Philip had invaded central Greece to 'free' in the previous decade, was once again in the headlines. Its temple had been destroyed by an earthquake back in 373 BC. The temple's reconstruction had been funded by donations sent from all over Greece. Yet the rebuilding had been interrupted by the occupation of the sanctuary and the subsequent war for its freedom. The temple's completion had been spurred on by a massive injection of new cash raised as part of the punishment meted out to the city which had unjustly taken over the sanctuary. Now complete, the new temple stood as Delphi's brightest crown jewel, glittering in its brilliance against the rough-hewn stone of the steep Parnassian mountains behind it (Fig. 5). Athens moved to rehang shields on the temple, shields which Athens had placed on the previous temple over 100 years before as a dedication to the god Apollo. The small town of Amphissa nearby objected to Athens' 'occupation' of the temple and brought the matter before the assembly of cities and states that governed Delphi. Athens had to choose whom to send as its ambassador. Normally, they never bothered to send anyone of note. The governing council was a talking shop rather than a heavyweight political body. But now, with the fate of Greece hanging in the balance, and with Philip sitting on the council, it was crucial that Athens had a good man on the ground. They chose to send Aeschines, Philip's man in Athens, recently acquitted and still arch-rival of Demosthenes.

Aeschines' speech, so he himself claimed in a later law court trial, was outstanding. He managed in a single speech not only to reject Amphissa's charge of wrongdoing, but to turn the tables on the poor defenceless city of Amphissa by claiming that it had committed a much more serious act of sacrilege: it had cultivated sacred land. It was the same reason used to declare the last sacred war which had brought Philip marching down into central Greece. Before the poor city of Amphissa could have known what was happening, the general council of Delphi had declared war on the city and asked Philip to be its general. Suddenly Philip was on the march south again to take part in yet another sacred war.

It was clear this time, however, that Philip was having none of Athens', or rather Demosthenes', cheek. Exasperated by this mosquito constantly biting at his side and feeding on his blood, by the constant rebuffs of his attempts to conclude some sort of peace with Athens, and perhaps frightened by the possible implications of his inability to take Byzantium lest Athens use it to stir up central Greece against him, Philip moved south determined to sort out the problem of Athens one way or another. Marching straight over the hapless city of Amphissa, Philip seized the city of Elatea. This city was just two days' march from Athenian territory. At the same time, Philip delivered an ultimatum to Thebes and to the surrounding territory of Boeotia. 'You can join me and join in the spoils of war or you can suffer the ravages of war yourselves.' It was a stark choice that echoes George W. Bush's formulation of world politics in the post-9/11, axis-of-evil world: 'You are either with us or against us.'

It was now, with the city in peril, as the only people standing between Philip and Athens decided whether to fight or fall over, that Demosthenes had his finest moment. Never a man to make impromptu speeches, Demosthenes now broke his rule. The Athenian assembly, when they heard the news that Philip was just two days' march away, was silent. No one knew what to say. Everyone was dumbstruck by the fact that their belligerent stinging of the Macedonian beast, which had seemed to be happening far away in the Black Sea, had now resulted in that beast being just two days away from their homes and families. Not since the Persian invasion of Greece some 142 years earlier had the city of Athens been threatened in the same way by such a massive invading force. Then the forces of Athens had risen up to defeat the barbarian invader. But now, no one seemed to have the stamina for the fight. The assembly was silent.

As Plutarch later recounts: 'Then it was that Demosthenes, and he alone, came forward and counselled the people to cling to Thebes.' In Athens' darkest hour, the man who had, in no small measure, been the architect of that darkness now advised allegiance with Thebes and confrontation with Philip. Demosthenes, Athens' own 'prince of darkness', had finally got what he wanted: an all-out fight with Philip.

Demosthenes was dispatched at once to Thebes to persuade the Thebans to strengthen their resolve and to fight with Athens against Philip. It was a gargantuan task. Athens had abandoned Thebes in its hour of need in 379 and 371 BC. What possible advantage was there to Thebans to fight against Philip that day? What possible tie to Athens, with which they had been at war for most of the century, could bind them tight enough to face up to the onslaught of Macedon? Demosthenes arrived in Thebes at the same time as the ambassadors from Macedon were arriving to hear the response of the Thebans to their ultimatum. Both sets of ambassadors courted the Thebans. The silence of the Athenian assembly extended all over Greece as every city turned to listen intently to what Thebes would decide. On that day, on that assembly, on the words spoken by those men, the future direction of Athens rested entirely.

We don't know exactly what Demosthenes said to the Thebans. He spoke, as he later himself recalled in the law courts of Athens, 'of the liberties and freedoms of the Greeks', but even he himself later also exclaimed: 'How I would give my life to recap the speech I made that day!' But whatever winged words he used, I doubt there have been many speeches so powerful and persuasive in the history of mankind.

Against all the odds, against every ounce of common sense and fibre of self-survival, Demosthenes convinced Thebes that day to stand with Athens. As Plutarch later said: 'Demosthenes fanned the flames of Theban courage and inflamed their upstanding ambition and obscured all other considerations so that, throwing to the winds their fear and rational minds ... they were swept up by his words into following a course of honour.'

Demosthenes returned to Athens like a giddy schoolboy. He was, said Plutarch, 'lifted into a state of glowing excitement by the eagerness of so many men for battle'. Ignoring every objection, squashing every attempt to save the moment by offering further peace terms to Philip, denouncing as a traitor to Athens anyone who questioned the need to fight, Demosthenes now used his new-found authority in the Athenian assembly to resolutely keep the juggernaut on course for an all-out battle with Philip. Phocion, the wise old Athenian general who had stopped Philip taking over Byzantium, tried his best now to stop Demosthenes, opposing his every move by arguing for peace with Philip. He became so unpopular with the Athenian people, now thirsty as vampires for the blood of war, that even Demosthenes is said to have warned him: 'The Athenians will kill you, Phocion, if they become any more worked-up.' 'Yes,' Phocion is said to have replied, 'but they will kill you if they come to their senses.' Swept aside by public hysteria, Phocion could do nothing but watch the gathering storm clouds. Demosthenes' supporters moved that all foreigners in the city should be made citizens and all slaves freed and armed so that the Athenians could put the maximum possible number of soldiers into the field. The prince of darkness had got his battle against his lifelong enemy. But what would be the cost?

The forces of Philip lined up against the forces of Athens and Thebes at a place called Chaeronea on 2 August 338 BC, in the middle, most appropriately, of the dancing-floor of Ares in central Greece (Map 2). Today, the plain of Chaeronea is a fertile patchwork of fields nestled in between the swelling mountains of Boeotia. The valley has an air of sanguine calm, so much so that it's hard to imagine a battle in such a place.

But a battle there certainly was. Philip took control of his infantry and his son, Alexander, now eighteen years of age, took control of the cavalry. Opposite him were the elite forces of Thebes, the 300-strong Sacred Band of male lovers, never defeated in battle, the rest of the Theban army, and the Athenian troops, among whom stood Demosthenes, who had fashioned this moment through his oratorical haranguing of Philip over the last fifteen years. In contrast, we don't know for certain where Aeschines was. Did his loyalty to his friend Philip, in the cold light of battle, outweigh his loyalty to his city, as Demosthenes had prophesied it would? Or did he reluctantly take up arms against his friend, putting his city before himself? We will never know.

The archaeological remains of the battle at Chaeronea tell us only too graphically of the horrors of the conflict. There are two monuments to the slaughter still visible in the valley of Chaeronea – one said to belong to the Thebans and one to the Macedonians. The Theban burial site is claimed to mark the spot where nearly every member of the Sacred Band was hacked down and killed. Archaeologists excavating the site have found 254 human skeletons, their bones scarred with wound marks still visible after more than 2,000 years: leg bones hacked by swords and broken by the sharp points of the Macedonian *sarissa* pikes, skulls fractured by multiple sword blows, one skull with the face chopped completely off it. The bodies of these broken men were dumped together in seven rows – their skulls and bones intermixed with the remains of shoes and weaponry. The mass grave stands as a testament to the rage and ferocity with which the Macedonians cut down their foe.

10,000 Athenians were also said to have died that day and another 2,000 were captured. The battlefield was strewn with slaughter so horrendous that the throng of decomposing bodies and hordes of flies, in the sweltering August heat, may well have become a breeding ground for the plague that swept through Greece the following winter. Across the valley floor, by the Athens–Thessaloniki train line that now bisects the valley, the Macedonian funeral mound reveals the greater attention

FROM DEMOCRATS TO KINGS

paid to the fallen victors. Here the bodies weren't thrown ignominiously into the ground but were all cremated in a funeral pyre to victory, the remaining white bones, cleansed by fire, piled up neatly and covered by a mound seven metres high and 70 metres across.

Above the bodies of the fallen Theban warriors stands the lion of Chaeronea (Fig. 13). Still visible right by the old national road that meanders north through Greece, this huge stone lion, made out of local Chaeronean stone, stands alert and proud, looking out over the battlefield directly towards the Macedonian burial mound. It's the calling card of Philip, similar to another lion he set up after an equally monumental victory in northern Greece. Philip, the lion of Greece, stands triumphant to this day, surveying the location of his victory. Cypress trees, often used to mark cemeteries in modern Greece, have been planted in a row behind the lion, giving it an appropriate backdrop of death and foreboding. I dare anyone to go to Chaeronea today and not be moved by the haunting majesty of Philip's muscular lion, its deep-set, penetrating eyes and its bared teeth, sitting on its taut haunches above the broken remains of the butchered Theban Sacred Band.

What of Demosthenes? The man who had done more than any other to bring about this conflict ran from the battlefield like a coward. As Plutarch, who himself would live at Chaeronea some 400 years later, recounted: 'Demosthenes acted without courage, honour, and in flagrant breach of his own exhortations, abandoning his post, throwing away his weapons and running away in disgrace.' The 'hero' of Athens, the champion of Athens' and Greece's 'liberty', the prince of Athens' darkness, fled the battle which decided Greece's fate.

In the aftermath of the battle, the surviving Athenians, including the stylish natural orator Demades, retreated to their city. Aeschines, Philip's man in Athens, along with Demades and the old, wise and sullen general Phocion, were sent now to beg for peace from the undisputed ruler of Greece. Philip could not but laugh at Athens' plucky determination to punch above its weight. Following the battle, the defeated Athenians who had been captured were released magnanimously by Philip without ransom. Despite being given their lives, they turned to Philip and asked for their clothing and bedding back as well. Philip is said to have laughed, turning to his officers and saying: 'Does it not seem to you that the Athenians think they have only been beaten in a board game?' The Athenians were packed off home without their bedding and Aeschines, Demades and Phocion were left to minimise the damage.

Yet Philip, who was said to have been drunk with happiness at his victory at Chaeronea, was also badly shaken by it. Though the battle had gone his way, the stakes had been dizzyingly high. If he had lost, his reputation and ability to control Greece would have been in tatters. After years of planning, reform, careful diplomacy and military inter-vention, he had been forced to gamble everything on a single battle. The man who had made him do so was Demosthenes. The man who had fled Philip in battle was the man who had come closest to bringing him down.

It's no surprise that Philip now wanted Demosthenes' head on a platter. It would have been no surprise if the people of Athens, led into this catastrophe by his oratory and deserted by him in battle, had now wanted exactly the same thing. Which makes it even more surprising that Athens not only protected Demosthenes from Philip's rage, but gave him the honour, in the immediate aftermath of the battle, of ask-ing him to speak the funeral eulogy on behalf of the Athenian dead. The prince of darkness, the deserter, the coward, the man responsible for the deaths of fellow Athenians and for Athens' present predicament, was now given the honour of speaking on behalf of the city at one of its most important soul-searching moments. In the graveyard of Athens, at the entrance to the city, Demosthenes stood and faced his fellow citizens to eulogise over the dead he really should have been among. How did he hold his head up high that day? His speech, still surviving, is a tart mix of 'I told you so' and forlorn prognosis of the end of the world: 'There was folly among the Greeks and a slackness, which failed to understand the dangers and do anything about it at a time when it was still possible to have averted disaster ... but now, as when the light of day is removed out of this world and everything left becomes harsh and difficult, so now, with these brave men dead, all the former beauty and radiance of Greece is drowned in gloom and utter blackness.'

For Demosthenes, it must have seemed like the end of everything. The magnificent marble Parthenon temple, etched against the skyline of Athens on its Acropolis and dominating the ancient city below it, constructed with money extracted from Athens' empire in its glory days of the previous century, now looked down piteously on Demosthenes and what his Athens had become. For our political commentator Isocrates, however, it was the beginning of everything he had hoped for. He had lived a long life. He had begged Athens repeatedly to step up and lead Greece. Now he saw that Greece was at a fork in the road. In the run-up to the battle at Chaeronea, Isocrates had at last given up hope of the city ever fulfilling its potential. In the final year of his extraordinary long life, Isocrates had transferred his allegiance fully to Philip. For him, Philip represented Greece's best chance of unity and glory in its fight against Persia. At the age of 98, Isocrates it seems had had enough of Athens and its flip-flop democracy. He wrote to thank Philip for showing him, in his last moments, some of his dreams come true and hoped that Philip would in time bring the rest to reality. Looking around him in Athens, he was disgusted at how few shared his sentiment. It was this disgust that may have prompted Isocrates to make his final statement on the state of Greece, not in the form of another political pamphlet, but by his own death. Refusing food for four days, Isocrates finally dropped dead. In 338 BC, just after Philip's victory at Chaeronea, the old, withered and exhausted body of Athens' longest-serving political commentator was buried with those of his mother and father near the Ilissos river in Athens (Map 1). He would never know that every one of his dreams was indeed about to become a reality.

CHAPTER 14

❦

From Father to Son

King Philip of Macedon moved quickly after his victory at Chaeronea to establish his dominance over Greece. He punished the city of Thebes, which had chosen to fight against him with Athens that fateful August day. Then he turned his eyes to Athens itself. Everyone waited for what would surely come next: the punishing of the city which had been a thorn in Philip's side, which had brought him to the point of having to risk everything in a single battle. Surely, the time for Athens' destruction had come? Phocion, its trusted general for much of the century, spoke out to harangue Athens in the silence left by Demosthenes, who had suddenly gone very quiet in the assembly. Phocion lamented that the Athenians didn't listen to him when he told them not to follow Demosthenes. Now they would have to face the consequences.

Standing in Athens late in 338 BC, as summer turned to autumn and a difficult, plague-filled and grain-short winter loomed, Athenians must have been surprised and relieved to see not the many phalanxes of Macedonian infantry marching towards them, but two men accompanied by a bodyguard. These two Macedonians themselves accompanied a much longer train of newly released Athenian prisoners of war and the ashes of their dead counterparts. As those two Macedonians entered the city, the Athenians would have seen for themselves that they were two of the most powerful men in the Macedonian court: Alexander, Philip's son, and Philip's most trusted general, a man called Antipater.

The older, wiser statesman and general Antipater accompanied Alexander, the young, virile son of the king. Together they constituted the power and future of Macedonian hegemony. It was a sign to Athens, not of impending doom but of the honour in which Philip held the Athenians, that he had sent his most precious commodities to accompany the Athenian dead back home. All he asked in return was peace. The Athenians, jubilant at having escaped the hangman's noose, not only gave him peace, but put up a statue of Philip immediately in the Agora, at the heart of their city.

Such magnanimity by Philip is at first hard to understand. Plutarch, perhaps in an attempt to explain it, would later portray him as a man of true altruism. When asked after Chaeronea why he didn't simply put military garrisons all over Greece, Philip is said to have replied that he would prefer to be remembered as a good man for a long time rather than as a master for a short time. The truth is perhaps less poetic. Philip had plans, and those plans needed Athens, and particularly its fleet, to be in good shape and to be well disposed towards him. Whatever Athens had done to him in the past, he could not afford to destroy the city now.

Philip's plan had two stages. The first was to heal the wounds of internal war, which had plagued Greece for most of the century. He brought all the cities of Greece together and bound them into a new alliance, which has become known as the League of Corinth. Immediately after Chaeronea, as 338 gave way to 337 BC, almost every single city of worth in Greece became part of a single alliance, with Philip as its leader and general. Philip had achieved what no Greek city had been able to achieve that century. The text of the league charter still survives on stone to this day. Every member took the following oath:

I swear to abide by the peace, and I shall not break the agreement with Philip nor take up weapons against any of those who keep these oaths ... nor shall I overthrow the kingdom of Philip or his descendants.

In just one year, Philip had given the Greeks peace, he had given them a leader (a king in all but name), and he had given them unity. Now, in the second stage of his plan, he gave them purpose. The League of Corinth had but one aim – to take the fight to Greece's old enemy: Persia. What our political pamphleteer Isocrates, now resting in his grave, had always dreamed of had come true: a powerful leader uniting Greece in a war against Persia. In one fell swoop, Philip turned the clock back on Greek history. Gone were the internal conflicts of the previous 90 years since the start of the Peloponnesian war. Gone was the threatening and meddling influence of the Persian king and Persian money in Greek affairs. Gone was the ability of the Persian king to make peace terms in Greece. Back in was the one thing which had always proved successful in uniting the warring cities of Greece in the past: a joint campaign against their old enemy across the Aegean sea. Nothing brings people together like a war. Philip was ready to begin a whole new (or rather dust off an old) chapter in Greece's history.

Persia seemed ripe for the picking. It was in the midst of its own leadership crisis. In the same month as the battle of Chaeronea, yet another Persian king had been murdered and a new king had taken the throne. All the major Greek cities signed up for the expedition against this new monarch – except one: Sparta. Sparta refused to sign up to the league and went home once again, just like old times, to stick its head in the sand. It was having none of the league, none of Philip and none of the campaign against Persia. Perhaps Philip should have realised then that this would be a harder task than he had first imagined.

In the spring of 336 BC, less than two years after Chaeronea, Philip sent advance forces marching around the top of the Aegean to prepare for his invasion of Persia. It seemed that the task of toppling Persia would be even easier: the new Persian king, in power for less than two years, had himself been murdered and replaced by another monarch, Darius III. In autumn 336, Philip returned to Macedon to attend his daughter's wedding. Drunk with the giddiness of what he had achieved and the enormity of the task he was about to set out on, he declared that his own statue would be carried in the procession of the statues of the gods during the festival accompanying the wedding. Philip himself would also walk, dressed as the figures of the gods would be, without his armour. He would walk alone – as a man no longer needing earthly protection, as a living god among men. As he walked out, unprotected and unarmed behind the procession of the gods, one of his own body-guards rushed out of the crowd and stabbed him to death. King Philip of Macedon, the leader and general of Greece, was killed by one of his own, just as he was about to set out on his greatest adventure.

The assassin, a Macedonian called Pausanias, was later said to have killed Philip because of a private grievance between himself, Philip and a fellow military commander. But it's impossible to know if the assassin realised the enormity of what he had done. Within weeks, news of Philip's death had spread across Greece and Philip's peace, his unity, his league, his vision for the future of Greece were haemorrhaging life-blood.

It's no surprise to find out where the haemorrhaging was worst: Athens. Demosthenes, whose contacts were better than anyone's, heard about Philip's death before it was announced in the Athenian assembly. Sensing his chance to gain favour with the people once again, he quickly went to the assembly and, rising to speak, declared that he had had a dream of impending good fortune for Athens. Not long afterwards, the official messengers arrived to announce Philip's death. Demosthenes looked like he had been inspired with a dream of the future sent by the gods. He was, once again, launched into the driving seat of Athenian policy.

As a result, not only did Athens not stay silent about Philip's murder, but instead of condemning the assassin, it voted him public honours. Soon enough, Athens' example had fractured the league for good. The city of Thebes, still smarting at Philip's harsh treatment of it following Chaeronea, began to riot. Soon whole regions of Greece – Ambracia, Thessaly, Arcadia and Aetolia – followed. In 335, just a year after Philip's death, Thebes began an open revolt against Macedon. Inviting the

Persian king back into Greek affairs to help them, the Thebans fought for the freedom of the Greeks: 'Anyone who wishes to join the Persian king and the city of Thebes in freeing the Greeks and destroying the tyrant of Greece should come to them.' Greece's whole new page of history was ripped apart before the first sentence had been written. Demosthenes was, of course, the central protagonist behind all of this. Though his own daughter had died only six days earlier, he left his grief, his wife, his house and his family behind to take his place on the public stage and to lead the rebellion against Macedon. Demosthenes was back in his element, touting his old line: Macedon and its kings are the enemy of Athens and of Greece. Phocion, the wise old Athenian general, was one of the only figures to oppose him in the assembly. 'You rash idiot,' he is supposed to have cried, 'why are you seeking to provoke a man who is so savage? Can you really wish, when so great a bush fire is so near by, to fan our own city with its flames?'

Who was this savage man Phocion warned of? None other than Philip's son, Alexander, just twenty years old and propelled into the kingship of Macedon by the untimely death of his father (Fig. 1). Now king, he faced the immediate and total disintegration of everything his father had worked to achieve. Alexander's reputation, and his own life, hung on what he could accomplish in his first 100 days on the throne. He had to stamp his authority onto Greece or be left impotent and most probably dead. Surrounded by threatening rivals for the throne, by former allies now in open rebellion, Alexander had to show what kind of a man he really was.

Phocion's description of Alexander as savage reveals how Alexander responded to the challenge. Killing rivals in Macedon left, right and centre, he moved immediately to secure his kingdom. Turning his attentions to Thessaly, Alexander stunned the ancient world by capturing the forces cocooned on top of the almost 2,000-metre-high Mount Ossa – by cutting a stairway into the rock face so that his troops could climb up to make their attack. Reclaiming the title of *tagos*, supreme leader, of Thessaly, he moved north to quell his troublesome neighbours. It was then, while he was far away by the Danube river, that he received word of Thebes' open rebellion. In less than two weeks, he and his army were standing at the gates of Thebes (Map 4). No one could believe it was really him: he had covered an enormous distance, over 700 kilometres, on foot and horseback, in impossible time. As Franklin Roosevelt would say after the bombing of Pearl Harbor centuries later: 'We can't measure our safety in terms of miles on a map any more.' Nowhere was safe from Alexander's grasp. With the savagery and power of the stone lion that stood marking the spot of his father's great victory at Chaeronea only 20 kilometres away, Alexander tore the city of Thebes apart. He not only took the city, he burnt it to the ground, erasing its existence, squashing it under his feet, killing its citizens – the children of the generation of heroes like Pelopidas and Epaminondas who had helped Thebes become supreme in Greece – and selling the rest into slavery until there was nothing left of the once-proud city but its burning embers. Alexander declared that the city had been destroyed as punishment for 'a century and a half of collusion with the Persians'. The saddest part of this tale is that members of several other Greek cities, who were only too glad to stamp on Thebes themselves, helped Alexander in this annihilation. There was no love lost between the cities of Greece, even in the face of impending Macedonian hegemony. Isocrates' dream of a united Greece looked further away than ever. Now Alexander turned his attentions to Athens.

By the end of 335 BC, just over a year since the death of his father, king Alexander III of Macedon was back in control of Greece. In his first 100 days, he had quelled internal rebellion. In his first year, he had subdued an entire country. But Alexander, just like his father, didn't visit Athens with the same penalty as Thebes. Athens, true to its slippery self, though it had honoured Philip's assassin and followed Demosthenes in stirring up rebellion, had sent people to help Alexander destroy Thebes, the city which had chosen to stand with Athens against Philip at Chaeronea, and now quickly distanced itself from any notion of the revolution. Though it didn't deserve it, not least because of its two-faced cowardice and desertion of its former ally, Athens would be spared, principally because Alexander still needed its fleet if he was to follow in his father's footsteps.

But what about Demosthenes himself? Demosthenes had been sent on an embassy to seek peace for Athens with Alexander, but had turned back without meeting the king through fear for his own life. Now safely back in Athens, his belligerence seems to have returned. Alexander demanded nothing from Athens except ten prisoners – chief among whom was Demosthenes. To the assembly, Demosthenes cried out, with astonishing arrogance, that Athens should never be forced to give up its best hope of salvation. Athens, teetering in indecision, called upon the one man it always relied on in times of dire distress: the wise old general Phocion. He advised them to make peace with Alexander and send someone to negotiate terms. Athens sent the smooth-talking, wine-drinking, on-off friend of Macedon, the orator Demades, to plead its case with the Macedonian king. Demades, although we have no idea how, managed to persuade Alexander to let Demosthenes live and stay in Athens. Unbelievably, the cause of so much trouble once again walked free.

By the end of 335 BC, Alexander had proved himself equal to his father. Greece was firmly back under his control. His reputation as a man of military genius and astonishing, almost superhuman, ability was brewing nicely. Many scholars have sought to compare father and son, to think about the relationship between the two and to make a judgement on which was the more extraordinary. What were these two kings really like, and how did they get on with one another?

Philip has often suffered in comparison with his son – just look in any bookshop at books on the ancient world, and Alexander's shelf always out-groans his dad's. There's a Hollywood film about Alexander but not about his father. This is in part because Alexander's achievements were much more dramatic and widespread than his father's – Alexander would go on to conquer much of the Persian empire, the very thing his father had set out to do before he was cut down at his daughter's wedding. But Alexander would never have been able to achieve any of it if it weren't for the cultural, political and particularly military reforms put in place by his father, which turned Macedon from barbarian backwater into the powerhouse of Greece. Philip, in no small part, set up his son's success.

Philip's reputation among the historians of the ancient world was much higher than perhaps it is today. The ancient historian Polybius thought that Europe had never produced another man like Philip. The historian Diodorus marked Philip as the first individual to truly shape history, a man who combined military strength with diplomatic agility and a thorough knowledge of human weakness. Philip, for example, as Plutarch also later put it, knew that a donkey laden with gold could take any city impregnable to military might. He was also said to have once fired a man from his service for dyeing his hair, stating that a man who tried to disguise his true hair colour was untrustworthy in the business of the state. Several ancient historians wrote entire treatises about Philip's life and character; but, because his reputation has dimmed over the centuries in comparison with that of his son, those texts have simply been lost into the ether through the generations of scholars standing between then and now. Chief among the surviving sources we do have about Philip are the speeches of his arch-enemy, Demosthenes, who is always keen to give us Philip's bad side. But even Demosthenes, Philip's most vociferous opponent, marvelled at Philip's restless activity, his insatiable ambition and his skill in making the most of opportunities thrown his way.

Alexander, in contrast, whose reputation has only grown since antiquity, has a patchwork of sources about him surviving from different time periods, which creates something of a mythic-magical aura around his life and character. But these sources also reveal something of the relationship between him and his father. Unlike Dionysius I of Syracuse, so worried about his own life that he refused to let his son be educated lest he became a threat to him, Philip ensured that Alexander was given the best tuition possible. His tutor was no less than the great philosopher Aristotle, and Alexander was schooled in every possible kind of skill. Isocrates, the political commentator on the period, had even written publicly to the young Alexander with a long list of tips on how to be a good leader. Philip ensured that he was given experience early on in running the kingdom, making him regent of Macedonia at the age of sixteen and fighting alongside him at Chaeronea when he was eighteen. Plutarch recounts how Philip passed on wise words to his son about governing, telling Alexander to make as many friends as possible before he came into a position of power, because he would make plenty of enemies once there.

Yet Alexander, perhaps because of his education and his famous father, was also a man on a mission to prove himself. He was, says Plutarch, from the beginning intent on carving himself into history, forgoing all pleasures and weaknesses of the flesh (don't believe Plutarch for one minute). Stung by the criticism, for example, that Alexander was, like his father, a heavy drinker, Plutarch responded that Alexander didn't drink much – he just made each cup of wine last a long time so that it looked like he was drinking a lot. But the story of Alexander's youth also reveals a real tension between father and son. Philip, having failed to tame a wild horse, was begged by Alexander to let him have a go. The horse, which would become Alexander's constant companion, and in honour of which he would one day found a city in Asia, responded to Alexander's touch. Philip's reply was a mix of pride and jealousy: 'Son, seek out a kingdom equal to yourself – Macedon does not have room for both of us.'

The tension between father and son came to a head in the years immediately preceding Philip's death. Philip had taken many wives, but Alexander was the son of his first, the cunning, brave and vicious Olympias (played by Angelina Jolie in the recent film). As such, Alexander had a strong claim to the throne. But in his final years, Philip, who had always married for strategic reasons, is said to have fallen in love. Marrying late in his life for love, to a woman of Macedonian blood rather than to a foreigner (Olympias had come from Epirus), was a real threat to Olympias and Alexander – any offspring from this new 'Macedonian love' union could claim to supersede Alexander's right to the throne. Alexander had always argued with his father about the fact that he kept on having children with a number of different women, which meant too much competition for Alexander for the throne. Philip is supposed to have slapped his son down, suggesting that, if Alexander did succeed in taking the throne, it would at least be because he had earned it, rather than because he had been the only choice. But now, in the final year of Philip's life, spurred on by his mother who was bitterly angry at Philip's latest love conquest, as well as by insults that he wasn't a legitimate heir, Alexander took Philip to task one evening at dinner for marrying afresh when he was, as Alexander put it, 'quite simply past it'. Philip rose to challenge his son to a bare-knuckle fight, and promptly tripped drunkenly over the dining couch. Alexander just laughed at the sprawled figure of his famous father: 'Look, here is a man preparing to cross from Europe into Asia, and he can't even cross from couch to couch.'

Philip's inability, even if he could control Greece, to put his own house in order was his weak point and was made a joke of all over Greece. He tried to restrain Alexander by exiling his close friends, but relations with him and his mother were increasingly strained. Philip even exiled them both for a time. Olympias, whose influence over her son would remain unusually strong all his life, may now have pushed for them to take matters into their own hands. The sources are hesitant and uncertain, but the hint is strong: Alexander's mother, Olympias, may well have murdered the new love of Philip's life and her infant son to protect her own son Alexander's right to the throne. But even more startling, the bodyguard who killed Philip in 336 BC may have been bribed to do so by none other than Alexander and his mother. Philip, who conquered Greece and stood on the threshold of conquering Asia, may well have been murdered on the orders of his own wife and child. It was, after all, the Macedonian way.

Whether Alexander did or did not begin his reign by ordering the killing of his father, he certainly moved to scotch any rumours of their difficult relationship by lavishing honours on him after his death. At the great sanctuary of Olympia, where Philip had come to fame as the winner of the horse race in 356, Alexander now ensured the completion of a new building, still to be seen today, which housed statues of Philip, himself, his mother and Philip's parents: the new 'first family' of Greece. The sanctuary at Olympia was full of statues, but these were separated from the rest of *hoi polloi*, encased in a circular marble structure which only added mystique and emphasis to the extraordinary nature of these individuals who now ruled Greece (Fig. 6). While Philip was honoured at the sanctuary of Olympia, Alexander also moved to ensure that he was remembered closer to home. In Macedon, at a place called Vergina, archaeologists have discovered an extraordinarily sumptuous burial mound, so big it looks like a natural hill in the landscape. Inside is an array of burial chambers, each ornately built and decorated. Laid out in these chambers was found a staggering amount of armour, jewellery, gold and precious items. The tomb complex is thought to be for none other than the kings of Macedon, including Philip II. As you proceed out of the natural light into the dark silence of this complex, you can stand opposite the entrance to the supposed tomb of Philip himself. The silence and blackness encase you in awe as you stand so close to the brightly-coloured front entrance of what is possibly the final resting place of one of the greatest figures of history. It was a fitting tribute to a great father from a son who may have had more than a little guilt on his conscience.

Alexander's dream had always been to take on the might of the Persian empire, a dream now urged on by Athenian generals like Phocion, to whom Alexander had taken quite a shine (Phocion was the only Athenian to receive letters from Alexander which began with 'Greetings' rather than just barking orders). As a boy, while talking with ambassadors from the Persian court, Alexander had quizzed them on the road system and what the king was like. He had been terrified that if Philip had gone to Asia and conquered the Persian king himself, there would have been nothing amazing left for Alexander to accomplish. Now, with his father out of the way, and Greece once more under his thumb, Alexander had the chance to outshine his father and he wasn't going to miss it.

Alexander had as much flair for theatrics as he did for military strategy – his education had taught him the value of signs, portents and appearances in winning over both enemies and friends. His career, as related to us with awe by the hotch-potch of later sources, would take such 'meaningful moments' to a new level. He began by proceeding to the great oracle at Delphi, to ask the oracular priestess who passed on knowledge of the future from the god Apollo, son of Zeus, about his mission against Persia. He arrived in Delphi on a day when the priestess wasn't supposed to be working (she could offer prophecies on only a couple of days per month – the ancient Greek equivalent of the 35-hour working week). For centuries, Greeks had respected this tradition – as it was the will of the gods – and sat patiently at the sanctuary waiting for the correct days to come, then taking their place in a long line which zigzagged through the sanctuary. But not Alexander, the new leader of Greece. Taking the priestess roughly by the arm, he started to drag her into the temple to force her to answer his question. While being dragged, she cried out, 'You are invincible, my son!' That was good enough for Alexander. He took the answer as the word of the gods and left for Asia.

Alexander spent his life on the knife-edge between, on the one hand, inspiring admiration for his brute strength, military audacity, dangerous pride and supreme arrogance, and, on the other, attracting criticism and denunciation for his lack of proper respect, particularly for the gods. He lived in the twilight between the human and divine worlds (the sea was even supposed to have receded at his coming, unlike for poor king Canute who tried the same trick centuries later). He put himself above ordinary mortals and almost on a par with the gods, but as a consequence, brought himself dangerously close to being burnt by both. His character and actions were always in excess: too enthusiastic, too daring, too drunken, too arrogant, too brilliant. Later historians attempted to sum up what made this man so unlike any other the Greek world had produced. Some put it down to his *pothos*, his unbending desire for, his deep-seated need of, his all-conquering addiction to, success. Like conquerors of all ages, nationalities and centuries, psychologically speaking, Alexander had to prove himself. He had a chip on his shoulder the size, it would seem, of a small asteroid.

Alexander crossed the Hellespont – the narrow channel of water between Europe and Asia now known as the Dardanelles – in spring 334 BC (Map 4). With him he had approximately 32,000 men to take on an empire that stretched to the boundaries of the known world. His first moves exemplified his complex and highly successful mix of military intimidation, theatrical ability and sense of propaganda. He set about reaffirming his relationships with (and reiterating his military might to) Greek cities on the coast of Asia Minor which had been wavering in their support between Greece and Persia as the likelihood of a new war between these two great adversaries drew near. To add to his military impact, he began his invasion of Asia with a symbolic message: he was the first to set foot on Persian soil, and he threw a spear deep into the sandy beach as if claiming that the territory was already his. The conqueror had come.

In ancient times, a point could be made through military and diplomatic means, and even by a spear-throwing PR stunt, but nothing worked as well as making the present an echo of the past. The past for the Greeks was a time of myths and legends, of men greater than the people of today, a real golden age in which Greeks did extraordinary things. These legends, these myths, were the moral stories and proverbs of the Greek world. They were a code by which present-day behaviour was regulated and judged. Alexander, who occupied that twilight zone between human and more than human, was determined not just to echo that past, but to bring it to life. His first stop in Asia was none other than the great citadel of Troy, taken by the Greek heroes of a bygone age. Among these heroes, none was greater than Achilles, the son of a god and warrior of legend (and Brad Pitt in the movie). Alexander could not but mirror his own image on such a man. He anointed the gravestone of Achilles with oil, ran a race around it naked, crowned it in garlands, and then exchanged his own armour for armour which had lain there in splendid reverence since the time of the Trojan war. The new Achilles, the new superman, had been born.

Alexander would later justify his invasion in a letter to the Persian king: 'Your ancestors invaded Macedon and Greece and did us much harm. I have invaded Asia to take vengeance on Persia, but it was you who began this strife: you murdered my father, you stirred up the Greeks in rebellion, you unjustly and illegally usurped the Persian throne.' We can note the guilty attempt to pin the murder of his father on the Persian monarch, but note also the attempt to make Alexander out to be the one fighting for Persia's freedom against its king. Alexander, the invader trying to conquer Persia, makes himself out to be the man freeing Persia from its unjust usurper. Once again, Alexander had proved himself a master strategist, making the Persian king, who had indeed only just come to the throne two years before, look like a foreign tyrant in his own land.

But it would be some time before Alexander would have his chance to come face to face with the Persian king. The new monarch, Darius III, wouldn't dare to risk – or be seen to credit his adversary with the necessity of – putting the royal presence into battle unless absolutely necessary. For now, Alexander, for all his con-tricks and military acumen, was little more, so the Persian king thought, than an annoying tick biting at the hide of his empire, another of a succession of Greeks to land on the coast of Asia Minor. All who had invaded this coast before had been either defeated by his local governors or bought off. The Persian king, sitting over 2,600 kilometres away in his capital of Persepolis (Map 4), understandably felt that there was no need, yet, to engage in the expensive and time-consuming business of mobilising his empire to squash this new Greek upstart.

Underestimating Alexander was probably the Persian king's fatal error. Engaging the local governors of Persia in open battle at a place called Granicus, not far from the ancient city of Troy, in spring 334 BC, Alexander jumped headlong into the fray. His tempestuous nature surprised even his own, older, more experienced generals. Seeing his enemy across a raging river, instead of waiting for a more appropriate place to cross, Alexander charged on his beloved horse straight into the surging waters and through the other side. Immediately recognisable by the shining, white-feathered plume of his helmet, he was attacked repeatedly. One Persian even managed to bring an axe thundering down on his head, which split the metal of his helmet and even cut into his curly hair. But Alexander survived, and more than survived – he decimated the opposing forces. According to Plutarch, 22,500 Persians died, and only 34 Greeks. Ever with an eye to the value of letting people know about his successes, Alexander sent the captured shields back to Athens inscribed with a message: 'From Alexander, son of Philip and from all the Greeks, except the Spartans.' The Spartans would never be allowed to forget that they had refused to join his father's alliance.

Nor did Alexander forget to send his dear mother something as well. He sent her the captured drinking vessels and purple robes of his enemies. In fact, Alexander, throughout his campaign, was in constant communication with his mother, telling her what he was doing and receiving advice from her, even though he (supposedly) rarely listened to it. She was probably the most important relationship in Alexander's life. When his generals later complained about his mother's influence over him, Alexander is said to have replied simply: 'One tear from a mother is worth ten thousand of your complaints.'

But despite being something of a mummy's boy, Alexander also mixed military strength with diplomatic agility and brutal vengeance as required. Greeks found fighting on the Persian side as mercenaries were shown no mercy, but were exported back to Greece, stripped of their rights, to work in hard labour camps. Some Persian cities, terrified at his approach, surrendered quickly. Others proved trickier. Keen to extricate himself quickly from the complex political wranglings of the different mini-dynasties of the coast of Asia Minor, Alexander often made a deal to give local rulers control over a city in return for absolute loyalty to him. Wherever Alexander went, he did what would steal him the allegiance of the people away from the Persian king. If they wanted democracy, he gave them democracy. If they wanted a ruler, he gave them a ruler. All he asked in return was their unswerving loyalty. As one modern historian has put it: 'All cities were free, as long as they obeyed.'

In the spring of 333 BC, a year after he had entered Asia, Alexander moved to increase the value of his mythical image once more. Attracted by the promise of performing a task no human had ever yet been able to achieve, he arrived at the small city of Gordium, about 70 kilometres south-west of modern-day Ankara in Turkey. In this city was an old ox-cart tethered with an impenetrable knotted rope. There was a prophecy that whoever could loosen the knot would be lord of all Asia. The knot was, so the story goes, unfathomable to even the most agile mind. Alexander took out his sword and simply slashed through it. Unorthodox, rebellious thinking had loosened the Gordian knot and made Alexander the prophesied lord of Asia.

On 1 November 333, Alexander finally got what he wanted: a battle with the Persian king himself. Having realised that Alexander was more than just a fly on his hide, the king had moved to gather a significant percentage of his troops spread across the empire to meet Alexander at a place called Issus, a strategic river crossing near the modern-day Turkish town of Iskenderun (Map 4). Once again, the odds were all on the Persian side – massive Persian forces with a large number of Greek mercenaries choosing to fight against Alexander. Alexander himself had been taken ill just before the battle. But once again, the Persian king underestimated Alexander and the inherent weaknesses of his own army. Alexander, as the celebrated mosaic of the battle from a later Roman villa still shows, came face to face with the king, perhaps even receiving a sword wound in the thigh from the king himself (see cover image of this book). The mosaic highlights Alexander's savage and keen thirst for battle in his eyes, face and body, and Darius' startled surprise at the power of his adversary. There's a hint also in Darius' face of the panic that was soon to follow. The king was forced to turn tail and flee, leaving behind his troops, his baggage, his royal tent and even his wife and children.

Alexander, still covered in the dirt and stink of battle, walked into the tent of the Persian king. It was the king's most private space while on campaign, the ultimate sign of his power, an extraordinarily ornate moveable palace. Alexander moved through it, drinking in the riches and power he now possessed. He bathed himself in the king's own bath. 'This is what it is to be a king', he is said to have murmured to himself.

His victory at Issus broke the myth of the might of the Persian empire. Cities fell over themselves to congratulate him and surrender to him. The capture of so much opulence and wealth gave his troops both the courage and the blood-thirst for more. Like wolves, their nostrils filled with the scent of their prey, they bayed for more conquest. The humiliated Persian king, retreating further into the depths of his empire, continued to make his most basic mistake: underestimating his enemy. He offered to split the Persian empire with Alexander. But Alexander, never a man of moderation, a man who supposedly thought weariness and even pleasure were human weaknesses, wanted it all. In attacking an empire where power was concentrated in the hands of the sole ruler, what mattered was the capture or death of the king himself. Alexander would stop at nothing less.

Alexander, though, faced a problem. He was marching deep into the interior of Asia. His supply lines were stretched across thousands of kilometres, and he couldn't always trust that the people he had conquered and put to his back wouldn't rise up and knife him in it. The Persian fleet was also still sailing the seas, landing and striking his flank. He needed to secure the territory he already had, particularly the coast, and make sure his power base was secure. Once again, to do so, he employed a heady mix of military strength, superhuman ability, vicious vengeance and powerful myth-creation. His siege of the city of

Tyre, on the coast of modern-day Lebanon, around January 332 BC passed quickly into legend. Sited on an island half a mile off the coast in Alexander's day, the fortified citadel of Tyre thought itself impregnable even to Alexander. But Alexander, through seven months of tireless siege, with the help of cunning, ingenuity and dogged determination, took the untouchable city. Besieging the ancient city of Gaza not much later, he took that city after just two months and made an example of its leader by dragging him around the city walls attached to the back of his chariot, just like the mythical hero Achilles had done to his enemy Hector around the walls of Troy.

Egypt, in contrast, welcomed Alexander with open arms. Never a fan of the Persian king, Egypt welcomed its 'liberator' and made him its Pharaoh. It was here that Alexander made an unexpected diversion about 500 kilometres into the desert to visit the sacred oracle of the Egyptian god Ammon at Siwah (Fig. 14). There he's said to have been told that the murderers of his father had been justly punished (so it couldn't have been Alexander, then) and that, anyway, his father wasn't Philip but the god Ammon himself (Alexander's mother really had struck lucky – she was said to have had sex with the god while he was in the form of a snake). Returning from the desert, Alexander was now not just a man who acted like a superhuman, but half-man, half-god, with a lineage to prove it.

He was also a man of mercy. He apparently didn't lay a finger on the Persian king's wife and children, although, as they were captured in war, he was within his rights to do with them as he pleased. On the wife's death, Alexander ensured that she was buried with great ritual and fanfare. A spy escaping to the Persian king reported that 'Alexander was as gentle in victory as he is terrible in battle'. King Darius, in terrible grief and increasingly isolated and powerless, prayed that he might have the strength to defeat such a man, but that if he didn't, that no man less worthy than Alexander should take his throne. Attempting to bribe him one more time with unlimited riches, the Persian king met with

Alexander's final warning: 'Surrender to me and you shall receive every courtesy. But otherwise I shall march at once against you.'

Alexander soon marched again, this time encountering the king, who had summoned a fresh army, at a place called Gaugamela, east of Mosul in modern-day Iraq (Map 4). The king threw everything he had at Alexander: every fighter from strange barbarian lands, scythe chariots (chariots with rotating blades attached to the wheels), and even elephants. In the days before the battle, Alexander witnessed a total eclipse. Always superstitious, Alexander surrounded himself with diviners and soothsayers, from whom he now demanded an interpretation of this supernatural sign. Together with his personal soothsayer, he celebrated rites and sacrifices for the god of fear. Sleeping like a baby, he had to be woken by his generals for the battle on 1 October 331 BC. Emerging from his slumber, Alexander, the son of a god, rose to meet his adversary.

Once more, Alexander drove straight into the enemy's lines, looking for his prey. Once more, he came face to face with the Persian king, close enough to see the whites of his eyes, to admire his fine and lofty countenance, but not close enough to land the mortal blow. The Persian king again turned tail, his chariot wheels ripping through the fallen bodies of his bodyguard in his haste to escape certain death. Abandoning his chariot, its wheels stuck fast in piles of torn flesh, the Persian king jumped on a solitary horse and rode off. King Darius III, the man who had commanded the greatest empire the world had ever known, was reduced to riding alone as he fled into the distance.

The great cities of Persia fell now to Alexander. Babylon, in modern-day Iraq, welcomed him as 'king of the universe'. Susa, the financial and administrative capital, was taken. Finally, in May 330 BC, the great symbolic capital of Persia, the city of Persepolis in modern-day Iran, over 2,600 kilometres away from where Alexander had entered Asia, now stood undefended (Map 4). Alexander took control of the central city of the Persian empire. His quest to right the wrongs Persia had done to

Greece was complete. Sending back to Greece the cultural treasures that Persia had stolen from them and hidden in Persepolis over the years, Alexander declared that Greece was now the supreme power in the ancient world. That night, at a banquet held in Persepolis to celebrate their victory, Alexander was baited by an Athenian woman, the mistress of one of his generals, about how delicious an irony it would be if she, a female courtesan, who was one of the least important figures in Greek society, were to set fire to the mighty city of the once-mighty Persian king, the most powerful individual in the Persian empire. Alexander, taken by the neatness of the gesture, gave permission for the great city to be burned (Fig. 15).

But as he watched the flames lick around the lovingly crafted architecture of this magnificent palace and destroy its rich history, even Alexander, the undefeated and perhaps undefeatable one, must have sensed that he was at a crossroads. The invasion of Persia, the original rallying call of his father's League of Corinth and Alexander's campaign, was now almost complete. With the original mission so far a resounding success, should he now halt his advance, disband the league, take his army home and allow everyone to go their separate ways? Was he the leader chosen by the Greeks to lead them in their campaign to right past wrongs and who must now, job done, listen to them if they wished to return home – or was he the leader who could do whatever he pleased, and whom the Greeks must slavishly follow? Alexander sat at the junction of several different worlds – he was leader of the cities of ancient Greece, a king of Macedon, soon to become absolute monarch of the Persian empire – and now he had to decide what to do with all this power. What kind of king was he? What kind did he want to be? What kind would the people and cities of Greece let him be?

CHAPTER 15

≈≈≈

Ruling the Ancient World

By 330 BC, just one year after his crushing victory at Gaugamela, the soaring gap between Alexander as Greek leader and Alexander as Persian king had become even starker. King Darius, fleeing for his life from the battle at Gaugamela on horseback with, ironically, only his Greek mercenary troops still loyal to him, had finally been murdered by his own subjects in July 330. The great king had been arrested and forced into chains of gold, before being brutally speared and left in the dust by the side of the long road that stretched like a spine throughout the length of the Persian empire and beyond. Alexander, forcing his men to pursue Darius through the scorching heat of the summer, found the king's body pierced by javelins. Darius was still just breathing. Seeing this Greek who had managed to topple his world empire, who had respected his wife and children until death, he asked Alexander for a little water and gave Alexander his blessing as his successor. The handover between the two most powerful men in the ancient world took place on the dusty hard shoulder of the trading spine of Persia. Alexander placed his own cloak over Darius and covered his face with it when the great king eventually left this world. Alexander now declared himself Darius' legitimate successor and ruler of the Persian empire.

The body was buried in a lavish funeral. Alexander would pursue the king's murderer, a Persian man called Bessus, who had attempted to declare himself also king of what was left of the Persian empire, over the course of the next year. Finally catching up with him in modern-day Afghanistan in spring 329 BC, Bessus was sentenced to death for the murder of king Darius. He was executed according to Persian custom: by tying his body to two trees which had been forcibly bent towards one another, and allowing the power of nature to slowly rip the man apart as the trees straightened themselves. It was a horrifyingly excruciating death that proceeded slowly, as skin, muscles, tendons, ligaments, arteries and organs were slowly torn apart.

As Alexander moved towards becoming undisputed king of Persia, as well as leader of Greece and king of Macedon, he became the most important man in the largest empire the ancient world had ever known. As the Persian empire's final great city, Ecbatana, the modern city of Hamadan in Iran, fell into Alexander's hands in the summer of 330 BC, his mission to bring vengeance to Persia on behalf of Greece was indisputably complete (Map 4). Now he was in control. But just as his grasp over Persia strengthened, it seems that his grasp over Greece was weakening. In 331, the same year as his great triumph at Gaugamela, Sparta, the one city in Greece not to sign up to his father's league and which Alexander had continually snubbed, attempted to rebel from Macedonian control. The revolt was paid for with Persian money – the Persian king's last throw of the dice to upset Alexander's campaign. It was brutally suppressed by Alexander's lieutenant, Antipater, the man who had served Alexander's father well and by whose side Alexander had fought at Chaeronea back in 338 BC, and whom Alexander had left behind to keep control of Greece. Antipater had been busy dealing with a similar revolt in Thrace in northern Greece when he was forced to head south to deal with the Spartan threat. The two armies finally met at the recently built city of Megalopolis in the Peloponnese, in a battle which – though Antipater won, having killed the Spartan king – left 3,500 Macedonians dead.

The rebellion, though it caused significant Macedonian losses, had perhaps always been bound to fail. Even Demosthenes, still loitering in Athens and spitting quiet hatred against Alexander, didn't jump up in the assembly and advise the Athenians to support this rebellion. Yet though Sparta was the most obvious sign of disquiet in Alexander's Greece, it wasn't the only one. Athens had itself for several years been conducting a subtle anti-Alexander foreign policy and Alexander had never completely put his trust in the troops and ships provided by the cities of Greece. The Athenian navy, for instance, which had been the reason both Philip and Alexander had spared Athens twice before, was never really used in battle by Alexander for fear it would betray him. As Alexander became undisputed ruler of Persia, he had to face up to the increasingly clear fact that there were many back in Greece not content with his rule.

As the year 330 BC progressed, it had also become clear that there were many, much closer to Alexander, who had similar reservations. His victory at Gaugamela, and the end of the quest for Greek vengeance, had brought with it calls from his battle-hardened, but weary and homesick, Greek troops to return home. They had been on constant campaign away from their families, cities and fields for three years. Arriving at Ecbatana, the last enemy stronghold, 2,400 kilometres from Greek shores in summer 330, Alexander took the decision to dismiss his allied troops and fleet. No longer relying on the rest of Greece, Alexander stood in the heart of Asia with only his Macedonian warriors and mercenaries around him. But even they were starting to whisper against him. In the autumn of 330, one of his senior officers, a man called Philotas, was accused of conspiring to murder king Alexander the Great. Philotas' copybook had already recently been blotted when he had foolishly bragged to his mistress that Alexander was successful only because he had a brilliant general (Philotas' father) to guide him. Alexander, furious at the insult to his ability and reputation, though he made a play of investigating the accusation fully, in reality immediately sent an assassin to murder Philotas. Soon enough, Philotas' dad, Alexander's trusty general, was also assassinated. Alexander would have no subordination in his world. By the end of 330 BC, it was increasingly clear what kind of king Alexander intended to be.

The question of whom Alexander could trust in his own ranks wasn't a new one. Had not many Macedonian kings been killed by members of their own family? Had not Alexander perhaps murdered his own father? From the very start of his campaign, Alexander had had to make decisions on whom to trust. When he was ill before the battle of Issus, one of his men had prepared a special medicine to help him recover, while another of his subordinates had written him a letter telling him not to trust the man who prepared the medicine. Alexander drank the medicine at the same moment as he forced the man to read the letter accusing him of treason. Working out whom to trust in the ancient world often involved putting your life on the line.

But now it wasn't just a question of whom to trust, it was a question of how to govern. Alexander faced a dilemma. To govern such a vast territory as the Persian empire, thousands of kilometres in length, he needed more than his small contingent of Macedonian troops. Alexander, despite his superhuman abilities, couldn't be everywhere at once. He needed to employ the vast bureaucracy created by the Persian kings into whose shoes he was stepping. It was only natural as a result that he kept in place the systems of provincial governors and employed senior trustworthy Persians in his court. It was also only sensible that he began to recruit and train local army units to supplement his numbers. These Persian fighters, as Alexander had proved only too well in battle, were not all-powerful. Alexander knew better than any their weaknesses and their strengths. As a result he set about training Persian fighters in Macedonian military tactics and weaponry. At the same time, just as his father had done in Macedonia to secure relations with neighbouring tribes, he set out to secure alliances with local tribes through marriage. In 329, 328 and 327 BC, Alexander was occupied with particularly violent and difficult guerrilla warfare, first against the killer of Darius and would-be Persian king Bessus in Bactria, and subsequently with the tribes of neighbouring rocky Sogdiana (both in modern-day Afghanistan; Map 4). Just as in more recent history, Alexander's large army was held up by the rocky mountain landscape, the enemy strongholds perched high on the hilltops, and the local militia hidden in caves and deep valleys. In late 328 or early 327 BC, to help his somewhat successful military conquest of Sogdiana and to celebrate the recent capitulation of its last local ruler, he agreed to marry Roxane, the ruler's daughter.

Much of this was galling to his original Macedonian troops and officers. Was this man a conqueror of the Persians or one of them? Alexander had replaced the assassinated Philotas and his father with new generals, one of whom agreed with his policy of integration and one of whom was very much on the Macedonian side. Together, these two men, though they argued bitterly between themselves about Alexander's choices, represented the different faces of Alexander to his fellow Greeks and to the native Persians. But there were two issues that couldn't be resolved through this policy of divide and rule.

The first was Alexander's clothes. You could always tell a Greek from his clothes. They were, just as today, a clear marker of culture and origin. Alexander had always been a macho Greek with clothes to match. But now, as he assumed the role of Persian king, and continued to march further into Asia, soaking up the Persian bureaucracy as he went, his clothes became more and more Persian. At first, as Plutarch later recounted, he mixed the two fashions, and then wore local dress only when he met Persians rather than Greeks. But this constant costume change soon morphed into a permanent new wardrobe. Alexander, king of Macedon, leader of the Greeks, conqueror of the Persians, was now dressing as the enemy.

The Greek fighters, were, it seems, just about willing to put up with their cross-dressing king. But they wouldn't put up with another Persian custom he adopted. As a rule, all Persians had to prostrate themselves on the ground before the king every time they came into his presence. Not to do so was to insult the ruler in the most serious way and to undermine the entire basis of the authority of Persian kingship. Alexander, if he wanted to be the Persian king, had to receive this treatment, known as *proskynesis*. But no Greek, king or otherwise, had ever been honoured in the same way – for Greeks, such honour was reserved only for the gods. One or two Greek leaders had been worshipped as a god while still alive, most recently Alexander's father, Philip, but he had been killed on the day he chose to walk in procession with the gods. To behave like, or to be treated as, a living god was to invite divine vengeance on everyone. No Greek prostrated himself to another Greek, not even a Macedonian whose king he was. To do so would be a betrayal of the very fabric of Greek religion, culture and society. It was the ultimate treason.

The Greeks not only refused to prostrate themselves to Alexander, they disliked him intensely for receiving such homage from his Persian courtiers, because they believed such actions constituted a dishonour of the gods. Alexander was caught in the gaping no man's land between two very different cultures. To rule one, he had to act in a way that made him unacceptable to the other. Alexander's response was, as Plutarch recounted, to try 'to mix the lives and customs of men in a loving cup', in the hope that such mixing of 'race and cultures would go far towards softening the hearts of men'. It was a worthy aim and plan of action – something that, even in our globalised world today, we're still struggling to make a reality.

In summer 328 BC, the tension in Alexander's camp came to a head once again. One of his newly elected generals, who had saved Alexander's life back in the first battle for control of Asia at Granicus six years earlier, now turned on his master. His speech thick with alcohol at a drinking party one evening, this man, nicknamed 'Black' Cleitus, shouted at Alexander: 'It is by the blood of Macedonians, and by these wounds on me, that you have become so great as to disown your father and make yourself the son of a god!' Despite whispers for him to shut up, Cleitus would not be silenced. He shouted that it was a disgrace that Macedonians had to ask Persians for permission to see a Greek king. It was better to be dead than dishonoured in such a way. Alexander sprang from his drinking couch to silence his upstart subordinate. Such a reaction, to silence free talk, was just what one expected of a Persian barbarian, Cleitus retorted. He added: 'If you don't want to do things in the Greek way, then surround yourself with barbarian sycophants'. Alexander, furious, threw an apple at Cleitus' head. While Alexander demanded his personal bodyguard, his supporters tried to calm him and to stop the trumpeter from sounding the alert. Alexander punched the trumpeter in the face for disobeying his orders. Cleitus was bundled out of the dining room, but forced his way back in, shouting: 'This is an evil government for Greece!' Alexander seized a spear from a guard and ran Cleitus clean through with it.

Alexander, prone to fits of passion and anger, immediately regretted his actions and may even have tried to kill himself (his men had to find him a philosopher who could allay his guilt by explaining to him that, as such a powerful man, he had the right to do these things). He spent the night bitterly weeping for the loss of the friend who had once saved his own life. But the loss didn't stop his tendency to kill those who disagreed with him. Another subordinate, Callisthenes, who had objected to the Persian tradition of bowing to the king and who may have been involved in another plot to kill Alexander, found this out at the cost of his own life the following year.

It's around this time, as 327 gave way to 326 BC, that a new phase of Alexander's adventures seems to have begun. Instead of turning back towards home, Alexander struck out further east. Leaving behind many of his soldiers as permanent garrisons to keep control over the garrulous tribal region of Sogdiana, which he had only partially quelled with his marriage to the local princess Roxane, in 327 Alexander proceeded with his core of Macedonian infantry, as well as a vast new local army, to cross into ancient India and continue his campaign of conquest to the very edges of the earth. It seems that Alexander, despite the growing opposition, had once and for all made his decision about what type of king he wanted to be: a king of conquest, a king of the universe, 'a king', as he would later be given the title, 'of kings'.

The march into India was a tough and gruelling one. Alexander faced the mighty king Porus, who rode around on an elephant like a Greek man would do on a horse, and who commanded even vaster armies than Alexander's. Yet Alexander once again proved his invincibility in battle, bringing the great Porus finally to the negotiating table. Once again, Alexander proved his savvy by mixing military superiority with diplomatic brilliance – rather than destroying Porus, which would take time, money and men, Alexander made him his ally and friend. Two such different men, from such different worlds and cultures, agreed to treat one another like the kings they were (although Alexander was, of course, the superior king). It was a gentleman's agreement, backed up by force, which delivered Alexander his first foothold in India.

It was at about the time of this battle and subsequent alliance that Alexander's horse – which he had tamed as a young man back in Macedonia in front of his jealous and proud father, which had carried him much of the way across Persia and which had been ridden by Alexander into every battle he had ever fought – now finally passed away. It was a great personal loss to the king. Alexander not only buried the horse, called Bucephalus, with great ceremony, he also founded a city in the horse's honour: the city of Bucephala in modern-day Pakistan.

It wasn't long after this moving tribute to the close relationship of man and animal (Alexander may also have named a city after his beloved dog Peritas) that Alexander was reminded once more that relationships between men weren't always so fulfilling. At the banks of the Beas (also known as the Hyphasis) river, which has its origins in the Himalayas, the ancient sources indicate that Alexander's weary troops, who had covered something in the region of 20,000 kilometres marching back and forth all over Asia, refused finally to follow their great leader any further (Map 4). Alexander is said to have returned to his tent at the nearby Hydaspes river and sulked for days before emerging to speak to his battle-hardened soldiers of fortune. First, he attempted to woo them with hopes of further conquest: to continue east and 'to add to this Macedonian empire of ours'. The men, their treasures of conquest already once burnt by their unforgiving leader to lighten the baggage train as they were about to cross the mountainous Hindu Kush back in 329, were having none of it. Next Alexander tried to inspire them with divine parallels: they were doing deeds in the likeness of gods and heroes, he cried. No luck. They were almost at the edges of the world, and it would be a shame, and indeed dangerous, to leave its last vestiges unconquered, he continued. Still no luck. Finally, Alexander reminded them of the inglorious life they had left behind and what little awaited them back at home: 'merely keeping in check Thracians … and those Greeks, who are not well disposed to us.' Alexander left them with a choice: be policemen at home or men of glory and fortune at the ends of the world.

Replying to his speech, his men reminded him that Alexander had promised to be not a dictator, but a man who led by persuasion. They were not persuaded. They wanted to return home where Alexander, if he so wanted, could gather new troops, young rather than old, fresh rather than weary, and continue his conquest of the world. Alexander, whatever king he may have wanted to be, whatever the truth of what he wanted at that moment, couldn't be any kind of king without his army. Standing on the banks of the Hydaspes river, in modern-day Pakistan, Alexander was forced to stare across the raging rapids at the land stretching into the distance and turn his back to it. Almost 5,000 kilometres from home – so close to what he had thought was the last stretch of land before the great sea that encircled the world, but which he was now realising actually stretched much further into unknown worlds and lands – Alexander had finally reached what would be the limits of his new world empire.

Despite his disappointment, Alexander didn't lose his flair for theatrics. Keen to impress his authority upon any tribe, king or invader who might one day think about crossing the river from the other side and encroaching upon his territory, Alexander gave orders for huge statues to be created, great altars to be fashioned, armour to fit giants to be cast, and horse tack constructed for horses larger than life. These he left strewn on the banks of the Hydaspes. The misleading, but brilliant, message was clear to any potential invader: 'Do not approach this land, for there be giants here within …'

But Alexander wasn't quite finished with conquest. He turned back and agreed to march his men home, but he didn't promise how, when, or how quickly. Giving orders for a fleet to be constructed, he sailed and marched his men south towards the modern-day Arabian sea, following the path of the Hydaspes which flows into the mighty Indus, the arterial life-blood of the region then as now (Map 4). On his way, he encountered his fiercest enemy yet: the tribes of the Punjab. The ensuing battles almost cost Alexander his life. In one siege, Alexander, eager as ever for the fray, jumped alone onto the enemy's city walls. Single-handedly defending himself from attack, he was wounded several times, but fell to the ground only when an arrow became lodged deep in his chest. Pulled back to safety by his men, his generals and doctors fretted over what to do. To leave the arrow there would mean certain death through infection. To remove it would mean certain agony and possible death through loss of blood and the tearing of organs. Alexander's men couldn't bring themselves to pull it out. Grasping at the arrow shaft, Alexander, half delirious with pain, attempted to pull the arrow from his own body. Only then, his hands shaking so much with pain that he was sure to kill himself if he continued, did his men lay hold and, despite the sound of metal arrowhead scraping against bone, find the courage to dislodge it from his chest.

Not only recovering swiftly from his near-death experience, Alexander was soon once again leading his troops south, until they were near the open sea. Alexander made sacrifices to the same gods he had honoured when he had set out on his mission to conquer Persia almost ten years earlier, and prayed that no man might ever better his record of conquest. Turning his back finally on the rising of the sun, he began the long journey back home.

But the fleet he had built was not for all his troops to sail easily homewards in. Ahead of him lay the Gedrosian desert, a barren, mountainous region on the north coast of the Arabian sea. Some say that Alexander wanted to march his men home through this inhospitable place as a punishment for them not being willing to follow him any further east. Others say he wanted to cross this region because, so the locals told him, no one had yet been able to make it across alive, and Alexander relished the opportunity to once again put himself into legend. Whatever the reason, the fact remains that Alexander now marched his tired troops for 60 days across this wasteland. For 60 days, they battled scorching heat and sinking sands which swallowed up, literally in some cases, both men and animals. For 60 days, his men were forced to secretly butcher their own horses and mules to feed themselves.

For 60 days, they were driven crazy by thirst to the point that men, on finding water, would drink so much of it that they actually killed themselves through water intoxication (nowadays known as hyponatremia). If drinking too much water didn't kill them, Alexander's men were also sometimes overwhelmed by the sudden sheer presence of it. Camping by what they thought were small trickles of water, the army would occasionally find these trickles swelling overnight into raging torrents crashing down from the mountains after heavy rainfall, sweeping away their belongings, supplies, women, children, and even on one occasion the royal tent.

Sixty days later, a beleaguered column of survivors emerged from this gruelling suicide march, putting Alexander once again into the history books, to continue west towards the setting sun and back into Persia. Returning to the heart of his new Persian empire in 324 BC, almost two years after his men had demanded to return home (and they were still a long way from Macedon), Alexander celebrated their safe return with a massive festival in honour of the god Dionysus, which became almost as famous as his horrendous desert march (this time for its licentiousness rather than its hardship). Alexander also took the opportunity to take stock of his new world. What he found wasn't pleasant reading. A significant percentage of the provinces of his new kingdom were showing varying degrees of disloyalty. Restlessness was rife and his Greek generals and soldiers were still not content with his policy of Persian and Greek integration. But if his Greek soldiers thought they had seen the last of this policy, they were very much mistaken. Alexander, returning from the east, now redoubled his efforts to mix lives and customs in a loving cup. His newly Macedonian-trained Persian soldiers were just coming on-line, and were introduced into the regular army as their own unit. More Persian governors were imported into Alexander's command structure. In February 324 BC, at the sumptuous Persian city of Susa in modern-day Iran, Alexander attempted to push his integration campaign to the next level by forcibly marrying off many of his men to a native bride, irrespective of whether or not they already had wives at home. Though many thousands married, many of his elite companions also flatly rejected their commander's wishes. 'All this aggrieved the Macedonians,' the historian Arrian later recounts, 'who thought that Alexander was going utterly barbarian at heart, treating Macedonian customs and the Macedonians themselves without the proper respect.'

But Alexander was similarly aggrieved at the Macedonians' lack of loyalty. In the summer of 324, just a couple of months after his attempts at the mass-wedding at Susa, Alexander began the process of retiring and sending home his core Macedonian troops who had followed him from his first footsteps on Asian soil. At a place called Opis, not far from what is now Baghdad in Iraq, Alexander offered the chance, for those 'unfit for service', to go home. The men protested bitterly at this dishonour: even though they wanted to go home, to be discharged by their leader as 'unfit for service' was a bitter blow. Protesting about this and about all Alexander's recent attempts at integration, they drove their king into a rage by sarcastically calling his bluff: if he didn't need them because he was now so divine and all-powerful, he could go off on campaign alone with his supposed father, the god Ammon. Alexander, the ruler of so great a swathe of the ancient world, was taunted by his troops into a fury. Executing the ringleaders, he lectured the shocked Macedonians on how much they owed to him and his father: 'My father found you wandering aimlessly about, clothed in sheepskins and working as farmers in the mountains ... he gave you proper clothes to wear

... made you fighting men ..., he gave you cities to dwell in and laws to live by. He made you rulers of your enemies ... he made you governors of Thessaly ... helped you to humble the Phocians and ... the Athenians and Thebans ... and settled matters in the Peloponnese ... I defeated the Persian king and gave to your rule the whole of Ionia ... All the wealth of Egypt and Cyrene ... are now yours. Syria, Palestine and Mesopotamia are yours to own, Babylonia and Bactria and Elam belong to you, you own the riches of Lydia, the jewels of Persia, the wealth of India and the outer ocean. You are the rulers, the governors, the generals. As for me, what do I have left from all these labours?'

Alexander's men were stunned by this outburst and begged for Alexander's forgiveness, refusing to move from outside his tent until he had seen fit to forgive them. In their honour, Alexander held a massive banquet. Yet his problems were far from over. Many veteran warriors (maybe 10,000 or more), despite Alexander's speeches and hospitality, still took the opportunity to leave the army and return home to Macedonia. By the end of 324 BC, Alexander may have had as few as 2,000 Macedonian cavalry and 13,000 infantry left, in comparison to his growing tens of thousands of local troops. At the same time, Alexander's minister of finance, the man he had trusted to manage the wealth of the empire, had squandered a large amount of it on his prostitute mistress and now fled to Athens with a large amount more. At the same time again, many Greek cities and states began to complain seriously against Alexander's recent order that all Greek cities should be forced to accept back at home those previously exiled abroad. Every rumour of Alexander's death feeding back to Greece brought the seeds of rebellion to the point of germination. Antipater, Alexander's trusted lieutenant in Greece, was constantly on the move to keep control. Worse for Alexander, in the same summer of 324 BC, one of his generals, his closest friend (and perhaps more than a friend), a man called Hephaisteion, died from a fever after excessive drinking at Ecbatana. Alexander, journeying to the city, beside himself with grief unbecoming for such a divine ruler, ordered all flute-playing in the city to be silenced, and horses' tails and manes to be bound up in mourning; and he' slaughtered the doctor who had failed to save his friend. Hephaisteion was honoured as a mythical hero, to whom Alexander offered the bodies of slaughtered local youths and for whom he spent countless amounts of gold on his tomb.

As 324 gave way to 323 BC, Alexander became increasingly removed, unmanageable and violent. He may have given the order for his own deification – for him to be worshipped as a living god – at Susa in 324. Macedonians arriving from Greece to pay him honour at the city of Babylon, 85 kilometres south of modern Baghdad, laughed at the sight of men prostrating themselves on the floor in his honour. Alexander grabbed them by the hair and dashed their brains out against the wall. He began to dream of even bigger and greater campaigns of conquest, this time against Carthage in north Africa, and Arabia. He began to see evil omens at every turn. He took to constant sacrifices and drink for his protection. Following one particularly heavy drinking bout, he contracted a fever on 2 June 323 BC and drank more wine instead of water to cure it. Continuing with his plans for campaign through his fever, his illness, in no small part thanks to his continued alcohol consumption, turned violent and he started to become delirious. Within days he was left unable to speak, and on 10 June 323 BC, just one month short of his 33rd birthday, king Alexander III of Macedon, Alexander the Great – *megas Alexandros*, the 'great king', the 'king of the universe', the 'king of kings', the divine son of the god Ammon, living god – died. The heroic fighter, the scheming strategist, the diplomatic mastermind, the drunkard, the sadistic leader, the seemingly unstoppable and unkillable military terminator, the man driven by a volcanic desperation to prove himself, the individual who changed the ancient world forever, had breathed his last.

He left behind him no male heir, but instead a pregnant wife and a host of ambitious subordinates. Just what, everyone asked, would happen now?

CHAPTER 16

❦

You've Never Had it So Good

It's one of the ironies of ancient history that the captivating and inspiring story of Philip and Alexander the Great, which has made Alexander renowned as perhaps the most famous Greek in history, is represented to us, in the majority of the ancient Athenian written sources at least, as something bad for the health of ancient Greece. The vociferous and high-profile attacks particularly by Demosthenes, whose opinions still often hold great authority with modern readers as they did with his ancient Athenian listeners, portray Athens and Greece losing their freedom and right to self-control, their *autonomia*, under the tyrannical control of these two kings. We in the modern world are thus caught between admiration for the heroic, if flawed, 'kings of kings' and sadness that their arrival marked the 'death' of Greek liberty.

Nowhere is this impression of Macedonian rule as bad for Greece imprinted on our minds more clearly than in the law court debates going on in Athens in the late 330s BC. At this point, Alexander was riding the crest of a wave of success in his campaign to conquer the Persian empire. The Persian king had been defeated by Alexander not once but twice and had been forced to flee on horseback alone, eventually to be murdered by his own men. By 330, Alexander was in control of most of the Persian empire, had his hands on the great Persian palace of Persepolis (or what was left of it after he allowed it to be burnt) and was on the verge of his next phase of campaign to the east. 330 BC marked the watershed when many realised that Alexander was not just a leader of a Greek league, but a man who would brook no insubordination or debate, a king who would be king of kings.

In 330 BC in Athens, Demosthenes, who had already managed to escape the anger of Macedon several times, now came once again into the public spotlight. Six years earlier, a man called Ctesiphon had proposed a motion in the assembly that Demosthenes be honoured with a gold crown for his services to Athens. Demosthenes' old enemy Aeschines, the supporter and friend of Philip, was appalled. He immediately brought a charge against Ctesiphon that his actions were illegal. The trial, however, was delayed for many years and didn't finally come to court until 330 BC. In standing to make their speeches, Demosthenes and Aeschines were not only rehashing (by now) old news. They were not only defending or prosecuting a particular individual's actions. Nor were they only engaging (once again) in their celebrated enmity, which had polarised the Athenian political scene for well over the past two decades. They were also, much more importantly, fighting for the right to give the authoritative account of what Alexander's conquests meant for Athens. They were fighting to tell the story of how Athens had come to the position it was now in. They were fighting to shape the message of Athenian history and to predict its future.

It's in Demosthenes' speech in 330 BC that Philip's victory at the battle of Chaeronea back in 338 BC, in which he defeated the Athenian and Theban forces, and from which Demosthenes ran away a coward, is forever cast as *the* critical turning point in Greek history, the point at which Greek liberty died and tyranny took over. Aeschines, of course arguing a very different line, lost his case in the law courts of Athens. Humiliated, his political reputation in tatters, he left Athens overwhelmed with shame and fled to the Greek island of Samos, where he later died (Map 2). The great battle of egos, beliefs and visions between Aeschines and Demosthenes was over. Demosthenes had emerged the victor and, as a result, his version of how to read the history of Greece has emerged triumphant.

But was Demosthenes right to argue that such a moment heralded the beginning of the end for Athens and for Greece? Out of that battle, and the settling of yet another sacred war over Delphi, came about the League of Corinth. Philip's umbrella organisation for the cities of Greece brought everyone together in a peaceful pact which achieved the kind of stability that many Greek cities had been attempting to create through their own supremacy for much of the century. The league reasserted the primacy of Greek cities in settling Greek affairs and rejected the continued (and occasionally unhelpful) influence of the king of Persia (if only to replace it with a Greek king of Macedon). Philip's league gave the cities of Greece a unified purpose that they had not felt for well over 100 years, just as Isocrates had argued it would.

Philip's league, and his efforts to communicate with the cities across Greece, also brought great investment to the places where Greek cities had historically met in peace: the international sanctuaries. While Delphi and Olympia were rich enough to look after themselves, two other sanctuaries that hosted international athletic and musical games and attracted international audiences, the sanctuaries of Isthmia and Nemea in central mainland Greece, were in a much worse state (Map 2). Isthmia had suffered financially since the beginning of the 4th century and Nemea had been all but closed since the bigger nearby city of Argos had taken it upon itself to host the Nemean games. It's no accident that both these sanctuaries saw massive investment in the period immediately surrounding Philip's creation of the League of Corinth (not least because the city of Corinth wasn't far from Isthmia or Nemea). At Nemea, Philip may even have paid for some of the rebuilding. Soon enough, Nemea was operating once again as a centre for international athletic games with a new temple, hostel, gymnasium and stadium, playing host to large gatherings of Greeks from across Greece. Isthmia too received a makeover, which not only saw it rebuild its theatre, but also saw the sanctuary become the noticeboard for Philip's league. In the place of many of the monuments to battle victories erected by Greek cities over the preceding centuries (which were often victories over other Greek cities) now stood the public announcements of the League of Corinth – representing the peaceful alliance of Greek cities under Philip (all except Sparta, of course).

These sanctuaries benefited hugely from Philip and Alexander's investment (it's no coincidence that Nemea would fall into disrepair again after Alexander's death). Why did Philip invest so much time and money in them? These sanctuaries provided the Macedonian kings with exactly what they required: places in which messages could be communicated to large gatherings of Greeks. In a world without internet and mass media, these places were the megaphones through which Philip and Alexander could be heard. Alexander, while on campaign in the heart of Asia, ensured that his victories were announced at each meeting of the Olympic games at the sanctuary of Olympia, and it was at Olympia that he had his rules and regulations read out (including the one in 324 BC that required all cities to take back their exiles, which caused so much animosity against him). But despite the negative reactions these pronouncements sometimes incurred, their existence, and the investment in the places that enabled them to be heard, also heralded a new chapter in the co-ordination of the disparate cities of Greece.

It could thus well be argued that ancient Greece, never a single country or unit in the ancient world, but since time immemorial a loosely-tied community of sharply differentiated, often warring, cities and ethnic groups, came as close as it ever would in ancient times to being a single unit under Philip and Alexander. The common identity of the Greeks, if there was one, had always been a provocative issue for the cities and peoples of ancient Greece (just remember the initial disquiet over whether Macedonian rulers were 'Greek' enough to enter the Olympic games). In the 4th century, as the Greek world expanded with increasing integration at its boundaries and immigration at its core, debates over the nature of Greek identity (or rather identities) burned only brighter. On the international stage, as recent scholarship has shown, those debates focused more keenly than ever on the nature and importance of relationships between individuals and communities and the degree to which unity supported or collided with the equally important notions of freedom and autonomy. Macedon, and particularly its rulers, was the touch-paper for all of these issues. The dominance of these kings both increased the potential for unity and threatened the survival of autonomy. What side you took in the debate depended almost entirely on what you had at stake to lose or gain.

Yet even Athens, the city, Demosthenes would have us believe, which had the most to lose under Macedon, benefited greatly during the period of Macedonian hegemony in Greece. Athens, as we have seen, was in financial crisis in the 350s. Yet, in the aftermath of that crisis, thanks to the canny financial policies of one Athenian, a man called Eubulus, who would make today's 'iron chancellors' look like shopaholics, Athens soon managed to turn its finances around. That financial security, though threatened when the Athenian assembly, spurred on by Demosthenes, raided Eubulus' coffers to fight Philip at Chaeronea, was quickly restored in the aftermath of the battle by Eubulus' successor Lycurgus (who was himself a pupil of the political commentator Isocrates). Within the more settled environment of Greece post-338 BC, as a member of Philip's League of Corinth, Athens, under the watchful eye of Lycurgus, enjoyed its most stable period of prosperity that century. Athens' GDP doubled to an amount higher than it had ever been under the Athenian empire of the previous century, and crucially, a large percentage of that income was generated internally rather than being harvested in the form of tax from abroad. The city's sacred temple vaults, standing near-empty since the time of the Peloponnesian war almost a century before, were slowly refilled. Banking families, many of whom had started life as immigrants in the city, now spurred on by Athens' pro-rich-foreigners policy, rose to prominence in an ancient version of the American dream. The average daily wage increased between 50 and 100 per cent by the end of the century. It turns out that people living in Athens under Philip and Alexander, economically at least, may well have never had it so good their whole lives.

But it wasn't just an economic boom that Athens enjoyed under Philip and Alexander. Physically, the city grew during this period as well. The first half of the 4th century had been a time of limited building for Athens, but following its recovery from the economic crisis of the 350s, and the ascent of Philip's control over Greece, Athens enjoyed a renewed period of architectural growth. In part, that growth was military in nature: first to improve Athens' chances against Philip, but subsequently both to supply Alexander's army and to rebuild Athens' status within Greece. Lycurgus, the great mastermind of Athens' prosperity, oversaw improvements to the walls of the city immediately after Chaeronea, and increased the size of the Athenian navy, as a result increasing the amount of employment and building surrounding the service and maintenance of the fleet. Great new buildings for housing military equipment and huge ship-sheds were constructed, along with improvements to the system of forts throughout Athens' territory of Attica.

But not all the building was military. Lycurgus was also deeply interested in the religious and theatrical life of the city. According to Plutarch, it was Lycurgus who oversaw the building of Athens' first stone theatre of Dionysus at the foot of the Acropolis, housing up to 17,000 people, which you can still visit today (Map 1). He also ensured that the sanctuary of Dionysus surrounding the theatre was furnished with a new temple. It was Lycurgus who continued Athens' policy of making foreigners (particularly economically important foreigners) welcome by willingly giving them land in Athens on which to build sanctuaries to worship their own gods and cults. It was also Lycurgus who built a new stadium to be used for athletic competitions during Athens' own annual international festival to celebrate the city, the *Panathenaia*. It was under Lycurgus' auspices that the philosopher Aristotle opened up a second philosophical school in Athens, the Lyceum (Map 1), to complement Plato's Academy, and it was Lycurgus who authorised further additions to Aristotle's institution. It was during this time too that the sanctuary of Asclepius on the slopes of the Acropolis in Athens was completely refurbished, improvements to Athens' great sanctuary of the mystery cult at Eleusis were finally completed, and new temples and altars were constructed around the city.

Athens, under the extremely competent direction of Lycurgus, was able to take advantage of the general peace within Greece created by Philip and Alexander, to rebuild itself so that the city shone brighter than at any other time that century. Far from being the beginning of the end, as Demosthenes portrayed the battle of Chaeronea in 338 BC, this was the beginning of a new period of prosperity for Athens, which revelled in the atmosphere of the league and the establishment of a new balance of power across the ancient world. Even Athens' democracy, its cherished system of government, benefited under the new 'tyrannical' world order. The Athenian assembly place, the Pnyx, was remodelled to create a permanent speaker's platform, the same platform still to be seen today on the Pnyx hill (Fig. 2). The Agora, the heart of the city, was embellished with more buildings at this time and also played host to a new system of government–citizen communication. A public notice-board was set up, which detailed the duties of each citizen on a month-by-month basis, watched over by statues of Athens' tribal founders, the remains of which can still be seen in the Agora today. The Agora, the beating heart of democratic Athens, was beating faster than ever under the Macedonian kings.

In the aftermath of 330 BC, as Demosthenes had finished his down-beat assessment of Athens' history and future fortunes, Alexander went to the effort of returning to the city its most prized possession: the statue of Athens' democratic founders, the two men who had murdered the former tyrants of the city and paved the way for the 'birth' of democracy (Fig. 16). This statue group, which had stood originally in the Agora, had been stolen by the Persians over 150 years before and carried off to their palace at Persepolis. Returned by Alexander after he had captured the palace, the statue group, known as the *Tyrannicides* ('tyrant-killers'), now once again took pride of place in the heart of the city. It symbolised more than anything else the resurgence of Athens to its former glory and the beginning of a new period of prosperity for the city and its democracy. The statues, ironically, were a gift from the son of a man who, as Demosthenes had put it in his recent law court speech (given not far from where the statues would be set up), 'wanted to enforce his supremacy over Greece and annihilate the glories and rights of our ancestors'.

But even this new prosperous Athens couldn't avoid being implicated in the events leading up to the death of Alexander. Particularly serious for Athens was the case of Alexander's miscreant finance minister, a man called Harpalus, who squandered Alexander's money on his prostitute mistress and then, in 324 BC, fled to Athens with a load more. Athens was in a difficult position. Did it protect Harpalus or send him packing? Demosthenes, who hadn't suggested that Athens join Sparta in its rebellion against Alexander in 331, was initially against giving support to Harpalus. But Harpalus had a way of knowing a man's weaknesses. As Plutarch later recounted: 'Harpalus knew how to sense when a man had a consuming passion for gold, by judging the look that crossed his face and the twitches of his eyes.' Demosthenes had just that twitch, and fell in love with a particularly fine gold cup. Harpalus bought the support of Athens' most vociferous statesman by offering it to him. Suddenly, with Demosthenes in support, Athens invited Harpalus and his money into the city.

Antipater, Alexander's lieutenant in Greece, was soon on the case, demanding the return of Harpalus and the money that came with him. Demosthenes managed to persuade the Athenians not to acquiesce until they had heard the request from Alexander himself (and as he was deep in Asia, this would take some time). In the meantime, Harpalus escaped from Athens to Crete, supposedly out of Alexander's reach, but in reality to be murdered there eventually. It was only later, while investigating the whole sordid affair, that the Athenians found out that Demosthenes had been bribed with his gold cup. Like a modern-day politician consumed by a media storm over some financial or personal scandal, Demosthenes now felt the wrath of the Athenians. They jeered at him in the assembly, sneering: 'Men of Athens, shall we not listen to the man who holds the cup?' Even Demosthenes' old friend and supporter, the orator Hyperides, now turned against him and publicly denounced him for his actions.

Demosthenes had made a fundamental miscalculation. In all his previous advice to the city, whether the outcome had been good or bad for Athens, the people had believed he had sincerely argued for what he thought best for the city. This time, however, it was clear that Demosthenes had forsaken Athens for his own greed, and that was something that the Athenians wouldn't forgive. Things only got worse as the investigation into the affair continued. A disparity in the numbers was found between the amount of gold Harpalus claimed to have brought with him and the amount actually deposited on the Acropolis in Athens. Demosthenes at the time hadn't investigated this disparity. The Areopagus, the most senior and most ancient court in Athens, decided to prosecute the individuals who were said to have been the beneficiaries of this discrepancy. Demosthenes and his fellow orator Demades, the smooth-talking, on-off friend of Macedon who had boasted of taking Macedonian gold all his life, were among those found guilty.

Athens had washed its dirty laundry in the most public way: ten public prosecutors – one of whom was Demosthenes' old friend, now turned enemy, Hyperides – led the case against the defendants in front of a jury of 1,500 people in the most prestigious law court of Athens. Demosthenes was the first man to be tried. 'Do not,' cried another of the prosecutors, the orator Dinarchus, in his speech *Against Demosthenes* composed for this very trial, 'let go unpunished this man who embraced the misfortunes of his city and the rest of Greece, when he has been caught red-handed with bribes against Athens.' Demosthenes, who had been himself the exhorting voice of Athens for so many years, was now exiled from his home city and only narrowly escaped being executed for treason. Banished to the island of Aegina just off the coast of the Athenian territory of Attica (Map 2), he was forced to gaze across the sea towards his homeland, as Plutarch later wrote, with tears welling up in his eyes. Demosthenes, for all his misdeeds, loved Athens more than anything. Exiled in his old age, with no prospect of redemption, he became a bitter old man who told anyone who would listen that they should avoid public life, that the *demos*, the people, were a wretched beast, and that if he had had a choice in life between a road that led to the speaker's platform in the assembly and a road that led to certain destruction, he would have picked destruction.

The history of Athens in this period underlines the fact that, though the city is often thought of as a microcosm of ancient Greece, it was, in reality, more often than not the exception rather than the rule. Having stood perhaps to lose most by the ascent of Philip and Alexander, in reality, compared to many Greek cities, Athens benefited hugely in economic, social, architectural and even political terms from the peace and general stability of their reigns. Yet Athens also, thanks to Demosthenes, played no small role in disrupting that stability, particularly during Philip's lifetime and in the immediate aftermath of his death. It was only during Alexander's lifetime that even Demosthenes, though he could still argue successfully in the courts about Athens' sad plight and the lost 'golden age', could no longer persuade Athens to support publicly others who *did* rebel against Alexander's rule. Athens had begun to believe perhaps that Macedonian power was now a permanent feature of the political landscape and, at any rate, it was enjoying too much the fruits of the stability it brought – an enhanced economy and a strengthened democracy. It's perhaps no accident (and again not without irony) that it was during Alexander's reign, in the 320s BC, that the great philosopher Aristotle, living in Athens, wrote his detailed analysis of the history of the Athenian democratic political system (the *Constitution of the Athenians*), from where we get much of our information about the workings of ancient Athenian democracy today. We learn most about democracy, it turns out, from when it was successfully operating under the auspices of absolute monarchy.

But here again is another of the ironies of ancient Greece, and another reason why Athens is often the exception rather than the rule. Despite the fact that this was a time in which, in many parts of the ancient world, individuals were gaining power, in Athens individuals seemed to be, if anything, losing it. Demosthenes' ability to persuade the people of Athens to particular courses of action became increasingly mitigated during Alexander's time by the presence of other powerful voices within the democratic system, like those of Lycurgus and the old but wise Phocion, who advocated a much more profitable course of unity and peace. Indeed, as had been the case several times previously in Athens, powerful individuals not only lost the ear of the people, but ended up being cut down by them. Even Demosthenes, the central voice of Athens for so long, eventually fell foul of the Athenian body politic and was hung out to dry for his crimes. As a result, despite the fact that much of the surviving anti-Macedonian rhetoric comes from Athens, it wasn't from Athens that Alexander had the most trouble in the last years of his life, but, paradoxically, from his own Macedonian people. Within a year of Demosthenes' exile, Alexander was dead, supposedly of a fever – but some sources suggest his own men poisoned him. Peace and stability were brought to an abrupt end and the ancient world was once again in flux. What would Athens and the rest of the ancient world do now?

CHAPTER 17

～～

A New World

A lexander's shoes were hard to fill. No one, to begin with, was convinced that he was dead. Not only had there been so many rumours of his death over the years that few believed them any more, but also this was the man who always seemed to look death in the face and walk away smiling. In Plutarch's later account of Alexander's fortunes, he reels off the list of wounds Alexander sustained on campaign: a head wound and stone pounding in the neck, his head being cut open, his thigh pierced with a sword, his ankle wounded with an arrow, his shoulder dislocated, the bone of his leg split open by an arrow, his shoulder wounded by an arrow, an arrow buried deep in his chest and organs. All of these Alexander had survived, not to mention marching thousands of kilometres, several fevers, and a 60-day desert march. He was, by all accounts, the son of a god and most likely receiving sacrifices in his last years as if he were a living god himself. How could such a man, 'king of the universe' who had conquered the ancient world, and who was only 32 years old, actually die?

His generals, to make it clear to the remaining Macedonian troops in Babylon that the king really was on his death-bed this time, ensured that, in the last days of his life while Alexander lay unable to speak on the bed in his tent, each Macedonian soldier was allowed to enter and see the king for himself. Alexander is said to have been able only to move his hand in response to their tears and sadness at the state of their great leader. In his final days, Alexander was able to witness his own lying-in-state.

When he died of his alcohol-induced fever (later whispered to be the result of poisoning) on 10 June 323 BC, it wasn't just Athens that didn't know where to turn or what would happen next. Whereas Philip had lived to a much riper old age and ensured that he had several children ready to succeed (and even murder) him, Alexander died in the prime of his life, not quite 33 years old, leaving behind only a pregnant (foreign) wife. He had created a world united around him as its prime leader, as the king of kings. It was a world littered with new cities bearing his name or cities that he had himself founded (perhaps as many as 57), that spread across continents, cultures and modern-day time zones. It was a world obsessed with the cult of the individual. And now there was no one obvious individual who could take Alexander's place.

The result was that Alexander's world, which was enjoying the benefits of a period of relative stability, began to fragment once again. Athens, the city which had long been in opposition to Macedon but which had recently gone very quiet under Alexander while it enjoyed the fruits of that stability, now once again reverted to its old tricks. Who did Athens turn to but the man who had managed to ride the rough waves of public life with consummate skill, who had directed and managed every aspect of anti-Macedonian Athenian activity and who had, until just recently, been the darling of the city? None other than Demosthenes. Wiping the tears from his eyes, Demosthenes sailed triumphantly out of exile from the island of Aegina to be welcomed back to Athens. He was welcomed not like the convicted criminal he was, but instead like a conquering hero. The fickle Athenian crowd, forgetting their all-too-recent jeering of the man, lined up in a massive parade to welcome the orator back into the fold. The great philosopher Aristotle, seeing the Athenian people beginning to whip themselves up into an anti-Alexander frenzy, suddenly felt very uncomfortable living in Athens. As the old tutor to Alexander, he was a prime target for retribution. Well aware of what Athens had done to one of its previous great philosophers, Socrates, at the beginning of the century, Aristotle quickly left Athens, muttering that the city must not be allowed to sin twice against philosophy. A year later, he died of natural causes in his home town.

Demosthenes lost no time, as news of Alexander's death spread, in heading out to the cities of Greece to try to secure their alliance with Athens in a new league against Macedon. On his journey, he met with his old friend, the Athenian orator Hyperides. Hyperides had disowned Demosthenes for his role in the Harpalus affair and had even stood as one of the public prosecutors at Demosthenes' trial. Not more than two years later, they found themselves both deep in the Peloponnese, both looking for allies against Macedon, both, once again, on the same side. Burying the past, they joined forces and continued their hunt for allies in Athens' new quest to be at the head of Greece once more.

What was the response from Macedon? Just a few days after Alexander's death, his generals had gathered in Babylon at a crisis meeting to end all crisis meetings, to decide on how to rule Alexander's empire. They were faced with a very difficult task. Alexander had made unbelievable conquests across vast swathes of the ancient world, but he had only just begun to work in earnest on fashioning a bureaucracy capable of administering it all. What made matters worse was that, in the final years of his life, he had returned to the heart of the former Persian empire and had struck dead any local governors who seemed to be disloyal. As a result, almost half of the provincial governors of Asia had been executed in the previous year or were awaiting judgement on their fate. The machinery of government had been gutted just at the same moment as the machine had also lost its own head. Without local governors, without a permanent machinery of governance, without a leader, Alexander's generals met to decide what should be done with Alexander's vast empire.

The problem was compounded by the fact that each of Alexander's generals saw the potential for his own advancement out of the crisis. One of these generals, Perdiccas, who convened the meeting, said that

Alexander, in his final moments, had given him the royal signet ring of power. Perdiccas claimed that he thus had the power and authority to rule. But there were no witnesses to the handover, and none of the other generals were keen to let the matter be solved so easily. Another of Alexander's generals, Ptolemy, argued that all those present at the meeting should form a council which could lead the empire until they knew whether Alexander's unborn child, blissfully unaware of the crisis brewing around it, was a boy and could thus be king. Another general suggested that they shouldn't wait for Roxane to give birth, but put one of Alexander's bastard children on the throne straight away.

While this debate between generals was still ongoing, Alexander's remaining Macedonian army acted of its own accord. Still fearful and resentful of Alexander's attempts to integrate Persians into their Macedonian empire and infantry, they were even more fearful of the idea that the mixed-blood offspring of Alexander and his barbarian Sogdian queen would one day rule over them all. Picking their own candidate, a true-blooded but simple Macedonian with a good Macedonian name (after they had renamed him Philip III), the army demanded that their man be crowned king.

Faced with the mutiny of the army, the one thing no king or general could do without, the alternatives produced by the crisis meeting of generals were put to one side. In its place, a constitutional fudge was created. This new Philip was crowned king, with provision for a joint kingship if Alexander's barbarian wife Roxane produced a son. Two of Alexander's generals, the ones who had sought power for themselves, were named as the future infant's legal guardians. In the meantime, the council of generals and the new king Philip were to staff the empire by naming new local governors and army commanders. Sections of the empire were given to different generals for overall control. It was a system that put a whole set of powerful and ambitious men in equally powerful positions, circling a woman and her unborn child. It was a system designed to explode.

Within months, Alexander's empire was haemorrhaging badly. In the east in Bactria, part of modern-day Afghanistan, the Macedonian mercenaries who had been left to keep control of the area mutinied and headed for home. The island of Rhodes in the Aegean declared its independence from the empire. In central Greece, Athens had gathered twenty Greek cities to its cause and now led them into battle against Alexander's, by now old, trusted lieutenant of Greece, Antipater. Antipater had been part of the rise of Macedon under Philip, controlled Greece under the expansion of Alexander's empire, and now was forced once again to fight to subdue Greece. This time, however, Greece was fighting back harder than expected. Antipater was forced to withdraw into Macedon and send word for reinforcements. The veterans of Alexander's campaign to subdue barbarians at the edge of the world were now called back to subdue neighbours in their own home country.

In late August 322, just over a year after Alexander had died, the war of rebellion came to an end at a place called Crannon in Thessaly in central Greece (Map 2). Antipater, armed with veteran men of war, was victorious. The Greek alliance came apart and Athens was, once again, left sitting in a very vulnerable position. Antipater arrived in Athens and put a Macedonian armed garrison on duty in the city. Never under Philip or Alexander had Athens been humiliated so badly. In its usual tradition, Athens chose a man to give the funeral speech on behalf of the dead in the battle. The man chosen was Hyperides, who had been responsible with Demosthenes for organising the rebellion. One of the men most responsible for the catastrophe was given the duty of honouring those who died because of it. 'Though they have failed to reach old age in life,' Hyperides orated over the dead in the public cemetery of Athens, 'they have achieved a glory which knows no bounds.'

Immediately after the funeral gathering, Athens did what it always did on these occasions: it tried its best to save its own skin. The city put the leaders of the rebellion to death. This included not only Hyperides, who had only just finished giving the funeral speech on behalf of the city, but also, of course, Demosthenes – the fearless orator turned criminal, turned hero again, now once again turned traitor and criminal. Condemned to death by their old friend and fellow orator, the smooth-talking, now friend of Macedon, Demades, these two men awaited execution not by fellow Athenians but by the Macedonian men under Antipater. Demosthenes, the man who had run away from the battlefield at Chaeronea, now once again turned tail and fled. Escaping Athens by stealth, he sought refuge in the temple of Poseidon on the island of Calauria (modern-day Poros) just off the coast of the Peloponnese in southern Greece (Map 2). He hoped that the religious sanctuary would give him protection from Antipater's men, perhaps even that they would forget about him. But Demosthenes, who so often had eluded the sword of fate, was now finally mistaken. Antipater's men surrounded the temple and demanded Demosthenes surrender for execution. Claiming that he wanted just a little time to write a letter to his family, Demosthenes was seen to bite on his pen as if concentrating hard on his letter. It wasn't until a few minutes later that Antipater's men realised that this act of feigned concentration had hidden what Demosthenes was really doing: taking poison. Demosthenes, the great orator, the fearless critic of Macedon who constantly steered Athens into the path of storms, who himself never faced up to their conse- quences on the battlefield but abandoned his position and fled, whose lust for gold persuaded him finally to betray his city, now, in his final moments, chose to take his own life rather than allow others to take it from him. Athens, forever in love with the man despite being only too aware of his faults, later honoured him with a statue in the city. Below the statue was inscribed the telling epitaph: 'If only your strength had been equal to your desire, Demosthenes, never would the Greeks have been ruled by the Macedonian god of war.'

The suppression of the revolts in both Greece and in the east of Alexander's empire still didn't bring stability to the ancient world. Alexander's barbarian queen, Roxane, had given birth to a son in late 323 BC, meaning that a joint kingship was on the cards and anyone who controlled the infant king would be ruling effectively in his stead for

some years. Not much later, in 321 BC, one of Alexander's generals had
hijacked Alexander's body while it was being carried back to Macedon
for burial and buried it instead within his own arena of control, in
Egypt, most probably to bolster his claim for overall kingship. This
general, Ptolemy, had during the previous year been in the process of
gathering other generals on his side. Alexander's empire split into two
coalitions: Ptolemy with his supporters in the west of the empire vs.
Perdiccas in the east, who was guardian to the recently born infant son
of Roxane and Alexander, as well as official co-regent with the army's
choice for king, the nice-but-dim Macedonian renamed as Philip III.

Perdiccas was no Alexander the Great. He was soon murdered by
his own officers for his inability to deal decisively with Ptolemy and his
supporters. Antipater, the man in charge of Greece with a long record of
military success, now took matters into his own hands. He marched into
Asia Minor, took control and kidnapped both the feeble king Philip III
and the infant son of Alexander, appropriately also named Alexander.
Control of Alexander the Great's empire was re-divided between the
surviving generals. The Athenian orator Demades, who had turned tail
to Macedon and condemned Demosthenes and Hyperides to death,
was now found by Antipater to have been a supporter of Perdiccas.
Demades was promptly executed in Athens for treason. Even the most
smooth-talking of men couldn't survive the turbulent seas of Greece.

But this settlement was not to last either. Antipater, now over 80,
ignored his own son Cassander (who may have been involved in poisoning Alexander the Great), and instead passed on his power to a
man called Polyperchon. In the ensuing tumult, Athens once again got
caught fighting for the wrong side. This time, however, the casualty was
perhaps the saddest of all. Phocion, the old and wise Athenian general
who had fearlessly advised Athens to the best of his ability for well over
half a century, was caught arguing for Athens against Polyperchon. As
this man was (for now) the dominant power in Greece, Athens couldn't
afford to offend him. Polyperchon now demanded that Phocion,
among others, be punished for treason. When they saw Phocion among

those indicted, the Athenians are said to have wept. But despite their tears, no man, however dear to the city of Athens, was safe if he stood in the way of Athens' survival. Turning on Phocion, the Athenians called for him to be executed, some even for him to be tortured right there in front of them. They ran alongside him, screaming abuse at him on his final journey to the place of execution. Old Phocion was forced to drink poison, and even to pay his executioner an additional fee to ensure that there was enough poison to kill him quickly, rather than leaving him to die in slow fits of agony. The great statesman and general of Athens, the survivor of so many power games in the ancient world, who had always given the best counsel to Athens, had finally been toppled by the brutal dawn of this new world.

Athens was left in a sorry state. No old and wise Phocion, no financially astute Lycurgus, who had also died in 324 BC (amazingly of natural causes), no fearless and encouraging Demosthenes, no smooth-talking Demades to soothe their problems with Macedon. Athens was left to be rocked by the power-struggle which was now engulfing the entire ancient world. To make matters worse, Alexander the Great's mother, Olympias, who had for so long been a crucial influence in Alexander's life, to the extent that she may have had a hand in her own husband's death to protect Alexander's inheritance, now continued to weigh in to support her grandson, the infant Alexander IV. Taking to the battlefield herself, this fearless woman not only murdered 100 Macedonian noblemen but also managed to kill the feeble joint-king Philip III. No wonder that when archaeologists looked to rebuild a full-size working version of an ancient battleship, the trireme, in Athens in the late 1980s, they named it in honour of this fearsome battleaxe of the ancient world: the first mother of Macedon, Olympias. She (the trireme, that is) can still be seen today in dry-dock in Athens.

But even the formidable, scheming Olympias was finally toppled: caught by one of the new powerful generals of Greece, the overlooked son of Antipater, Cassander (one of the possible poisoners of Alexander), who promptly had Olympias executed. Cassander was thus possibly responsible for the death of Alexander and certainly for that of his mother, but what would he do with Alexander's son, the infant Alexander IV, future king of the empire, whom he now had in his possession?

By 316 BC, the scarred battlefield of the ancient world, with many more key players now dead, was again re-divided: Antigonus 'the one-eyed' controlling Asia, Ptolemy 'the Saviour' ruling Egypt, Lysimachus (sadly lacking a descriptive title) in charge of Thrace, and Greece still split between Cassander and Polyperchon, one the son and the other the chosen successor of the now-dead Antipater. Throughout the continuing struggle of the coming years, the young Alexander IV was the ticking time-bomb. Peace treaties sworn between the different warring generals were all supposed to last until Alexander IV was sixteen years old. At that age, his father had been regent of Macedon and was gearing up for his first battle. Would Alexander IV be a new Alexander the Great? Would he be the man who could unite the ancient world once again under a single ruler? Would he be, like his father, man enough to become king of the universe?

We will never know. Cassander, who had murdered little Alexander's grandmother and possibly his father, now murdered the young Alexander IV and Roxane, his mother, before Alexander had the chance to reach his sixteenth birthday. In the aftermath of the death of the only legitimate progeny of Alexander the Great, all sides dropped the pretence of wanting to rule in the king's name. Now they all wanted to be king themselves. Unable ever to excel to the same level as Alexander 'king of kings', these generals slowly settled for a little less. By the end of the 4th century BC, Alexander's empire was cleaved apart into separate mini-empires, each with its own king. These kings created their own dynasties and royal families that dominated the map of the ancient world. It was a power framework that defined this area of the world for hundreds of years.

How did Athens fare in these years? Having executed old Phocion, Athens' democracy had gone into overdrive, but it was soon squashed not only by the continued presence of a Macedonian garrison in the city, but by the imposition after 317 BC of a single overlord: Demetrius of Phaleron. Appointed by the murderous Cassander to rule Athens, Demetrius became its tyrant for ten years. His rule may have started even-handedly enough, but Athens was soon bled dry by Demetrius' wanton excess as he squandered its precious reserves on little but wine, women and song. In 307, another Demetrius – Demetrius 'the Besieger', son of the general Antigonus 'the one-eyed' who ruled Alexander's empire in Asia – chased the original Demetrius out of the city. Freeing Athens from its military garrison and drunken tyrant, 'the Besieger' allowed the city its democracy as long as it gave him loyalty. Athens responded with countless statues and altars in his name, creating new Athenian tribes in his honour and decreeing that he should be called a god. Demetrius 'the Besieger' became Demetrius 'the Saviour' and was given the title of king by the Athenians. As the tumultuous century came to a close, Athens, the birthplace of democracy, had begun openly to worship a living man as a god, and had willingly given him the title of king. The dawn of a new world was complete.

~~~

From Democrats to Kings

W hat should we take from this story? A friend, quoting the philosopher Hegel, recently said to me that the only thing we learn from history is that we don't learn from history. There are examples enough in any period of the past to prove this paradox sadly only too true. Just as children can't be told everything by their parents, but have to experience it for themselves and often learn the hard way as a result, so humanity over time perhaps is bound to keep tripping over some of the same potholes as it evolves.

Yet, at the same time as we can't seem to learn from the past, we can't escape it either. The past may be a different country where they do things differently, but it's a different country which is forever all around us. With the ancient Greek world, that's especially the case. The physical remains, like the great temples and theatres that crowned the Greek landscape, still populate, enthral, and are used by our world. Everywhere you walk in Greece, as Cicero the Roman orator said, you are likely to be walking over history. The poet Lord Byron, one of the first great philhellenes ('lovers of Greece') who would die fighting for Greek independence in the 19th century, came upon Philip's stone lion at Chaeronea on his travels, fallen and buried in the ground. He marvelled at its majesty and power and buried it again for the safe keeping of future generations. Individual pieces of great ancient structures also turn up today in the most unexpected of places: blocks of stone from Mausolus' Mausoleum, the greatest funerary monument on the coast of Asia Minor and one of the seven wonders of the ancient world, for example, can today be found in the walls of the Bodrum underwater archaeology museum, which itself was originally built as the Church of St John by the Crusader knights.

But it's not just a case of recycling ancient stone. These remains and the legends that come with them, which have been passed down to us through millennia of careful recording and scholarship, still have a strong vital currency in our world. As I write, Greek TV is hosting a popular competition for the greatest Greek in history. It's a strong likelihood that Alexander the Great will win hands down. His figure, his story, sums up a lot of what Greeks like to think is best about Greece, just as Britain chose Winston Churchill in its 2002 greatest Briton competition, as America might choose Martin Luther King, or South Africa Nelson Mandela. We choose these figures, scattered through history, because they represent the essence of who we are, or want to be, today. Though we can't choose the country we're born in and the history it has had, just as we can't choose our own parents, we can make choices about the kind of historical examples we want to guide us in our future. Rather than trying to learn simply not to repeat the mistakes of history, it's better, in my view, to think of studying history as a preparation for understanding and shaping what we want our present and future to be like. The past can empower us to create what we believe to be important in our future.

Such an engagement with the past, however, requires a good deal of open-minded debate, not least because individual people will almost always have different historical heroes and different visions for the future. More importantly, people will also very often have different views of the same historical figure or event. For the west, Alexander is Alexander the Great. But in the Persian tradition, he is also known as Alexander the Accursed. Every time I teach Alexander the Great to students, we end up having to assess not who was Alexander, but who is *their* Alexander. Nor is this just the case with particular individuals, but also with cities, peoples, trends, ideas, wars, whole societies and individual monuments. There is, rightly, an intense and important debate in Greece, among both the Greek people and archaeologists from around the world, over what to expose from the ancient world and how, if at all, to reconstruct it – everyone has their own vision of the past and how they want to see it displayed in our present. Everyone has their version (and vision) of history. Such continued awareness of, and engagement in discussion about, those different modern understandings of the past is a vital part of the process of historical inquiry and of adjudicating what is and what is not a fair assessment (and use) of our history.

The story of this period, from democrats to kings, is an important part of that process and that debate. Not simply because it focuses on a lot of the places that still have significant, perhaps inappropriate, weight in our world (the traditional image of the 'glory' that was ancient Athens and its democracy, I think, needs to be complemented by a realisation of its cut-throat, often mob-like reality; and the notion of heroic Sparta needs to be paired with its overtly bullying attitude), nor because other cities and individuals in its story have, perhaps inadvisably, fallen out of the modern viewfinder (like Isocrates and ancient Thebes), nor even because parts of the world visited in this book are once again in the headlines of international diplomacy (Alexander marched through the modern-day countries of Iraq, Iran and Afghanistan, and indeed died in Iraq). Nor is it simply because many of the events and themes that occurred during the period of Isocrates' life, at the time of a brutal dawn of a new world, so eloquently reflect those we find ourselves facing today in our own changing world: economic turbulence, concerns over immigration, social cohesion, globalisation, a shifting balance of world power and a crisis in identity and sense of self. You need look no further than Barack Obama's book *The Audacity of Hope: thoughts on reclaiming the American Dream* – which has often struck me as not dissimilar to the kind of political exhortation Isocrates wrote 2,400 years ago – to see just how much America, and societies across the globe, need to face up to many of the same dilemmas as those living in Isocrates' own time.

All of this is important, but where I think the story of the transition from democrats to kings helps most is with a slightly different problem of history. Though we may realise that each of us takes a different modern view of ancient historical events, history can too often be thought of as an uncomforting support in uncertain times like ours. While we're unsure of where to turn or how to react in our own world, we too often see the narrative of historical events as having a debilitating certainty and decisiveness, in which people *did* this and *thought* that. But *From Democrats to Kings* is a story not just of Athens at the height of its power and Alexander at his, but of the turbulent times of transition in between these two powerful extremes. It highlights how at every stage individuals, groups and cities had to weigh the options and proceed not knowing what would happen next; how different actions and events were simultaneously perceived as meaning very different things (to pursue freedom, then as now, was an irregular verb: I fight for control of Greece for its freedom, but you fight to be its tyrant). This phase of ancient history underlines how it's not just our own modern times that are 'uncertain', compared to a past 'golden age' when everything was somehow easier, better and more certain. It emphasises that all periods of history are just as uncertain as one another: there were no undisputed facts, inevitable events or agreed conclusions, not least because no one at the time knew what would happen next. In many ways, the past is just like now, but earlier.

More importantly, our story also spotlights how the ancients were, just like us, having to engage with their own past at the same time as they were negotiating their uncertain present. For Greece as a whole, that meant engagement with the heavy weight of their myths and legends. For Athens, there was the sometimes useful, sometimes bludgeoning, reputation of their powerful role in the previous century. For Alexander, there were his father's achievements to outdo. But it wasn't just a case of living up to your past. The Greeks during Isocrates' lifetime also began in earnest to manipulate that past for present ends, just as we often do with the story of ancient Greece for own uses today. The Spartan general Lysander's attempts at revolution were literally buried with him and his reputation sanitised because Sparta needed a hero. Athens chose to forget its turbulent revolution at the beginning of the century to ensure the strength of its new democracy. History, even in the ancient world, was what you made of it. And all this complicated intertwining of what happened, what people thought happened, what people made it look like had happened, not to mention what was actually happening, is told to us today through a myriad of different surviving sources, which present haphazard windows into the ancient world, each with its own take on the past. Xenophon, for example, wrote his history of Greece as a grumpy and disillusioned old man, looking back with occasionally sadistic irony on the century. Diodorus was writing about 300 years after Isocrates' lifetime. Plutarch was writing his biographies 400 years later. The story of Alexander the Great is a confusing tussle between often conflicting histories by writers of different times. We have to be aware, as we engage with what we want to take with us from history into our own present and future, not only of how we constantly manipulate our past, but also of how the past was constantly being re-viewed, re-presented and re-invented in the past as well. Delving into history is to delve into a world of shifting sands, but one that we can't afford to ignore.

That said, I want to leave the final words to a man who did his best to ignore it all as it was happening. In the ancient city of Corinth during Isocrates' lifetime, there lived a man called Diogenes. He was a philosopher who believed in the rejection of the material world and engaged in the ultimate quest for individual self-sufficiency and isolationism. He lived in a barrel, owned little, urinated on people in public, defecated in the theatre, masturbated in the bustling heart of the city's Agora and, worst of all, pointed at people with his middle finger (a grievous insult). On his death, he told people to throw his body to the dogs, not least because his nickname was Diogenes 'the dog'. Diogenes cared for no man. Alexander the Great, on the eve of setting out for his conquest of the Persian empire, came up to Diogenes while he was sunbathing and asked why he had ignored him, and if he wanted anything. Diogenes replied: 'Yes, get out of the way of my sun.' Alexander walked away, apparently saying: 'Truly, if I were not Alexander, I would be Diogenes.'

This man was admired by Alexander supposedly for his arrogance (something Alexander could certainly identify with). But I admire Diogenes because, ironically for a man who ignored the world around him, he summed up the greatest change that this world had gone through better than most. Any Greek asked where he was from would give his name and his home city. But Diogenes, when asked where he was from, replied simply: 'I am *cosmopolites*' – I am 'a citizen of the world', the first cosmopolitan. The man who had rejected it all – who died in the same year as Alexander, one of the men responsible for changing it all – had realised more clearly than anyone that a new world, not just of politics, but also of ideas, perceptions and identities, had come.

Select Bibliography

All ancient texts cited can be read in English in either Penguin or Loeb editions, unless otherwise stated.

Introduction: One Man's Dream
For the character of Isocrates, try: T. Papillon (2007), 'Isocrates', in I. Worthington ed., *A companion to Greek rhetoric*; Y. Too (1995), *The rhetoric of identity in Isocrates: text, power, pedagogy*; T. Poulakos (1997), *Speaking for the polis: Isocrates' rhetorical education*; P. Cloché (1963), *Isocrate et son temps*. For the two speeches made at the end of his life, see Isocrates' *Panathenaicus* and *The second letter to Philip*. For some studies of Athenian democracy and its link to the modern world, try: L.J. Samons III (2004), *What's wrong with Democracy: from Athenian practice to American worship*; M. Meckler (2006), *Classical antiquity and the politics of America: from George Washington to George W. Bush*; P.J. Rhodes (2003), *Ancient democracy and modern ideology*; J.K. Davies (1978), *Democracy and Classical Greece*. For studies of Alexander the Great, see: Chapters 16 and 17; W. Heckel and L. Tritle eds (2009), *Alexander the Great: a new history*, and (2003), *Crossroads of history: the age of Alexander*; P. Cartledge (2003), *Alexander the Great: the hunt for a new past*; A.B. Bosworth and E. Baynham eds (2000), *Alexander the Great in fact and fiction*. For recent attention paid to the 4th century, see the bibliographies for subsequent chapters and in particular: L. Tritle ed. (1997), *The Greek world in the fourth century BC: from the fall of the Athenian empire to the successors of Alexander*; Cambridge Ancient History, Vol. 6 (1994), *The fourth century BC*. For further reading on the relationship of ancient Greece and the modern world, try: A. Pomeroy (2008), *Then it was destroyed by the volcano: the ancient world in film and on television*; C. Higgins (2008), *It's all Greek to me*; S. Settis (2006), *The future of the Classical*; S. Goldhill (2004), *Love, Sex and Tragedy: how the ancient world shapes our lives*; N. Morley (2009), *Antiquity and Modernity*; P. Cartledge (2001), *Greeks: crucible of civilization*; L. Hardwick

and C. Stray eds (2008), *A companion to classical receptions*. For past scholarly focus on events in the 5th century BC: T. Holland (2005), *Persian Fire: the first world empire and the battle for the West*; P. Cartledge (2006), *Thermopylae: the battle that changed the world*; B. Strauss (2004), *Salamis: the greatest battle of the ancient world, 480 BC*. For the concept of the 4th century as 'decline', see for example: J. Fine (1983), *The Ancient Greeks: a critical history*; C. Mosse (1973), *Athens in decline 404–86 BC*.

Chapter 1: Flute Players and Pick Axes

The ancient historian Thucydides gives a full account of the Peloponnesian war 431–411 BC (Thucydides' *History of the Peloponnesian War*); after which Xenophon gives us a record down to 362 BC (Xenophon's *Hellenica*). There are also several law-court speeches surviving from cases brought against members of the 30 Tyrants, e.g. Lysias' *Eratosthenes* (Lysias XII). For secondary material: D. Kagan (2003), *The Peloponnesian war: Athens and Sparta in savage conflict 431–403 BC*; N. Bagnall (2004), *The Peloponnesian war: Athens, Sparta and the struggle for Greece*; B. Strauss (1986), *Athens after the Peloponnesian war: class faction and policy 403–386 BC*; R. Osborne (2008), *Debating the Athenian cultural revolution 420–380 BC*; N. Loraux (2002), *The divided city: on memory and forgetting in ancient Athens*; J.L. Shear (2009), *Polis, Demos and Revolution: Responding to Oligarchy in Athens 411–380 BC*. For the life and death of Socrates, have a look at Xenophon's *Apology of Socrates*. For Plato's account of Socrates' law-court defence, see Plato's *Apology*, and for the account of his death, see Plato's *Phaedo* and *Crito*. For some more recent works: J. Colaiaco (2001), *Socrates against Athens: philosophy on trial*; R. Waterfield (2009), *Why Socrates died: dispelling the myths*; P. Cartledge (2009), *Ancient Greek Political Thought in Practice*. For Xenophon's march with Cyrus and the return of the 10,000 Greeks, see Xenophon's *Anabasis*; T. Rood (2004), *The shout of the ten thousand in the modern imagination: The Sea! The Sea!*; R. Lane Fox ed. (2004), *The Long March: Xenophon and the ten thousand*; R. Waterfield (2006), *Xenophon's retreat: Greece, Persia and the end of the golden age*. For a history of the Persian empire, try: J.M. Cook (1983), *The Persian Empire*. For Dionysius I of Syracuse, try: L.J. Sanders (1987), *Dionysios I of Syracuse and Greek tyranny*; B. Caven (1990), *Dionysios I: war lord of Sicily*.

Chapter 2: The City of (Crass) Long-Haired Warriors
For the ancient sources relating to this period, see among others Xenophon's *Hellenica*. For an ancient discussion of the Spartan constitution: Xenophon's *Constitution of the Spartans*. For Lysander, see Plutarch's *Life of Lysander*. For secondary reading on the Spartans, try: P. Cartledge (2002), *Sparta and Lakonia: a regional history 1300–362 BC*; P. Cartledge (2001), *Spartan reflections*; P. Cartledge (1987), *Agesilaos and the crisis of Sparta*; C. Hamilton (1991), *Agesilaos and the crisis of Spartan hegemony*; A. Powell and S. Hodkinson eds (1994), *The shadow of Sparta*, and (2002), *Sparta beyond the mirage*. For the role of women in ancient Greece: P. Brulé (2003), *Women of ancient Greece*; H. Middleton (2002), *Ancient Greek women*; J. Connelly (2007), *Portrait of a priestess: women and ritual in ancient Greece*; D. Lyons (1996), *Gender and immortality: heroines in ancient Greek myth and cult*; S. Pomeroy (1976), *Goddesses, whores, wives and slaves: women in classical antiquity*; S. Pomeroy (2002), *Spartan women*. For more detail on the war which enveloped Greece after 395 BC (the 'Corinthian war'): C. Hamilton (1979), *Sparta's bitter victories: politics and diplomacy in the Corinthian war*; J. Buckler (2003), *Aegean Greece in the fourth century BC*; S. Hornblower (2002), *The Greek world 479–323 BC*. For the different ancient opinions of king Agesilaus: Plutarch's *Life of Agesilaos* and Xenophon's *Agesilaos*.

Chapter 3: Dancing with the Persian King
For Pericles' funeral speech in the 5th century, see Thucydides' *History of the Peloponnesian War* (2.35ff). For Lysias' funeral speech (his *epitaphios*), see Lysias' *Funeral Oration* (Lysias II). For discussion of funeral orations in Athens: N. Loraux (1986), *The invention of Athens: the funeral oration in the classical city*. For the end phases of the Corinthian war, see the bibliography for Chapter 2. For Xenophon's account of the king's peace: Xenophon's *Hellenica* (5.1.3–5.3.27). For a modern study: T.T.B. Ryder (1965), *Koine Eirene: General peace and local independence in ancient Greece*. For inter-city relations in Greece more generally in this period: P. Low (2007), *Interstate relations in classical Greece 411–322 BC*. For accounts of the Boeotian confederacy, see the bibliography for Chapter 5. For Persia, see S. Hornblower (1994), 'Persia', in *Cambridge Ancient History, Vol. 6: The fourth century BC*. For accounts of Sparta's enforcing of the peace and its social instability, see the bibliography for Chapter 2. For the political events of the 380s BC: J. Buckler (2003), *Aegean Greece in the fourth century BC*; J. Buckler and H. Beck (2008), *Central*

Greece and the politics of power in the fourth century BC; P. Rhodes (2006), *A history of the classical Greek world 478–322* BC. For Lysias' speech at Olympia, see Lysias' *Olympic Oration* (Lysias XXXIII). For Isocrates' published essay at Olympia, see Isocrates' *Panegyricus*. For the importance of the Olympic games in Greece: J. Swaddling (1999), *The ancient Olympic games*; N. Spivey (2005), *The ancient Olympics*.

Chapter 4: 'Serious Business for Tomorrow'

For the ancient sources relating to the tale of the Theban rebellion, see Plutarch's *Life of Pelopidas* and Plutarch's *On the daimon of Socrates* (contained in his *Moralia* (575B–598F)); Xenophon's *Hellenica* (5.4.1–13) and Nepos' *Pelopidas* (2.1–4.1). For scholarly discussion of the Theban rebellion, see J. Buckler (2003), *Aegean Greece in the fourth century*; J. Buckler and H. Beck (2008), *Central Greece and the politics of power in the fourth century BC*; M. Munn (1997), 'Thebes', in L. Tritle ed., *The Greek world in the fourth century BC: from the fall of the Athenian empire to the successors of Alexander.*

Chapter 5: The Vegetarian Philosopher and the Body-Building Philanthropist

For the ancient sources relating to the lives of Pelopidas and Epaminondas, see the bibliography for Chapter 4 and Plutarch's *Moralia* (192C–194C); Nepos' *Epaminondas*; Polyaneus' *On Stratagems*, Pausanias' *Description of Greece* (9.13–15). For scholarly discussion of these characters: P. Cartledge (2001), *The Greeks: crucible of civilization*; V. Hanson (1999), *The soul of battle: from ancient times to the present day, how three great liberators vanquished tyranny*. For discussion of the Sphodrias incident and the run-up to the Boeotian war in 378 BC, see J. Buckler (2003), *Aegean Greece in the fourth century BC*; J. Buckler and H. Beck (2008), *Central Greece and the politics of power in the fourth century BC*; P. Cartledge (1987), *Agesilaos and the crisis of Sparta*; P. Cloché (1952), *Thèbes de Béotie, des origines à la conquête romaine.* For discussion of the Boeotian confederacy, see R. Buck (1994), *Boiotia and the Boiotian League 423–371 BC*; R. Buck (1979), *A history of Boeotia*. For the beginning of the Theban hegemony, see J. Buckler (1980), *The Theban hegemony 371–362 BC*. For the ancient accounts of the peace conference of 371 BC and the battle of Leuctra, see Xenophon's *Hellenica* (6.3.1–4.22); Diodorus' *Library of history* (15.50.4–6).

Chapter 6: The Slippery Fish

For discussion of Athens in the early years of the 4th century: B. Strauss (1986), *Athens after the Peloponnesian war: class faction and policy 403–386 BC*; R. Osborne ed. (2008), *Debating the Athenian cultural revolution 420–380 BC*. For discussion of Greek military practices: W. Pritchett (1971), *Ancient Greek military practices* (also known as *The Greek state at war Part 1*). For discussion of Attica's defensive wall built in 378 BC: M. Munn (1993), *The defence of Attika: the Dema wall and the Boiotian war of 378–75 BC*. For discussion of Athenian imperialist intentions in the 4th century and the Second Athenian League, see: J. Cargill (1981), *The Second Athenian League: empire or free alliance?*; G.T. Griffith (1978), 'Athens in the 4th century', in P. Garnsey and C. Whittaker eds, *Imperialism in the ancient world*. For discussion of the Greek colonies in the Black Sea: S. Burstein (2006), 'The Greek cities of the Black Sea', in K. Kinzl ed., *Companion to the classical world*; D. Grammenos and E. Petropoulos eds (2003), *Ancient Greek colonies in the Black Sea (Vols 1–2)*; C. Tuplin (2004), *Pontus and the outside world: studies in Black Sea history, historiography and archaeology*; S. Burstein (1976), *Outpost of Hellenism: the emergence of Heracleia on the Black Sea*; V. Gabrielsen and J. Lund eds (2007), *The Black Sea in antiquity*. For discussions of Cyrene: M. Luni (2006), *Cirene – Atene d'Africa*. For what would become the battleground of the north Aegean coast: J. Heskel (1997), *The north Aegean wars 371–360 BC*. For discussions of Greek colonies in France, Spain and Italy: J. Boardman (1999), *The Greeks overseas*; R. Talbert (1997), 'The Greeks in South Italy and Sicily', in L. Tritle ed., *The Greek world in the 4th century BC: from the fall of the Athenian empire to the successors of Alexander*; A. Trevor-Hodge (1998), *Ancient Greek France*; G. Pugliese-Carratelli ed. (1996), *The Western Greeks*; K. Lomas (2004), *Greek identity in the western Mediterranean*. For discussions of the development of Thessaly and Macedon: H. Westlake (1969), *Thessaly in the 4th century BC*; E. Borza (1990), *In the shadow of Olympus: the emergence of Macedon*.

Chapter 7: The Clash of Philosopher and Tyrant

For the ancient sources relating to Plato's visits to Sicily and Sicily's history in the 4th century, see Diodorus' *Library of history* (Books 13 and 14); Plutarch's *Life of Dion* and *Life of Timoleon*. For modern discussion of Dionysius I, Dionysius II, Dion and Plato's visits: M. Finley (1979), *Ancient Sicily*; L. Sanders (1987), *Dionysios I of Syracuse and Greek tyranny*; B. Caven (1990), *Dionysios I: warlord of Sicily*; G. Levy (1956), *Plato in Sicily*. For discussion of

Plato's Academy in Athens: D. Nails (1995), *Agora, academy and the conduct of philosophy;* G. Fine (2008), *Oxford handbook of Plato.*

Chapter 8: The Implosion of Greece

For the ancient evidence of the campaigns of Pelopidas and Epaminondas and their trial after Leuctra until the battle of Mantinea in 362 BC, see: Xenophon's *Hellenica* (Books 6 and 7); Plutarch's *Moralia* (194c); Plutarch's *Life of Pelopidas;* Diodorus' *Library of history* (Book 15). For some modern scholarship, try: J. Buckler (1980), *The Theban hegemony 371–362 BC;* J. Buckler (2003), *Aegean Greece in the 4th century BC;* J. Buckler and H. Beck (2008), *Central Greece and the politics of power in the 4th century BC;* P. Cartledge (1987), *Agesilaos and the crisis of Sparta;* J. Roy (1994), 'Thebes in the 360s', in *Cambridge Ancient History, Vol. 6: the fourth century BC;* J. Heskel (1997), 'Macedonia and the North: 400–336 BC', in L. Tritle ed., *The Greek world in the 4th century BC: from the fall of the Athenian empire to the successors of Alexander.* For developments in the north Aegean during the 360s: J. Heskel (1997), *The north Aegean wars 371–360 BC.* On Epaminondas at Mantinea, see V. Hanson (1999), *The soul of battle: from ancient times to the present day, how three great liberators vanquished tyranny.* For discussion of Xenophon and his history of Greece (*Hellenica*), see J. Wickersham (1994), *Hegemony and Greek historians;* J. Dillery (1995), *Xenophon and the history of his times;* V. Gray (1989), *The character of Xenophon's Hellenica.*

Chapter 9: The Cow's Bladder, the Love Curse and the Caricature

For Aeneas the Tactician, see: D. Whitehead (1990), *Aineias the Tactician: how to survive under siege.* For discussion of some of the literary and artistic output of the 4th century, try: R. Osborne ed. (2008), *Debating the Athenian cultural revolution 420–380 BC;* T. Webster (1956), *Art and literature in the 4th century;* B. Ridgway (1997), *Fourth century styles in Greek sculpture.* For some discussions of the nature of Greek religion: J. Bremmer (1994), *Greek religion;* J. Mikalson (2005), *Ancient Greek religion;* R. Buxton (2000), *Oxford readings in Greek religion;* D. Ogden ed. (2007), *Companion to Greek religion.* For discussions of temple-building in Greece during the 4th century and the sites of Bassae, Epidaurus, Oropus and Delphi, try: A. Spawforth (2006), *The complete Greek temples;* J. Pedley (2005), *Sanctuaries and the sacred in the Greek world.* For discussion of the surviving documents relating to the building of the temple at Epidaurus, see: A. Burford (1969), *The Greek temple builders at Epidauros: a social and economic study of building in the Asklepian sanctuary, during the fourth and early third centuries B.C.* For the oracle questions at Dodona, oracular consultations of the dead, and curse tablets, see: E. Eidinow (2007), *Oracles, curses and risk among the ancient Greeks*; C. Faraone (1999), *Ancient Greek love magic*; D. Ogden (2001), *Greek and Roman necromancy*. For discussions of Greek magic: J. Petropoulos (2008), *Greek magic: ancient, medieval and modern*. For the development of different religious beliefs in ancient Greece, try: R. Garland (1992), *Introducing new gods: the politics of Athenian religion*; R. Parker (1995), 'Early Orphism', in A. Powell ed., *The Greek world*; E. Kearns (2006), 'Religious practices and religious beliefs', in K. Kinzl ed., *Companion to the classical world*. For the development of medical writing, see: J. Longrigg (1998), *Greek medicine from the heroic to the Hellenistic age*. For the text of the Asclepius success stories, see P. Rhodes and R. Osborne (2003), *Greek historical inscriptions 404–323 BC* (No. 102). For 4th-century theatre, try: P. Easterling ed. (1997), *The Cambridge companion to Greek tragedy*. For Aristophanes and his later comic successor Menander, see: D. MacDowell (1995), *Aristophanes and Athens*; T. Webster (1974), *An introduction to Menander*. For Theophrastus, see Theophrastus' *Enquiry into Plants* and *Characters*. For the vast range of Aristotle's work, try Aristotle's *Politics, Poetics, Logic, Physics, Metaphysics* and *Nicomachean Ethics* among many others.

Chapter 10: Ten Years That Changed the Ancient World: 362–352 BC
For the situation in central Greece at the end of the 360s, see J. Buckler and H. Beck (2008), *Central Greece and the politics of power in the 4th century BC*. For the clash between Dion and Dionysius II, see: Plutarch's *Life of Dion*; R. Talbert (1997), 'The Greeks in South Italy and Sicily', in L. Tritle ed., *The Greek world in the 4th century BC: from the fall of the Athenian empire to the successors of Alexander*. For Athens' involvement in the war with Mausolus (the 'social war') and its involvement in wars on the north Aegean coast, see: J. Heskel (1997), *The north Aegean wars 371–360 BC*; C. Schwenk (1997), 'Athens', in L. Tritle ed., *The Greek world in the 4th century BC: from the fall of the Athenian empire to the successors of Alexander*; S. Hornblower (1982), *Mausolus*. For Isocrates' summation of Athens' position, see Isocrates' *Areopagiticus* and *On the Peace*. For king Philip and his reorganisation of Macedon: I. Worthington (2008), *Philip II of Macedon*; E. Borza (1990), *In the shadow of Olympos: the emergence of Macedon*; N. Hammond (1994), *Philip of Macedon*; G. Cawkwell

(1978), *Philip of Macedon*; N. Hammond and F. Walbank (1988), *History of Macedonia, Vol. 1*; J. Ellis (1976), *Philip II and Macedonian imperialism*; E. McQueen (1995), 'Why Philip won', in A. Powell ed., *The Greek world*. For discussion of the Olympic games and the need to prove Greek descent: N. Crowther (2004), *Athletika: studies on the Olympic games and Greek athletics*. For discussions of 'Greekness' and Greek identity, try: J. Hall (1997), *Ethnic identity in Greek antiquity*; I. Malkin ed. (2001), *Ancient perceptions of Greek ethnicity*; K. Zacharia ed. (2008), *Hellenismus: culture, identity and ethnicity from antiquity to modernity*. For the sacred war fought over Delphi: J. Buckler (1989), *Philip II and Sacred War*.

Chapter 11: Survival Strategies

For discussion of Athenian trade and economy in the 4th century, try: M. Finley and P. Millett (1985), *Studies in land and credit in ancient Athens 500–200 BC*; P. Millett (1991), *Lending and borrowing in ancient Athens*; S. Isager and M. Hansen (1975), *Aspects of Athenian society in the 4th century*; K. Shipton (2000), *Leasing and lending: the cash economy in fourth-century BC Athens*; E. Cohen (1992), *Athenian economy and society: a banking perspective*; N. Ferguson (2008), *The ascent of money: a financial history of the world*; P. de Souza (1995), 'Greek Piracy', in A. Powell ed., *The Greek world*; G. Oliver (2007), *War, food, and politics in early Hellenistic Athens*. For Xenophon, see Xenophon's *Oikonomikos* and *Poroi*. For discussion of Athenian democracy in the 4th century: M. Hansen (1999), *The Athenian democracy in the age of Demosthenes*; J. Ober (1996), *The Athenian revolution: essays on ancient Greek democracy and political theory*; R. Osborne (2010), *Athens and Athenian democracy*. For discussions of Athenian law and order: V. Hunter and J. Edmondson eds (2000), *Law and social status in classical Athens*; V. Hunter (1994), *Policing Athens: social control in the Attic lawsuits 420–320 BC*; A. Lanni (2006), *Law and justice in the courts of classical Athens*; D. MacDowell (1978), *The law in classical Athens*; P. Cartledge, S. von Reden and P. Millett eds (1998), *Kosmos: essays in order, conflict and community in classical Athens*.

Chapter 12: Saviour or Tyrant?

For discussion of Demosthenes: R. Sealey (1993), *Demosthenes and his time: a study in defeat*; I. Worthington ed. (2000), *Demosthenes, statesman and orator*. For recent discussion of the law courts and other orators in Athens at this time: E. Carawan ed. (2007), *The Attic orators*; C. Carey (1997), *Trials from classical Athens.* For discussion of the importance and use of friendship as a key term: P. Millett (1989), 'Patronage and its avoidance in Classical Athens', in A. Wallace-Hadrill ed., *Patronage in ancient society*; L. Mitchell (1997), *Greeks bearing gifts: the public use of private relationships in the Greek world 435–323 BC.* For an example of the law-court and public speeches of Demosthenes and Aeschines over the issue of Philip, see Demosthenes' *First, Second and Third Philippics* and Aeschines' *Against Ctesiphon.* For some modern scholarship on the relationship of the two: T. Ryder (1975), *Introduction to Demosthenes and Aeschines.* For discussion of the impact of Demosthenes on Athens' policy: H. Montgomery (1983), *The way to Chaeronea: foreign policy, decision making and political influence in Demosthenes' speeches*; C. Gibson (2002), *Interpreting a classic: Demosthenes and his ancient commentators*; W. Jaeger (1963), *Demosthenes: the origin and growth of his policies.* For Timoleon and the Syracusan example, see: Plutarch's *Life of Timoleon*; R. Talbert (1974), *Timoleon and the revival of Greek Sicily 344–317 BC.* For Isocrates' final entries into the debate, see Isocrates' *Panathenaicus* and *Second Letter to Philip.*

Chapter 13: The Final Showdown

For discussion of the different tactics used by Demosthenes and Philip in the early 340s BC, see the books on Demosthenes in the bibliography for Chapters 10 and 12, and also S. Perlman ed. (1973), *Philip and Athens*; N. Hammond (1986), *A history of Greece to 322 BC*; T. Buckley (1996), *Aspects of Greek history 750–323 BC: a source-based approach.* For some of the ancient source material, see Diodorus' *Library of history* (Books 16 and 17). For commentary, see E. McQueen (1995), *Diodorus Siculus, the reign of Philip II: the Greek and Macedonian narrative from book XVI: a companion, translation and commentary.* For Demosthenes' invective against Philip, see Demosthenes' *First, Second and Third Olynthiacs* and *First, Second and Third Philippics.* For the debates in the law courts between Demosthenes and Aeschines over their joint embassy to Philip to secure peace between 346–343 BC, see Demosthenes' *On the False Embassy* and Aeschines' *Against Timarchus* and *On the Embassy.* For Demosthenes' role in Athens from 343 onwards, see Plutarch's *Life of Demosthenes.* For the sacred war against Amphissa and Aeschines' role at the assembly meeting of Delphi's governing council, see Aeschines' *Against Ctesiphon.* For the battle of Chaeronea: J. Heskel (1997), 'Macedonia and the North', in L. Tritle ed., *The Greek world in the 4th century BC: from the fall of the Athenian empire to the successors of Alexander*; J. Ma (2008), 'Chaironea

338: topographies of commemoration', in *Journal of Hellenic Studies*. For Philip's relationship with Demosthenes, see Plutarch's *Moralia* (177). For Demosthenes' funeral eulogy after the battle, see Demosthenes' *Funeral Speech*.

Chapter 14: From Father to Son

For the ancient biographies of Demosthenes, Phocion and Alexander, see Plutarch's *Life of Demosthenes*, *Life of Phocion* and *Life of Alexander*. For ancient commentary on Philip, see: Polybius' *Histories* and Diodorus' *Library of history* (Book 16); Plutarch's *Moralia* (177). The lost works on Philip: Satyros' *Life of Philip*; Theopompus' *Philippica*. For modern scholarship analysing Philip's character and achievements, see bibliography for Chapter 10. For the League of Corinth, see P. Low (2007), *International relations in classical Greece*; P. Rhodes and R. Osborne eds (2007), *Greek historical inscriptions 404–323 BC* (No. 76). For the ancient sources about Alexander the Great, see among others: Diodorus' *Library of history*; Arrian's *Anabasis*; Plutarch's *Life of Alexander*. For rumours that he may have killed his father: Plutarch's *Life of Alexander* (10.8); Pausanias' *Description of Greece* (8.7.5). For discussions of Alexander and Alexander's mother, Olympias, see P. Cartledge (2001), *The Greeks: crucible of civilisation*. For Philip's tomb at Vergina: M. Andronicos (1984), *Vergina: the royal tombs and the ancient city*. For the momument at Olympia: P. Schultz and R. von den Hoff eds (2007), *Early Hellenistic portraiture: image, style, context*. The bibliography on Alexander the Great, his personality and conquest of Asia is enormous. Try: S. Sebag-Montefiore (2009), *Heroes: History's greatest men and women*; R. Matthew (2009), *Alexander at the battle of Granicus: a campaign in context*; R. Stoneman (2008), *Alexander the Great: a life in legend*; P. Green (2007), *Alexander the Great and the Hellenistic age: a short history*; I. Worthington ed. (2003), *Alexander the Great: a reader*; J. Roisman ed. (2003), *Brill's companion to Alexander the Great*; A. Bosworth (1996), *Alexander and the East: the tragedy of triumph*; P. Cartledge (2003), *Alexander the Great: the hunt for a new past*; A. Bosworth (1988), *Conquest and empire: the reign of Alexander the Great*; A. Bosworth and E. Baynham ed. (2000), *Alexander the Great in fact and fiction*; P. Briant (1987), *Alexander the Great: the heroic ideal*; P. Green (1998), *Alexander of Macedon 356–323 BC*; J. Hamilton (1973), *Alexander the Great*.

Chapter 15: Ruling the Ancient World

For ancient and modern bibliography on Alexander and his campaigns, see the previous chapter. For discussion of resistance to Alexander, and his attempts to integrate Persian and Greek worlds and cultures, see: S. Hornblower (2002), *The Greek World 479–323 BC*; W. Heckel (1997), 'Resistance to Alexander the Great', in L. Tritle ed., *The Greek world in the 4th century BC: from the fall of the Athenian empire to the successors of Alexander*; L. Tritle, W. Heckel and P. Wheatley eds (2007), *Alexander's empire: formulation to decay*. For Alexander's attempt to declare himself a god, see E. Badian (1981), 'The deification of Alexander the Great', in H. Dell ed., *Ancient Macedonian studies in honor of Charles F. Edson*.

Chapter 16: You've Never Had it So Good

For Demosthenes' defence speech in 330 BC, see Demosthenes' *On the Crown*. For Aeschines' prosecution speech, see Aeschines' *Against Ctesiphon*. For discussion of how Demosthenes reframes the history of Greece and pinpoints Chaeronea as a vital turning point: P. Carlier (1996), *Le IVième siècle av. J.C.: approches historiographiques*. For discussion of the League of Corinth and international relations in 4th-century Greece: P. Low (2007), *International relations in classical Greece*; E. Badian (1982), 'Macedonians and Greeks', in B. Barr-Sharrar and E. Borza eds, *Macedonia and Greece in late classical and early Hellenistic times*. For discussion of financial reforms in Athens under Eubulus and Lycurgus, see: G. Oliver (2007), *War, food and politics in early Hellenistic Athens 404–323 BC*; G. Oliver (2006), 'The Economic Realities', in K. Kinzl ed., *Companion to the classical world*; S. Isager and M. Hansen (1975), *Aspects of Athenian society in the 4th century BC*. For discussion of the building programme in Athens in the second half of the 4th century, see J. Camp (2001), *The archaeology of Athens*. For discussion of Lycurgus' policy of allowing the worship of foreign gods in Athens: R. Garland (1992), *Introducing new gods: the politics of Athenian religion*. For the *Tyrannicides* statue-group: R. Osborne (1998), *Archaic and classical Greek art*. For the discussion of the importance of the Agora in Athens: M. Millett (1991), 'Encounters in the Agora', in P. Cartledge, M. Millett and S. von Reden eds, *Kosmos: essays in order, conflict and community in classical Athens*. For Aristotle's writings on democracy, see Aristotle's *Constitution of the Athenians*. If we want to talk appropriately about Athenian democracy, we have to talk about democracy in the time of Demosthenes: M. Hansen (2001), *Athenian democracy in the age of Demosthenes.* For discussion of the Harpalus affair: Plutarch's *Life of Demosthenes* and *Life of Alexander*; Hyperides' *Against Demosthenes* and Dinarchus' *Against Demosthenes*; I. Worthington (1994), 'The Harpalus affair and the Greek response to the Macedonian hegemony', in I. Worthington ed., *Ventures into Greek history*; R. Wallace (1989), *The Areopagus council to 307 BC.*

Chapter 17: A New World

For Alexander's injuries and good fortune, see Plutarch's *Moralia* (326Dff). For the many cities founded by Alexander, see P.M. Fraser (1996), *The cities of Alexander the Great.* For Demosthenes' redemption and final suicide, see Plutarch's *Life of Demosthenes.* For the rebellion led by Athens after Alexander's death (the Lamian war) and Hyperides' funeral oration for the war's dead, see Hyperides' *Funeral Speech.* For the final demise of Phocion, see Plutarch's *Life of Phocion.* For a discussion of the succession power struggle after Alexander's death, see: W. Lindsay (1997), 'The Successors of Alexander', in L. Tritle ed., *The Greek world in the 4th century BC: from the fall of the Athenian empire to the successors of Alexander.* For a discussion of Alexander's mother, Olympias, see P. Cartledge (2001), *The Greeks: crucible of civilization.* For the creation of the modern-day *Olympias* trireme, see J. Morrison, J. Coates and N. Rankov (2000), *The Athenian trireme: the history and reconstruction of an ancient Greek warship.* For the emergence of a new world, the 'Hellenistic' world after the death of Alexander the Great, see: D. Ogden ed. (2002), *The Hellenistic world: new perspectives*; R. Errington (2008), *A history of the Hellenistic world: 323–30 BC*; M. Austin (2006), *The Hellenistic world from Alexander to the Roman conquest: a selection of ancient sources in translation*; P. Green (2007), *The Hellenistic age: a short history*; P. Green (1990), *Alexander to Actium: the historical evolution of the Hellenistic age.* For Athens and its deification of Demetrius 'the Saviour', see Plutarch's *Life of Demetrius.*

Epilogue: From Democrats to Kings

For some works looking at how ancient historians have cast ancient events: J. Wickersham (1994), *Hegemony and Greek historians*; V. Gray (1989), *The character of Xenophon's Hellenica*; C. Tuplin and V. Azoulay eds (2004), *Xenophon and his world*; K. Sacks (1990), *Diodorus Siculus and the first century*; A. Stadter ed. (1992), *Plutarch and the historical tradition.* For Diogenes: L. Navia (1998), *Diogenes of Sinope: the man in the tub.*

Timeline

Date (BC)	Mainland Greece	Aegean sea, north Aegean coast, and Black Sea	Asia Minor and Persian empire	Western Mediterranean
480	Battle of Thermopylae			
440s	Height of Athenian empire. Construction work starts on the Parthenon in Athens			
436	Isocrates born			
431	Start of the Peloponnesian war			
406	Battle of Arginusae			
404	Defeat of Athens and imposition of 30 Tyrants		Death of Persian king Darius. Artaxerxes II proclaimed king	
403	Restoration of Athenian democracy			
401			Battle of Cunaxa. Cyrus killed. 10,000 Greeks stranded in Asia	Dionysius I strengthens his control over Syracuse and Sicily
400	Agesilaus ascends to Spartan throne Temple of Apollo at Bassae is completed			

Date (BC)	Mainland Greece	Aegean sea, north Aegean coast, and Black Sea	Asia Minor and Persian empire	Western Mediterranean
400 (cont.)	Xenophon's *Oikonomikos*			
399	Death of Socrates in Athens			
396	Cynisca, sister of Agesilaus, wins at the Olympic games		Spartan invasion of Persian empire	
395	Corinthian war breaks out in Greece between Sparta and Athens, Thebes, Argos and Corinth The Spartan general Lysander killed at the battle of Haliartus Aristophanes' *Ecclesiazusae* performed in Athens			
394	Battle at Coronea in Boeotia	Sea battle near Cnidus		
392	Rebuilding of Athens' city walls Lysias' funeral oration Cynisca wins for a second time at the Olympic games			
391	Attempt at peace killed off by Athens			
390	Isocrates opens his school in Athens			
388	Lysias' *Olympic Oration* Aristophanes' *Wealth* reperformed in Athens			Plato goes on his first visit to Dionysius I in Syracuse

Date (BC)	Mainland Greece	Aegean sea, north Aegean coast, and Black Sea	Asia Minor and Persian empire	Western Mediterranean
387	Plato opens his Academy in Athens			
386	Imposition of king's peace	Imposition of king's peace	Imposition of king's peace	
384	Demosthenes and Aristotle born Sparta destroys city of Mantinea			
382	Sparta occupies the city of Thebes			
380	Isocrates' *Panegyricus* Death of Lysias Building of temple of Apollo at Epidaurus begins Athens conducts reassessment of value of land in Attica			
379	Theban rebellion begins			
378	Sphodrias' failed attempt to march on Athens Boeotian war begins Boeotian confederacy is relaunched Second Athenian League is founded Athens constructs its defensive wall in Attica			
375	The Theban Sacred Band beats the Spartan army at Tegyra	King's peace is reaffirmed	King's peace is reaffirmed	

Date (BC)	Mainland Greece	Aegean sea, north Aegean coast, and Black Sea	Asia Minor and Persian empire	Western Mediterranean
375 (cont.)	King's peace is reaffirmed Jason of Pherae is confirmed as *tagos* of Thessaly	Second Athenian League has 75 members		
373	Thebans destroy city of Plataea Temple of Apollo at Delphi destroyed by earthquake. Restoration project begins (completed 340s)		Persian king undertakes unsuccessful expedition into Egypt	
371	Athens opens alliance negotiations with Sparta Failed peace conference at Sparta Battle of Leuctra Second failed peace conference in Athens			
370	Jason of Pherae assassinated. Alexander of Pherae takes over Alexander II becomes king of Macedon Epaminondas' and Pelopidas' first expedition into the Peloponnese begins			
369	Epaminondas and Pelopidas refound Mantinea, free Messenia, establish the city of Messene and threaten gates of Sparta			

Date (BC)	Mainland Greece	Aegean sea, north Aegean coast, and Black Sea	Asia Minor and Persian empire	Western Mediterranean
369 (cont.)	Epaminondas and Pelopidas put on trial and acquitted Athens and Sparta renew their alliance Epaminondas begins second invasion of Peloponnese Pelopidas begins first expedition north. Brings Macedonian hostage Philip back to Thebes			Dionysius I sends help to Sparta
368	Macedonian king assassinated. Succeeded by Ptolemy Pelopidas' second expedition north. Loses in battle with Ptolemy, king of Macedon Pelopidas' third expedition north against Alexander of Pherae. Pelopidas captured Epaminondas put on trial a second time and demoted Peace conference at Delphi organised by Persian king			Dionysius I becomes a citizen and ally of Athens

Date (BC)	Mainland Greece	Aegean sea, north Aegean coast, and Black Sea	Asia Minor and Persian empire	Western Mediterranean
367	Thebans' first attempt to free Pelopidas fails Epaminondas leads second attempt and frees Pelopidas Peace of Pelopidas rejected by Athens and Sparta		Pelopidas sent to Persian court to win king's favour. Returns with 'peace of Pelopidas'	Dionysius I dies. Dionysius II takes over as ruler of Syracuse
366	Epaminondas' third expedition into the Peloponnese. City of Megalopolis is founded Thebes regains control of Oropus from Athenians	Siege of Amphipolis on north Aegean coast by Athens		Plato's second visit to Syracuse to meet Dionysius II Dion exiled to Athens. Plato imprisoned and then released
365	Macedonian king Ptolemy assassinated. Perdiccas III now king Arcadian war with Elis over Olympia begins	Macedon forms an alliance with Amphipolis. Amphipolis hands itself over to Olynthus Athenians recapture island of Samos Timotheus sent to Amphipolis	Revolt against Persian king begins, led by governors of Asia Minor	

Date (BC)	Mainland Greece	Aegean sea, north Aegean coast, and Black Sea	Asia Minor and Persian empire	Western Mediterranean
364	Pelopidas' third expedition north. Pelopidas killed Thebes destroys city of Orchomenus	Epaminondas takes Theban navy to threaten Athenian allies in Aegean and entrance to Black Sea area Olynthus withdraws from Amphipolis Timotheus besieges Potidea		
363		Athens establish permanent colony in Potidea Athenian expedition sent to Chersonese peninsula		
362	Battle of Mantinea Death of Epaminondas A common peace is declared	Perdiccas installs garrison at Amphipolis	Mausolus joins rebellion against Persian king	

Date (BC)	Mainland Greece	Aegean sea, north Aegean coast, and Black Sea	Asia Minor and Persian empire	Western Mediterranean
362 (cont.)		Miltocythes, a rebel against the Thracian king, captures Sestos in the Chersonese peninsula and hands it over to the Persians		
361		Timotheus captures Sestos Olynthus attacks Potidea Athens' war against the king of Thrace begins		Plato's third visit to Syracuse
360	Perdiccas III dies. Philip II now king of Macedon Internal reform of Macedon begins Athens and Macedon agree terms over city of Amphipolis King Agesilaus of Sparta dies	Sestos besieged by Thracian king		
359			Death of Artaxerxes II, Persian king. Artaxerxes III becomes king	

Date (BC)	Mainland Greece	Aegean sea, north Aegean coast, and Black Sea	Asia Minor and Persian empire	Western Mediterranean
358	Theatre at Epidaurus built		Mausolus offers protection to cities of Asia Minor against Athens Social war against Athens begins	
357	Isocrates' *Areopagiticus* Philip marries Olympias Athens declares war on Macedon	Philip takes back control of Amphipolis		Dion returns to Syracuse
356	Alexander the Great born Philip wins horse race at Olympia Philip wins victory at Potidea and against the Illyrians Start of sacred war over sanctuary of Delphi		Artabazus, another Persian governor, revolts	
355	Isocrates' *On the Peace* Xenophon's *Poroi* Sacred war spreads to envelop whole of Greece Eubulus takes financial control of Athens		Social war ends Thebes sends support to Persian governor Artabazus	
354				Murder of Dion. Callippus takes control of Syracuse

Date (BC)	Mainland Greece	Aegean sea, north Aegean coast, and Black Sea	Asia Minor and Persian empire	Western Mediterranean
353		Athens sends permanent settlers to Chersonese peninsula Olynthus makes alliance with Athens	Death of Mausolus and completion of his Mausoleum by his wife Artemisia	
352	Philip annihilates Phocian force and forces 3,000 mercenaries into the sea Philip becomes *tagos* of Thessaly Philip repulsed at Thermopylae	Athenians send permanent settlers to Samos, exiling most Samians Philip makes alliance with Byzantium		Callippus killed
351	Demosthenes' *First Philippic*		Persian king begins another invasion of Egypt	
350	Temple of Amphiaraus at Oropus completed	Philip threatens Olynthus		
349	Demosthenes' *First, Second and Third Olynthiacs*	Philip attacks Olynthus		
348	Revolt in Euboea begins	Olynthus taken by Philip		
347	Plato's *Statesman* Plato dies. Aristotle leaves Athens			

Date (BC)	Mainland Greece	Aegean sea, north Aegean coast, and Black Sea	Asia Minor and Persian empire	Western Mediterranean
346	Demosthenes and Aeschines sent to conduct peace negotiations with Philip. Peace of Philocrates agreed Philip pushes past Thermopylae and frees Delphi Isocrates' *To Philip* Revision of Athenian citizenship lists Demosthenes and Timarchus bring a prosecution against Aeschines in Athens			Dionysius II recovers power in Syracuse
345	Aeschines' *Against Timarchus* counter-prosecution begins			
344	Philip protests about Athens' behaviour, while putting down revolts in Thessaly Philip and Demosthenes both looking for allies in Peloponnese Demosthenes' *Second Philippic*			Timoleon arrives in Syracuse and begins Syracuse's revival Dionysius II finally exiled to Corinth
343	Hyperides' *Against Philocrates* Demosthenes' *On the false embassy*. Aeschines' *On the embassy*. Aeschines acquitted		Persia continues to establish control over Egypt	

Date (BC)	Mainland Greece	Aegean sea, north Aegean coast, and Black Sea	Asia Minor and Persian empire	Western Mediterranean
343 (cont.)	Aristotle becomes tutor to Alexander in Macedon			
342	Isocrates' *First letter to Philip* and *Letter to Alexander* Eubulus dies in Athens			
341	Demosthenes' *Third and Fourth Philippic* Demosthenes again canvassing support in the Peloponnese	Philip campaigns on Black Sea coast Demosthenes sent to make alliance with Byzantium		Timoleon fights Carthaginians in Sicily
340	Demosthenes honoured by Athenians Philip sends final warning to Athens Athenians begin to build war chest Athens declares war on Philip	Philip makes unsuccessful attempt on Byzantium		
339	Aeschines defends Athens at Delphic council and persuades them to declare sacred war on Amphissa Philip chosen as general and seizes Elatea. Offers ultimatum to Thebes Athenians reject Phocion's advice and follow Demosthenes			

Date (BC)	Mainland Greece	Aegean sea, north Aegean coast, and Black Sea	Asia Minor and Persian empire	Western Mediterranean
339 (cont.)	Demosthenes persuades Thebans to stand with Athens Isocrates' *Panathenaicus*			
338	Battle of Chaeronea Isocrates' *Second letter to Philip* and death of Isocrates Athens' anti-tyranny law passed Demosthenes' *Funeral Oration* Thebes punished by Philip		Artaxerxes III murdered. Artaxerxes IV becomes Persian king	Timoelon and Carthage sign a peace treaty
337	League of Corinth founded Building work at international sanctuaries of Isthmia and Nemea begins Lycurgus appointed as manager of public revenue in Athens			Timoleon dies and is honoured in Syracuse
336	Ctesiphon moves that Demosthenes be honoured with a crown Philip assassinated. Alexander is crowned king Athens honours Philip's murderer Philip's tomb is created at Vergina		Philip's advance force sent to Asia Minor Artaxerxes IV murdered. Darius III becomes Persian king	

Date (BC)	Mainland Greece	Aegean sea, north Aegean coast, and Black Sea	Asia Minor and Persian empire	Western Mediterranean
335	Alexander subdues Thessaly after taking Mount Ossa Thebes revolts from Alexander and is destroyed Demades persuades Alexander to leave Demosthenes alive Philippeion begun at Olympia Alexander consults oracle at Delphi Alexander meets Diogenes Rebuilding of the Pnyx is finished in Athens Aristotle resettles in Athens and opens Lyceum	Alexander subdues revolts by Danube		
334			Alexander crosses the Hellespont. He takes Trojan armour from temple near Troy Battle of Granicus Alexander slashes Gordian knot	
333			Battle of Issus	

Date (BC)	Mainland Greece	Aegean sea, north Aegean coast, and Black Sea	Asia Minor and Persian empire	Western Mediterranean
332			Siege of Tyre Siege of Gaza Alexander made Pharaoh of Egypt Alexander's consultation of oracle of Ammon at Siwah	
331	Sparta revolts Battle at Megalopolis and death of Spartan king Agis	Thracian rebellion put down by Antipater	Battle of Gaugamela Babylon, Susa and Persepolis fall Burning of Persepolis	
330	Demosthenes' *On the Crown* and Aeschines' *Against Ctesiphon* Lycurgus finishes new building work at Eleusis *Tyrannicides* statue-group returned to Athens		Death of king Darius Ecbatana falls to Alexander Alexander dismisses allies' troops Philotas affair	
329	*Panathenaic* stadium built in Athens by Lycurgus		Death of Bessus Alexander burns his baggage train and crosses the Hindu Kush	

Date (BC)	Mainland Greece	Aegean sea, north Aegean coast, and Black Sea	Asia Minor and Persian empire	Western Mediterranean
329 (cont.)			Campaign in Bactria and Sogdiana begins	
328			Alexander murders Cleitus	
327			Alexander subdues Sogdiana and marries Roxane Callisthenes is murdered Alexander crosses into India	
326	Death of Lycurgus		Alexander concludes alliance with king Porus Alexander reaches Beas river. Agrees to turn back from camp at Hydaspes river. Gives order for fleet to be constructed	

Date (BC)	Mainland Greece	Aegean sea, north Aegean coast, and Black Sea	Asia Minor and Persian empire	Western Mediterranean
326 (cont.)			Alexander sets off south along Indus river and is almost killed fighting in the Punjab	
325	New monument of Eponymous Heroes is completed in the Agora at Athens		Alexander splits from fleet and marches across Gedrosian desert	
324	Restoration of Exiles decree read out at Olympia Harpalus arrives in Athens with Alexander's money Demosthenes and Demades put on trial. Dinarchus' and Hyperides' *Against Demosthenes* Demosthenes and Demades exiled		Alexander returns to Susa Mass wedding at Susa Hephaisteion dies at Ecbatana Mutiny of Alexander's Macedonian troops at Opis Alexander orders his own deification	
323	Demosthenes recalled from exile Demosthenes and Hyperides gather allies in the Peloponnese		Alexander contracts a fever and dies	

Date (BC)	Mainland Greece	Aegean sea, north Aegean coast, and Black Sea	Asia Minor and Persian empire	Western Mediterranean
323 (cont.)	Aristotle completes his *Constitution of the Athenians* Aristotle flees Athens Diogenes dies		Crisis meeting of generals in Bablyon. Army picks Philip III. First division of Alexander's empire Alexander IV is born	
322	Lamian war begins against Antipater Battle of Crannon in Thessaly Demades recalled from exile Hyperides' *Funeral Oration* Death of Demosthenes and Hyperides Macedonian garrison installed in Athens Aristotle dies	Island of Rhodes rebels	Mutiny of Greek mercenaries in Bactria Commanders line up behind Ptolemy or Perdiccas	
321			Alexander the Great's body stolen by Ptolemy and buried in Egypt Perdiccas killed	

Date (BC)	Mainland Greece	Aegean sea, north Aegean coast, and Black Sea	Asia Minor and Persian empire	Western Mediterranean
321 (cont.)			Antipater takes Alexander IV and Philip III hostage	
			Antigonus appointed to control Asia Minor	
			Agreement on power-sharing reached at Triparadisus	
319	Theophrastus' *Characters* written		Antigonus strengthens his control over Asia	
	Antipater dies, leaving Cassander and Polyperchon to fight for control of Greece			
	Demades killed			
	Roxane and Olympias flee to Epirus			
318	Phocion executed in Athens			
317	Demetrius of Phaleron imposed on Athens		Continued fighting for control of different parts of Asia	Agathocles makes himself tyrant of Syracuse
	Olympias joins forces with Polyperchon and fights in Macedonia. Murders Philip III and his wife Eurydice			
316	Olympias murdered by Cassander. Continued fighting for the next four years			

Date (BC)	Mainland Greece	Aegean sea, north Aegean coast, and Black Sea	Asia Minor and Persian empire	Western Mediterranean
312	Brief peace as Alexander IV soon to come of age			
309	Alexander IV killed by Cassander			
307	Demetrius 'the Besieger' takes control in Athens and is worshipped as a god			Agathocles becomes king of Sicily

Index